GEORGIA'S CIVIL WAR

Georgia Towns and Railroads, from *Goldthwait's Map of the United States* (1861).

GEORGIA'S CIVIL WAR

Conflict on the Home Front

David Williams

MERCER UNIVERSITY PRESS | *Macon, Georgia*

2017

MUP/ H942

Published by Mercer University Press
1501 Mercer University Drive
Macon, Georgia 31207

9 8 7 6 5 4 3 2 1

Books published by Mercer University Press are printed on acid-free paper that meets the requirements of the American National Standard for Information Sciences—Permanence of Paper for Printed Library Materials.

ISBN 978-0-88146-631-7
Cataloging-in-Publication Data is available from the Library of Congress

Contents

MERCER UNIVERSITY

MERCER UNIVERSITY PRESS

Endowed by

TOM WATSON BROWN

and

THE WATSON-BROWN FOUNDATION, INC.

For Teresa

Prologue: Two-Thirds of Our Men Are Absent

Just before dawn on Friday morning, September 23, 1864, an unexpected visitor stepped off the train in Macon. It was Confederate President Jefferson Davis. Atlanta had fallen three weeks earlier, and Davis was on his way to bolster the troops as best he could. When word spread that the president was in town, city leaders invited him to address a meeting called to organize relief for exiled Atlanta refugees. Davis agreed. Around eleven o'clock, he entered the Baptist church to polite applause. After taking a bow, Davis launched into a rambling speech that explained much, perhaps too much, about why the Confederacy was faltering. "Two-thirds of our men are absent," he lamented, "some sick, some wounded, but most of them absent without leave."[1]

It was astonishing to hear Davis openly admit that so many men had abandoned the ranks. One Milledgeville news editor called the statement an injustice. But it was hardly a secret. Desertion had plagued the Confederacy's war effort from near its beginning. By fall 1861, just a few months into the war, thousands of soldiers were going home with or without leave. Few were returning to the army, and fewer still were volunteering to take their places. In February 1862, Augusta's *Chronicle and Sentinel* reported that "one who walks Broad street and sees the number of young men, would come to the conclusion that no war...was now waging."[2]

Desperate for men, in April 1862 the Confederacy took a drastic step and enacted the first national draft in American history. It did little to stem the tide of desertion. In September, General Robert E. Lee wrote to President Davis that "desertion and straggling" were the main reasons for his army's defeat at the pivotal Battle of Sharpsburg, or Antietam as the Yankees called it.[3] Desertion rates continued to run so high

---

[1]*Macon Telegraph*, 24 September 1864.

[2]*Milledgeville Confederate Union*, 4 October 1864; *Augusta Chronicle and Sentinel*, 12 February 1862.

[3]*War of the Rebellion: A Compilation of the Official Records of the Union and Confederate Armies* (Washington, DC: Government Printing Office, 1880–1901) series 1, vol. 19, part 2, 622 (hereafter cited as *OR*).

that Lee finally issued a general amnesty for deserters who would return to their units voluntarily. All others, he warned, would "suffer the extreme penalty of the law."[4] Few responded to Lee's offer. The problem only became worse. Near war's end, J. T. Smith of Bibb County wrote to Governor Joe Brown that Georgia soldiers were "going home as fast as they can get there. The country is full of deserters and almost every man in the community will feed them and keep them from being arrested."[5]

Black folk were helping as well. Over many miles of traveling home, deserters found that slave cabins were a safe bet for food, shelter, and support. Nancy Johnson, enslaved on a Georgia plantation during the war, told how "some of the rebel soldiers deserted and came to our house and we fed them. They were opposed to the war and didn't own slaves and said they would die rather than fight."[6]

There was sympathy for deserters even among soldiers who remained at the front. They knew that their comrades had good reason for going home and knew why they were going in such numbers. Sergeant William Andrews of Clay County, serving in Lee's Army of Northern Virginia, wrote in his diary that it was "an everyday occurrence for men to get letters from home stating that their families are on the point of starvation. Many a poor soldier has deserted and gone home in answer to that appeal, to be brought back and shot for desertion." "Thank God," wrote Andrews, "I have no wife and children to suffer on account of an ungrateful government."[7]

Soldiers' families flooded Governor Brown's office with letters telling of starvation and begging for aid. Martha Tyler of Lowndes County, wife of a soldier who had not been paid in months, wrote that she and

---

[4]*OR*, series 1, vol. 42, part 2, 1169; *Early County News*, 14 September 1864.

[5]J. T. Smith to Joseph E. Brown, 25 February 1865, Governor's Incoming Correspondence, Georgia Department of Archives and History, Morrow.

[6]Ira Berlin et al., eds., *Freedom: A Documentary History of Emancipation, 1861–1867*, series 1, vol. 1, *The Destruction of Slavery* (New York: Cambridge University Press, 1985) 151.

[7]William H. Andrews, *Footprints of a Regiment: A Recollection of the First Georgia Regulars, 1861–1865*, annotated and introduction by Richard M. McMurry (Atlanta: Longstreet Press, 1992) 39.

her five children were "destitute of food and clothing and without help we will suffer." State relief efforts were largely ineffective, and women took matters into their own hands. They staged riots in all of Georgia's major cities and dozens of smaller towns, as the soldiers were well aware. In spring 1863, Daniel Snell of Harris County wrote from Virginia to his wife, Sarah, "You spoke of a riot in Columbus…it is no more than I expected. I understand there was also one in Augusta…. What will become of the women and children with the food situation?"[8]

Hunger plagued the army as well. Soldiers' letters, diaries, and reminiscences all speak of the Confederacy's inability to feed them properly—of scrounging and foraging just to stay alive. But it was for their families that the men were most concerned. One young soldier wrote to a friend in Columbus, "If it is the best our government can do, I am willing to live on dry bread for our cause; but I don't want mother to suffer for anything as long as I live…. when I hear she is in want of provisions and can't get them, I am going home."[9]

And so Confederate soldiers did go home, by the tens of thousands and ultimately hundreds of thousands. There were various reasons why they left. Many had opposed secession to begin with. Others came to see the conflict as a "rich man's war" and wanted nothing more to do with it. And, perhaps most significantly, it was hardship and hunger among their families that drew so many back home. But why was food scarce? The South was a vast agricultural region that should easily have been able to feed itself, yet soldiers and civilians alike struggled to keep themselves fed.

For more than a century and a half, historians have often ignored the South's home front difficulties, food shortages among them, which had so much to do with desertion and defeat. Anyone with even a passing knowledge of the Civil War knows that Confederate armies were nearly always outnumbered by roughly two to one. In a presumptive way, the South's manpower disparity is usually attributed to the North's larger

[8]Tyler to Brown, 11 October 1864, Governor's Incoming Correspondence; Louise Calhoun Barfield, *History of Harris County, Georgia, 1827–1961* (Columbus, GA: Columbus Office Supply Co., 1961) 758.

[9]*Columbus Sun*, 18 November 1863.

population. Lost in that simplistic view is the impact that desertion had on sapping the Confederacy's fighting strength. There was desertion in the Union army as well, but it paled in comparison to the Confederacy's desertion rate. This critical issue is but one of many that historians too often brush aside.

Why were Southerners so divided on secession? How were the foundations for those divisions laid in the antebellum South? How did secession happen if so many opposed it? Why did Confederate leaders feel compelled to impose a draft? Why did increasing numbers of Southerners call the conflict a rich man's war? What impact did slave resistance have on the war effort? What was the impact of women's experiences, attitudes, and actions? Why was the Confederacy unable to feed itself adequately? What role did cotton planters and speculating merchants play in that regard? Why were authorities unwilling or unable to sufficiently aid soldiers' families? And, finally, what impact did all this have on the war's course and outcome? Only by looking behind the lines with open eyes can we hope to find answers to these important but frequently overlooked questions.

***

In preparing this study and bringing it to print, I am very much indebted to the direction and clarity of Marc Jolley, Marsha Luttrell, Mary Beth Kosowski, and the staff of Mercer University Press. At every step, their professionalism and good humor made the process relatively easy and pleasant.

For their assistance in locating research material, I am most grateful to Kaye Minchew and Randy Allen of the Troup County Archives, Miriam Syler of the Cobb Memorial Archives, Craig Lloyd and David Daniel of the Columbus State University Archives, Mark Ellis of Albany State University's Pendergrast Library, Beverly Powers of the Auburn University Archives, Melissa Bush of the University of Georgia's Hargrett Rare Book and Manuscript Library, and Sally Mosely, Alice James, Andy Phrydas, and Anthony Winegar of the Georgia Department of Archives and History. Special thanks for help with research goes to Denise Montgomery of Valdosta State University's Odum Library for cheerfully tolerating my constant interlibrary loan requests.

For aid in obtaining and reproducing the illustrations, I wish to thank Rex Devane and his staff at Valdosta State University's media center, Gail Miller Deloach of the Georgia Department of Archives and History, Jody Norman of the Florida State Archives, and Bebe Overmiller of the Library of Congress.

Chris Meyers and Paul Riggs, both former heads of Valdosta State University's Department of History, were instrumental in securing and sustaining released time for work on the manuscript. I thank them both for their unwavering support of my scholarly efforts. Thanks also to James LaPlant, assistant vice president for research and dean of the graduate school at Valdosta State, who supported funding for the project.

For their continuing support in carving out a few daily writing and research hours, I wish to thank my current department head, John Dunn, and the chair of our scheduling committee, Jay Rickman.

David Carlson, long-ago graduate student, one-time collaborator, and currently a professor at Troy University, continues to influence my work with his own fine scholarship. He exemplifies the sort of student every professor hopes to encounter. He has made his old thesis director very proud.

Finally, my most heartfelt gratitude goes to my wife, Teresa, who has been the light of my life for almost forty years. I am very much looking forward to the next forty with her.

Chapter 1

Antebellum Georgia and the Road to Civil War

"Raining—raining—raining—pouring—pouring." That was how Alexander H. Stephens described the weather on January 2, 1861, the day Georgia voters chose delegates to the state's secession convention. Stephens called it "the worst day for an election I ever saw in Georgia." It was the same all over the state. "Wet and stormy" wrote a newspaper editor in Savannah. Augusta was "rainy, chilly and damp" with "very muddy" streets. The rain was so heavy in Macon that streets were "almost impassable." It was storming in Albany too. In Atlanta, "the rain came down in floods."[1]

Although he would soon be named Confederate vice president, Stephens was Georgia's leading voice against secession. Shortly after Abraham Lincoln became president-elect in November 1860, Stephens told a gathering at Milledgeville that "the election of no man, constitutionally chosen to that high office, is sufficient cause to justify any state to separate from the Union.... To make a point of resistance to the government, to withdraw from it because a man has been elected, puts us in the wrong." Stephens was concerned about much more than right and wrong. He knew that his neighbors were deeply divided on secession, and he worried that, should Georgia leave the Union, its citizens might "at no distant day commence cutting one another's throats."[2]

Stephens was right about divisions in Georgia's electorate. The balloting showed voters almost evenly split, with perhaps a slight majority opposing secession.[3] That majority would likely have been much greater

---

[1]Michael P. Johnson, *Toward a Patriarchal Republic: The Secession of Georgia* (Baton Rouge: Louisiana State University Press, 1977) 5.

[2]William W. Freehling and Craig M. Simpson, eds., *Secession Debated: Georgia's Showdown in 1860* (New York: Oxford University Press, 1992) 55, 68.

[3]In his seminal study of Georgia's secession, Michael Johnson concluded,

had it not been for the weather. Voting was heaviest in and around urban areas, mostly concentrated in the Cotton Belt of central and southern Georgia, where slaveholders and slavery held considerable influence. The polls there were more accessible, and opinions tended to favor secession. Stephens estimated that Georgia's election-day storm robbed the Union cause of at least ten thousand votes.[4]

That Georgia was a state divided came as no surprise to anyone at the time. For decades, there had been growing social and economic tensions that threatened the political power structure. The resulting divisions would have a profound effect not only on Civil War Georgia but also on the fate of the entire Confederacy.

Diverging Fortunes of Planters and Plain Folk

Georgia was among the South's most prosperous states in the late antebellum era, but that prosperity was by no means shared by all its people. Most lived in conditions that were regarded even at the time as abject poverty. Of Georgia's more than one million residents, nearly half were enslaved. Of Georgia's free inhabitants, the great majority were directly engaged in agriculture, but only slightly more than half owned three or more acres of land. Most of the rest were tenant farmers or sharecroppers, all working land owned by someone else. About half of land owners also held slaves, but only a few. Most small slaveholders worked the fields along with their slaves and had a lifestyle not so different from many of

---

"Using the most generous estimate of the vote for immediate secession, the result of the elections was a 44,152 to 41,632 victory for the secessionists, a popular majority of just over 51 percent of those voting. A less generous and more realistic estimate of the vote for immediate secession yields a 42,744 to 41,717 cooperationist victory, a majority of just over 50 percent" (Johnson, *Toward a Patriarchal Republic*, 63).

[4]Johnson, *Toward a Patriarchal Republic*, 73; Richard Malcolm Johnston and William Hand Browne, *Life of Alexander H. Stephens* (Philadelphia: J. B. Lippincott, 1883) 378. Johnson notes that "town counties gave secessionist candidates the overwhelming majority of 69 percent of their votes" while in rural areas "a 53 percent majority opposed secession" (Johnson, *Toward a Patriarchal Republic*, 73).

their nonslaveholding neighbors, roughly two-thirds of whom owned no slaves at all. It was mainly the planters, defined as those slaveholders owning at least twenty slaves, who benefited significantly from an economic system dominated by cotton and slavery. Ownership of twenty slaves was roughly the level at which slaveholders could afford to hire an overseer to manage the plantation and its slave labor force. Planters and their families made up less than 3 percent of Georgia's total population.[5]

Planter wealth rested largely on cotton production, which by 1860 had become the nation's leading export, accounting for nearly half the total value. Southern cotton output amounted to twice that of the rest of the world combined. Little wonder that the South came to be called the Cotton Kingdom.

The rise of King Cotton had been relatively recent. In 1791 the South produced just five thousand bales. Slaveholders devoted little of their labor force to cotton because it took too long to separate the seeds from the fibers by hand. Then came the cotton engine, commonly called a "gin" for short, which did the job mechanically and much more quickly. The gin's impact on cotton production was dramatic. By 1801 the output was up to one hundred thousand bales. In 1833 it was ten times that amount at 1,099,500. And in 1859, production had ballooned to 5,868,000 bales. Georgia's yield was 780,750 bales that year, accounting for more than 15 percent of the total. Only Alabama and Mississippi produced more cotton.[6] That production reflected the good prices cotton growers were getting for their crop. High prices encouraged producers to buy up as much good cotton land as they could, most of it in the Black Belt region, a broad swath of cotton land with a heavy slave population running from the Savannah River across central Georgia to the Chattahoochee and down into the state's southwestern quadrant. What money did not go into land went mostly into slaves to work it.

Much less of Georgia's investment capital went toward industrialization, a trend reflected in the state's overwhelmingly rural population. In

---

[5]U.S. Census, 1860.

[6]Christopher C. Meyers and David Williams, *Georgia: A Brief History* (Macon, GA: Mercer University Press, 2012) 76.

1860, less than 10 percent of Georgia's people lived in towns of a thousand or more. Savannah was Georgia's largest commercial and industrial center, with a population of more than twenty-two thousand. It manufactured goods worth almost $2 million annually and was Georgia's major port city. Augusta, Macon, and Columbus, each with about half Savannah's population, produced more than $1 million of goods a piece. Atlanta, with nearly ten thousand residents, produced about half that amount. But as a rapidly growing rail hub, Atlanta had one of the largest iron plants in the South, with a capacity to roll out eighteen thousand tons of rail a year. Georgia had twelve hundred miles of track, mostly connecting the cotton lands of central and southwestern Georgia to the coastal ports of Savannah and Brunswick. There were lines linking Georgia to South Carolina, Tennessee, and Alabama as well.[7]

Whether it was trade, manufacturing, or transportation, much of Georgia's economic activity was directly or indirectly driven by cotton. Towns depended on the plantations and served the needs of planters. Local cotton fed textile mills that were beginning to spring up in the state. Workers at train depots and river docks loaded cotton. Wagoners, steamer crews, and railroad workers hauled cotton. Carpenters and masons built cotton warehouses. Merchants and manufacturers sold their goods to townspeople and plantations. Cotton brokers, for an average 2.5 percent commission, provided planters with access to the textile mills of the North and Europe.

The cotton market's profitability ensured the dependence of so many people on cotton. Cotton prices rose steadily throughout the 1850s, reaching more than twelve cents a pound toward the end of the decade. With cotton leading the nation's exports, it is little wonder that so many planters thought of cotton as "king" and themselves as something of an aristocracy. One visitor to Georgia's Cotton Belt vividly described the planters' obsession with cotton: "People live in cotton houses and ride in cotton carriages. They buy cotton, sell cotton, think cotton, eat cotton, drink cotton, and dream cotton. They marry cotton wives, and unto them are born cotton children. In enumerating the charms of a fair widow, they begin by saying she makes so many

[7]U.S. Census, 1860.

bales of cotton." Cotton was, as this writer put it, "the great staple, sum and substance" of life for Georgia planters.[8]

Although cotton brought great wealth to Georgia, that wealth was concentrated in the hands of a very few. Only the planters traveled in "cotton carriages." The ox cart was much more common. Horses and mules were too expensive for most people. Personal transportation was only one reflection of what had by 1860 become a fairly rigid socioeconomic system headed by planters, along with a few industrialists and financiers. At the bottom were poor whites and slaves.

Little more than a third of Georgia whites were slaveholders. Planters constituted a much smaller group. In 1860, in the South as a whole, planters and their families made up about 2.5 percent of the white population. That figure was slightly higher for Georgia at 5.7 percent, or about thirty-four thousand people in planter families. But planter holdings in land and slaves represented a much greater percentage of the state's wealth. There were 6,363 heads of slaveholding households who owned at least twenty slaves, placing the planters at only 15.5 percent of the state's total slaveholders. Yet these few people held more than half of Georgia's slaves. Most of the planters, 5,049 of them, owned between 20 and 49 slaves; 1,102 held from 50 to 99. Only 212 planters owned more than 100 slaves. Of those, 181 owned from 100 to 199; 23 had between 200 and 299. Eight held between 300 and 500. The John Butler estate in McIntosh County headed the list at 505 slaves.[9]

For sheer ostentation, big planters were hard to beat. The most affluent modeled themselves after the landed gentry of Britain. Some, like the Shacklefords of Early County, were renowned for the extravagance they displayed at every opportunity. One overnight guest at "The Pines," as the Shackleford plantation was called, arrived by horseback at dusk and was "ushered to a room where a body servant prepared his bath and laid out fresh linen. Downstairs, candles and an open fire illuminated a

---

[8]Lynn Willoughby, *Fair to Middlin': The Antebellum Cotton Trade of the Apalachicola/Chattahoochee River Valley* (Tuscaloosa: University of Alabama Press, 1993) 13.

[9]U.S. Census, 1860.

large room with French windows opening onto a veranda. There were comfortable chairs, tables for reading by lamplight, a secretary for writing, a piano piled high with music. A dinner table laid with the finest silver, china and crystal." At "The Refuge" on the Flint River near Bainbridge, the Munnerlyns lived and entertained in similar high fashion at their "lovely mansion set in an English garden." Mrs. Munnerlyn was referred to by friends and family as "the Empress."[10]

Most planters did not live in such lavish surroundings as the Shacklefords and Munnerlyns. They generally owned homes of eight to ten rooms made of clapboard planks, usually painted with whitewash. Some, preferring the comforts and conveniences of town life, did not even reside on their plantations. Most were educated, but they often lacked the social and cultural refinement usually associated in popular media with the planter class. The great majority, especially the smaller planters, viewed themselves mainly as businessmen whose wealth and status happened to confer upon them a degree of social prestige.

On the next rung down Georgia's social ladder stood a comfortably well-to-do class of prosperous slaveholding farmers owning between five and nineteen slaves. These slaveholders and their families totaled about ninety thousand people, nearly a sixth of Georgia's white population of 591,550, or a little less than one-tenth the total of 1,057,248 by 1860 census figures. Their primary cash crop was cotton, but many also raised livestock and grew oats and corn for market. They lived in moderate homes of five or six rooms and were better fed, clothed, and educated than lesser farmers and poor whites.

Roughly 257,000 Georgia residents, nearly half the white population, made up a wide-ranging middle class of landholding farm families. Many of these folk, about ninety-five thousand, were members of small slaveholding households, owning one to four slaves. The other 162,000 belonged to families owning no slaves at all.

---

[10]Maxine Turner, *Navy Gray: A Story of the Confederate Navy on the Chattahoochee and Apalachicola Rivers* (Tuscaloosa: University of Alabama Press, 1988) 15.

Middling farmers generally lived in homes of two to four rooms made of unpainted planks or squared, rough-hewn logs. Few were formally educated. Many were functionally illiterate. They usually grew some form of cash crop, but much of their acreage was devoted to subsistence farming. This was especially true for nonslaveholders. Many depended more on small herds of free roaming (or open range) livestock than produce, particularly in the mountains of northern Georgia and the pine barrens of Georgia's south-central and southeast regions.

Whatever the family's economic focus, their main concern was having enough food on the table from day to day. For most nonslaveholders, cotton did not figure prominently in that effort. With few hands to work their land, cotton was a luxury they could not afford. It was unlikely that they ever would. There was only so much good farmland to go around, and by the 1840s most of it was already owned by planters and more affluent slaveholders. Land prices were so high that their chances of moving into the planter class or even reaching the ranks of the comfortably well-off were not good, especially among smaller landholders.

These small farmers were sometimes only marginally better off than landless or near-landless poor whites, often called "white trash" by planters and more prosperous slaveholders. Poor whites made up more than a quarter of Georgia's white population. They included nearly fifty thousand urban laborers and their families, whom one observer described as "in such a condition that, if temporarily thrown out of employment, great numbers of them are at once reduced to a state of destitution, and are dependent upon credit or charity for their daily food."[11]

Almost 150,000 poor whites belonged to rural families of tenant farmers and sharecroppers who did not own enough land to support their families or owned no land at all. Some hired themselves out to planters and other large landholders for meager wages. Others worked for a share of the crop. They lived mostly in plank or log structures with one or two rooms and plank or dirt floors. What vegetables they had were grown in small gardens. There were no vegetables at all out of season. What meat

[11]Frederick Law Olmsted, *The Cotton Kingdom*, 2 vols. (New York: Mason Brothers, 1861–1862) 1:273–74.

there was usually came from hunting or fishing. Illiteracy rates ran high among these people. Charged rent on the land they worked, the tools they used, and the seeds they planted, all at prices set by landowners, they commonly ended the year in debt and trapped in a state of economic enthrallment.

Wilie Poortwood, an indebted tenant farmer in Taliaferro County, tried to work a deal with Alexander H. Stephens to get a little land for himself and his family. His letter to Stephens reflects the condition of many a Georgia tenant. "Dear Sir," Poortwood began. "I am determ to try to make som outher Way of trying to liv and aultho I hav not pade you all that I owe yet I intend to doo it[.] [I] cannot make eney thing[;] I am on a nother man['s] land and cannot hav eney thing only what he ses and Whare he ses." Poortwood asked that Stephens sell to him on credit "a little cornor of land the som of thirty achors [acres].... I Will pay you for it and I Want you to hold it until I pay you for it." Poortwood closed his letter with a heartfelt plea that revealed what a bit of land could mean for someone who had none: "I Want a home for my Wife and little babys to have that no one can run them a Way from and to hav land enuff to bery them on Without intruding on mine or her connections in eney Way."[12]

Opportunities for upward mobility had been much better for men such as Poortwood only a generation before. Land prices in the late eighteenth and early nineteenth centuries had been relatively low as Creek and Cherokee Indians were forced out. Land speculators bought much of the land, but small farmers had little trouble getting loans to purchase land and sometimes slaves. Cotton prices were on the rise, and there was every expectation that loans could be repaid. Farmers who had enough good land might even hope to become affluent slaveholders or even planters.

A severe economic depression, the Panic of 1837, put an end to the dreams of many thousands of hopeful, hard-working farmers. Cotton

[12]J. William Harris, *Plain Folk and Gentry in a Slave Society: White Liberty and Black Slavery in Augusta's Hinterlands* (Middletown, CT: Wesleyan University Press, 1985) 79.

prices fell dramatically. Indebted farmers found it difficult or impossible to keep up with loan payments. Their land and slaves were repossessed and sold at auction, usually to better-established slaveholders. Some small farmers were able to keep a few acres and eke out a living as lesser landholders, but many lost everything and fell into tenancy and sharecropping. When the cotton market finally recovered, planters and affluent slaveholders held nearly all of Georgia's better lands. Most other farmers found opportunities increasingly limited.

The gap between rich and poor continued to grow through the 1840s, not only in Georgia but throughout the South. Larger slaveholders bought up more and more land, forcing a rapid rise in land prices. This made it nearly impossible for small farmers to increase their holdings or for tenant farmers to buy any land at all. Wealth in terms of slaveholding was also becoming concentrated in fewer hands. During the last decade of the antebellum period, the proportion of slaveholders in the white population dropped by 20 percent. Georgia historian Numan Bartley notes that "only the division of land and slaves of deceased planters among heirs prevented social mobility from being considerably more closed than it was." By 1860 at least 25 percent of farmers in Georgia and the South were tenants, and more were joining their landless ranks every day.[13]

Slavery without Submission

At the bottom of the social ladder in a caste of their own, separate and distinct from the white class structure, were black folk. Numbering 465,698 by 1860, they made up nearly 45 percent of Georgia's population. Almost all were enslaved. The census listed only 3,500 as "free colored." Yet these few people were not entirely free. They could not vote, testify against whites in court, or even hold property in their own names. Their property was held by a white person designated as their "guardian." To support the slaveholder argument that blacks could not take care of

[13]James Oakes, *Slavery and Freedom: An Interpretation of the Old South* (New York: Vintage, 1990) 118; Numan V. Bartley, *The Creation of Modern Georgia* (Athens: University of Georgia Press, 1990) 21.

themselves, free blacks, even those who held no property, were required by state law to have a white guardian.

Restrictions on blacks held as slaves were even tighter. In addition to those imposed on free blacks, Georgia's slave code dictated that no enslaved person could carry a gun, travel without a pass, or learn to read or write. Slave marriages had no legal standing, and slave gatherings, even for religious services, were forbidden without a white person present.

Such restrictions were born both of fear and a need for control. Despite slaveholder claims to the contrary, the "wise master," as historian Kenneth Stampp put it,

> did not take seriously the belief that Negroes were natural-born slaves. He knew better. He knew that Negroes freshly imported from Africa had to be broken into bondage; that each succeeding generation had to be carefully trained. This was no easy task, for the bondsman rarely submitted willingly. Moreover, he rarely submitted completely. In most cases there was no end to the need for control—at least not until old age reduced the slave to a condition of helplessness.[14]

Slave resistance took a variety of forms, ranging from work slowdowns and feigning illness or ignorance to engaging in sabotage. Sometimes slaves escaped to the North. Other times, torn between the burdens of slavery and the love of family, they stayed closer to home. "Slaves run away and hid out in caves," remembered former Georgia slave Benny Dillard. Other slaves "would slip 'em something to eat at night." Willis Earle ran off to the woods and dug a cave where he spent the next fifteen years.[15]

---

[14]Kenneth M. Stampp, *The Peculiar Institution: Slavery in the Ante-Bellum South* (New York: Vintage, 1956) 144.

[15]Benny Dillard, *Georgia Narratives*, part 1, 292, in *Slave Narratives: A Folk History of Slavery in the United States from Interviews with Former Slaves*, Manuscript Division, Library of Congress, Washington, DC; Tom Hawkins, *Georgia Narratives*, part 2, 131. The *Slave Narratives* collection is available online at the website *Born in Slavery: Slave Narratives from the Federal Writers' Project 1936–1938*. Interviews are collected into numbered volumes by state. In this book, I

When escape was unworkable and desperation too great, slaves occasionally resorted to suicide. In 1856, a Cuthbert slave belonging to Lizzie McWilliams took her own life by swallowing strychnine. Sometimes slaves took their owners' lives as well. A Georgia slave named Lash, after some "rough handling," murdered his owner. When the overseer on a Muscogee County plantation began beating an enslaved girl, one of the older slaves grabbed an axe and killed him. A Thomas County slave named Wade also attacked his overseer with an axe, yelling that the white man should have thought twice before "fooling with any of his little Georgia Negroes [a probable reference to rape]."[16]

More often, slaves were on the receiving end of violence. They were defined as property both by slave-state courts and finally, in the *Dred Scott* case of 1857, by the United States Supreme Court. As personal property, slaves were subject to the absolute authority of their owners and to whatever controls they chose to employ. According to the Georgia Supreme Court, "subordination can only be maintained by the right to give moderate correction—a right similar to that which exists in the father over his children." The definition of "moderate correction" was left entirely to the owner. "Should death ensue by accident, while this slave is thus receiving moderate correction," recalled one observer, "the constitution of Georgia kindly denominates the offence justifiable homicide."[17]

---

cite interviews by state, with the former slave's name appearing first. A more complete collection, which includes interviews from additional sources, is published as George P. Rawick et al., comp., *The American Slave: A Composite Autobiography*, series 1 and 2, and supplement, series 1 (Westport, CT: Greenwood Press, 1972 and 1977).

[16]*Cuthbert Reporter*, 23 September 1856; Jennie Kendricks, *Georgia Narratives*, part 3, 5; Charlie Pye, *Georgia Narratives*, part 3, 186; Susan E. O'Donovan, *Becoming Free in the Cotton South* (Cambridge, MA: Harvard University Press, 2007) 45.

[17]Thomas R. R. Cobb, comp., *Reports of Cases in Law and Equity, Argued and Determined in the Supreme Court of the State of Georgia* (Athens, GA: Reynolds and Bro., 1855) 15:542; James Stuart, *Three Years in North America* (Edinburgh, Scotland: Robert Cadell, 1833) 2:164. Stuart refers to that section of Georgia's constitution that purported to give slaves protection from murder "unless such death should happen by accident in giving such slave moderate cor-

Because slaves had monetary value, death as a direct result of discipline was rare. Even mutilation might decrease the slave's resale value or ability to work. The objective of physical abuse was to inflict pain without doing permanent damage. Owners and overseers frequently administered beatings in the "buck" or "rolling jim" positions. In each case the slave was stripped naked and bound tight. Rias Body, a former Harris County slave, remembered the buck as "making the Negro squat, running a stout stick under his bended knee, and then tying his hands firmly to the stick—between the knees. Then the lash was laid on his back parts."[18]

Another common method of abuse was to string slaves up by their thumbs with only their toes touching the ground and whip them. Former slave Rhodus Walton of Stewart County noted that the victim might be "further tormented by having his wounds 'doctored' with salt and red pepper." Walton belonged to an owner "whose favorite form of punishment was to take a man (or woman) to the edge of the plantation where a rail fence was located. His head was then placed between two rails so that escape was impossible and he was whipped until the overseer was exhausted. This was an almost daily occurrence, administered on the slightest provocation." After recalling the variety of tortures inflicted on slaves, W.B. Allen, a Columbus freedman, told an interviewer in the 1930s, "Sir, you can never know what some slaves endured."[19]

Little wonder that slaveholders lived in constant fear of slave resistance and rebellion. To mitigate that fear, they frequently hired poor whites to ride on slave patrols, designed to guard against everything from unlawful travel to insurrection. Slaves found away from their owners' lands without written permission could be given up to twenty lashes or more on the spot.

---

rection." See Christopher C. Meyers, ed., *Empire State of the South: Georgia History in Documents and Essays* (Macon, GA: Mercer University Press, 2008) 56.

[18]Rias Body in Rawick, *American Slave*, supplement, series 1, vol. 3, part 1, 71.

[19]Rhodus Walton, *Georgia Narratives*, part 4, 124; W. B. Allen in Rawick, *American Slave*, supplement, series 1, vol. 3, part 1, 6–7.

Along with the constant threat of physical abuse, slaveholders found that an effective means of intimidating slaves was by threatening their families. Any enslaved person might be pushed to the point of disregard for his or her own safety and attempt to fight back or escape. But when owners threatened loved ones, slaves were more likely to hold their anger in check. Slave marriages were, therefore, encouraged even though slaveholders refused to recognized such unions by law. To do so would establish a state-sanctioned bond between members of slave families, implicitly infringing on the "property" rights of the owner—specifically the right to deal with and dispose of property as the owner saw fit.

To further stress their authority, slaveholders used a variety of means to drive home the point that even within the slave family, the owner was still in control. Some personally presided over marriage ceremonies. Others did not even allow parents to name their own children. They reserved that right for themselves.

In naming the children of enslaved women, many owners were actually exercising their own parental rights. For a planter to have any number of rape victims among his slaves was fairly common. Some slaveholders viewed sexual abuse as another method of exercising physical and psychological dominance over the slave community. Others engaged in rape simply because they viewed slaves as property to be used at the owner's pleasure. Whatever the motive, slaves of light complexion were present on nearly every plantation. Fanny Kemble, wife of Georgia planter Pierce Butler, wrote that "Mr. [Butler] (and many others) speaks as if there were a natural repugnance in all whites to any alliance with the black race; and yet it is notorious, that almost every Southern planter has a family more or less numerous of illegitimate colored children."[20]

Some enslaved people used their light skin to good advantage. In 1833, the *Columbus Enquirer* ran an advertisement offering twenty dollars for the return of an escapee named Mabin. The ad described him as "a bright mulatto, with grey eyes—hair straight and sandy.... He will pass

---

[20]Frances Anne Kemble, *Journal of a Residence on a Georgian Plantation in 1838–1839* (New York: Harper and Brothers, 1863) 14–15.

for a white man where he is not known."[21] Ellen Craft, daughter of an enslaved mother and her white owner, also used her light complexion to escape. In December 1848, she and her husband, William, set out from Bibb County. Ellen, in male attire, posing as a slaveholder and William as her slave, boarded a train in Macon and headed for Savannah. Traveling several legs of their long and dangerous journey by steamship and railroad, they reached freedom in Philadelphia on Christmas morning.[22]

No matter how children were sired, owners usually encouraged slave women to have as many as possible. More children meant more field hands, but they also gave the owner an effective tool of control. Not only did slaves fear punishment for family members, there was also the concern that they might be sold off at any time. As the slaves well knew, any threat to sell a spouse or child was no idle one. One witness to the proceedings at a Georgia slave market wrote that "such separations as these are quite common, and appear to be no more thought of, by those who enforce them, than the separation of a calf from its brute parent."[23]

A Georgia woman recalled slave traders driving groups of children to market "the same as they would a herd of cattle."[24] Slaves constantly feared having their families put through such misery. They were also less likely to run away since that too would mean permanent separation from their loved ones. Of the tens of thousands of slaves who escaped bondage in the early nineteenth century, most were young, unmarried, and childless.

Still, as the slave population increased, so did resistance. In 1846, whites in the Augusta region frankly admitted that slaves and slaveholders were "beginning to look upon each other as natural enemies." They admitted also that physical abuse designed to control slaves was "harsh yet inefficient." In 1851, planters complained that the liberties slaves

---

[21] *Columbus Enquirer*, 9 February 1833.

[22] For the full account see William Craft, *Running a Thousand Miles for Freedom; or, The Escape of William and Ellen Craft from Slavery* (London: William Tweedie, 1860).

[23] James Silk Buckingham, *The Slave States of America*, 2 vols. (London: Fisher, Son, and Co., 1842) 1:249.

[24] Jennie Kendricks, *Georgia Narratives*, part 3, 1.

Ellen and William Craft, an enslaved couple from Bibb County, devised an escape plan in which Ellen would pose as a man and William as her slave. In December 1848, they boarded a train in Macon and headed for Savannah. Traveling several legs of their journey by steam ship and railroad, they reached Philadelphia on Christmas morning. That Ellen's light complexion allowed her to "pass" for white says much about the generations of sexual oppression enslaved women experienced. Image from William Still, *The Underground Rail Road* (1872).

were taking for themselves, especially in the forms of trade and travel, were endangering "the peace and tranquility of the country." Georgia's *Albany Patriot* called for more slave patrols and warned that whites "should always have their arms ready for service."[25]

Who Dares Advocate Slavery

Despite rising slave resistance, slavery remained firmly established in Georgia and the South. But it had not always been so. Lutherans at Ebenezer had argued strongly against slavery in Georgia's early colonial days. So had Presbyterians at Darien. "Freedom must be as dear to them as to us," they wrote in 1739 as they petitioned Georgia's Trustees to maintain the colony's ban on slavery. One passage was especially prophetic: "It is shocking to human Nature, that any Race of Mankind and their Posterity should be sentence'd to perpetual Slavery; nor in Justice can we think otherwise of it, than that they are thrown amongst us to be our Scourge one Day or other for our Sins."[26] In June 1863, black Union soldiers, many of them formerly enslaved along the Georgia-Carolina coast, ransacked Darien and set the town afire.

In the Western world generally, the eighteenth century was a time of rising arguments against slavery. The scientific revolution had shown that there were natural laws governing the physical universe. Some reasoned that there must also be natural laws governing human interactions, leading to concepts of natural rights. John Wesley, founder of Methodism and a resident of colonial Savannah, was sure of it. "Liberty," he insisted, "is the right of every human creature, as soon as he breaths the vital air; and no human law can deprive him of that right which he derives from the law of nature."[27]

Thomas Jefferson wrote in the Declaration of Independence, a document signed by three representatives from Georgia, that "life, liber-

---

[25]Harris, *Plain Folk and Gentry*, 60, 53; *Albany Patriot*, 25 December 1856.

[26]Meyers and Williams, *Georgia*, 27–28; "Darien Antislavery Petition," in Meyers, *Empire State*, 111–12.

[27]*The Works of the Reverend John Wesley*, vol. 6 (New York: Emory and Waugh, 1831) 292.

ty, and the pursuit of happiness" were unalienable rights endowed by the Creator. If true, was not slavery a violation of natural rights? The question troubled many slaveholders of Jefferson's generation, schooled as so many were in Enlightenment philosophy. Most, Jefferson included, were unwilling to give up slavery, but they did see it as an unnatural institution destined to end one day. Some, like George Washington, freed their slaves in their wills. Others freed their slaves long before their deaths. Georgia court records from the late eighteenth century are filled with manumission documents freeing hundreds of slaves.

Aside from the moral issues involved, most Americans of the Revolutionary generation tended to view slavery as an economic dead end. The institution thrived only in the tobacco fields of the Chesapeake region and the coastal rice country of the Carolinas and Georgia. As the nation expanded, slavery would become proportionally less important to the nation's economy and would eventually die a natural death. But in the 1790s, the cotton gin began to change all that. It soon became the vehicle by which slavery was carried westward across the Deep South. Not surprisingly, slaveholder attitudes changed with slavery's increasing profitability.

That change did not occur overnight. Antislavery sentiment in the South remained vigorous well into the nineteenth century. Several antislavery societies were active in the South, Georgia included. Robert Finley, president of the University of Georgia, was a founder of the American Colonization Society in 1816. Although some whites supported the society simply as a means of ridding the country of free blacks, many early members such as Finley had genuine antislavery motives. Even those who considered slavery at best a necessary evil were open about saying so. During debate on the Compromise of 1820, Congressman Robert Reid of Georgia, though he did not call for its immediate abolition, admitted that slavery was "an unnatural state; a dark cloud which obscures half the luster of our free institutions." The next year a leading state newspaper, the *Georgia Journal* of Milledgeville, wrote, "There is not a single editor in these States who dares advocate slavery as a principle."[28]

[28]Marion Mills Miller, ed., *Great Debates in American History*, vol. 4 (New

But this was also the era of Indian removal, which completed the transition in slaveholder attitudes begun a generation earlier by the cotton gin. Not only did they have the technology and labor force with which to make cotton king, they now had the land on which to do it. Slaveholders began to view slavery not as a temporary evil but as a permanent good for both slaveholder and slave. Attitudes of the Founding Fathers toward slavery, they now argued, were erroneous. Benjamin Hill, one of Georgia's leading planter-politicians, wrote that "in our early history the Southern statesmen were anti-slavery in feeling.... Washington, Jefferson, Madison, Randolph, and many of that day who never studied the argument of the cotton gin, nor heard the eloquent productions of the great Mississippi Valley. Now our people not only see the justice of slavery, but its providence too."[29]

Slaveholders' new attitudes were prompted by tremendous profits, but they also ran counter to prevailing trends. Just a quarter of whites in the South, and none outside the South, owned slaves. Aside from the United States, chattel slavery survived only in Brazil, Cuba, Puerto Rico, Dutch Guiana, and parts of Africa. How were Southern slaveholders to guarantee the survival of slavery in a country where most voters owned no slaves and in a world in which slavery was a dying institution?

In the 1830s slaveholders launched a campaign designed to educate their fellow citizens, and the world, on the virtues of slavery. In the first place, the world could not do without Southern cotton. Textile mills in Britain and the North depended too much upon it. Benjamin Hill insisted that "the world can never give up slavery until it is ready to give up clothing." Besides, slaveholders argued, people of African descent were content in slavery because it was, as Alexander Stephens put it, their "natural and normal condition." Dr. Samuel Cartwright of New Orleans claimed that their supposed child-like state of mind was due to a disease he called *dysesthesia*, defined as "defective hematosis, or atmospherization

York: Current Literature Publishing, 1913) 80; Ulrich Bonnell Phillips, *Georgia and State Rights* (Washington, DC: Government Printing Office, 1902) 159.

[29]Benjamin H. Hill, Jr., *Senator Benjamin H. Hill of Georgia* (Atlanta: H. C. Hudgins, 1891) 244.

of the blood, conjoined with a deficiency of cerebral matter in the cranium." If slaves were content in slavery, why did so many try to escape? Cartwright had an answer for that too—*drapetomania*, or simply an insane urge to run away.[30]

There was also the biblical defense. How could slavery be an evil institution when the Hebrew patriarchs had owned slaves? Was not slavery the result of Noah's curse on his younger son Ham and all his descendants, whose dark complexion was assumed to have been a result of the curse? The Reverend Patrick Hues Mell, a Georgia minister and later president of the Southern Baptist Convention, stressed that point in an 1844 tract titled *Slavery: A Treatise, Showing that Slavery is Neither a Moral, Political, nor Social Evil*: "From Ham were descended the nations…that now constitute the African or negro race. Their inheritance, according to prophecy, has and will *continue to be* slavery." Mell took it literally as gospel that "God, by the mouth of Noah…instituted slavery…it cannot be an immorality."[31]

Mell's fellow Georgian, Augustus Baldwin Longstreet, a leading apologist for slavery among Methodists, agreed with Mell's conclusion. In 1845, Longstreet authored what became a leading proslavery tract, *Letters on the Epistle of Paul to Philemon: Or, the Connection of Apostolical Christianity with Slavery*. Paul's instruction that servants should be obedient to their masters made clear that, in Longstreet's view, "there is no sin in holding slaves" and that "there is no *moral evil* in slavery." For those whose conscience might be bothered by slavery, Samuel Cassels of Georgia gave them comfort in an 1853 issue of the *Southern Presbyterian Review*: "God is our only true moral governor…. Our subjection, then, is

---

[30]Hill, *Senator Benjamin H. Hill*, 244; Henry Cleveland, *Alexander H. Stephens in Public and Private* (Philadelphia: National Publishing, 1866) 721; Samuel Cartwright, "Diseases and Peculiarities of the Negro Race," *De Bow's Review* (July 1851) 66; Stephen Jay Gould, *The Mismeasure of Man* (New York: Norton, 1981) 70–71.

[31]David Salter Williams, *From Mounds to Megachurches: Georgia's Religious Heritage* (Athens: University of Georgia Press, 2008) 58.

not to be a subjection of conscience…but a subjection to God." For Cassels, God clearly condoned slavery.[32]

Throughout the South, clergymen emerged as some of the most influential allies of slaveholders in defending slavery. Those ministers who held that Scripture must be taken literally had been for some time disturbed by a strong opposing trend in Christianity. Science had shown that the Bible contained many factual errors and omissions. By the eighteenth century, clergymen and laity alike began to argue that the Bible should be taken symbolically, not literally. But what might that mean for its treatment of slavery? Was that to be taken symbolically as well? Could Paul have been using the relationship of servant to master as a metaphor for the relationship of humanity to God? No, such symbolism would not do. If the Scriptures were to be used effectively as a defense of slavery, they had to be taken literally, and not just in part but in whole. As the slaveholding South changed its attitude toward slavery in the early nineteenth century, it became increasingly tied to a literalist view of the Bible.

Perhaps the most effective tactic slaveholders and their allies adopted was that of encouraging racist fears. By playing on such fears, slavery's defenders hoped to make all whites feel they had a stake in preserving the slave system whether they owned slaves or not. Poor whites were told to think of what slavery's end might mean for them. No longer would they be in a position of social superiority to blacks, or anyone else for that matter. A writer in the *Columbus Times* stated the case clearly: "It is African slavery that makes every white man in some sense a lord.… Here the division is between white free men and black slaves, and every white is, and feels that he is a MAN."[33] Without slavery, the rights guaranteed to whites might have to be shared with blacks, including perhaps the right to vote.

---

[32]Williams, *From Mounds to Megachurches*, 56, 59.
[33]Harris, *Plain Folk and Gentry*, 75.

For the Benefit of Slavery and Slaveholders

Though all adult white males could vote, there was little for them to decide in a practical sense. Then as now, any successful bid for high political office depended on money as well as votes, and planters were the South's wealthiest men. In Southern state politics, both major parties, Whig and Democrat, centered as much on personalities as issues, and both represented slaveholding interests. Whigs tended to attract larger slaveholders, whose wealth and wide investments gave them broader national concerns. Smaller slaveholders generally dominated the Democratic Party, which often differed with the Whigs on issues such as banking, infrastructure, and how best to use state revenues. But party leaders were firmly united when it came to slavery. Promoting racist fear, that traditional staple of Georgia politics, was always an area in which the candidates tried to out-do each other.

The influence of slaveholder wealth in politics was not lost on plain folk. As one farmer observed, the slaveholder, or slaveholder-backed candidate, "used money whenever he could. This fact usually elected him." The effect was easy to see. In the Georgia General Assembly's 1849–1850 session, though only a third of voters owned slaves, 80 percent of legislators were slaveholders. More than half owned at least ten slaves.[34]

Legislative apportionment had much to do with slaveholder dominance in the Assembly. Each county elected one state senator and up to four representatives, depending on population. But blacks, who could not vote, were counted as three-fifths of a person in awarding state representation, meaning that voters in high slaveholding counties carried much greater weight in the General Assembly. For example, coastal Glynn County and upcountry Campbell County (later part of Douglas and Fulton counties) had roughly the same total population and two representatives each. But Glynn's population was only 17 percent white while Campbell's was 84 percent white. The result was that Glynn's roughly

[34]Oakes, *Slavery and Freedom*, 80; Peter Wallenstein, *From Slave South to New South: Public Policy in Nineteenth-Century Georgia* (Chapel Hill: University of North Carolina Press, 1987) 21.

250 eligible voters had the same representation in the Assembly as Campbell's approximately 850.[35]

The poll tax gave slaveholders an edge as well. Though poll taxes might sometimes keep poor men from voting, they could also be used as a tool of political control, especially in an era when there was no secret ballot.[36] Landless whites and even small farmers who depended on larger landholders either for credit or employment or both could usually be counted on for political support, often with the wealthy landholder paying required poll taxes. It was also common for planters to hold expensive barbeques at election time, when good food and fine liquor proved politically influential. A similar tactic called "penning" was used in urban centers. Campaign workers rounded up men off the streets, got them drunk, and marched them to the polls. The party with the largest "pen" usually won. In his extensive study of antebellum Georgia politics, Donald DeBats concluded that "far from encouraging citizen participation in the party system, the leaders of both parties discouraged grassroots politics.... Beyond the simple casting of a ballot, the role of the citizen in the party system was passive by design."[37]

Slaveholder control of Southern state politics was near absolute. One Southerner observed that although most voters owned no slaves, "they have never yet had any part or lot in framing the laws under which they live. There is no legislation except for the benefit of slavery and slaveholders."[38] While it is true that some nonslaveholders held high public office, they were nearly always backed directly or indirectly by slaveholders. Some even married into planter families. During the 1850s,

---

[35]Wallenstein, *From Slave South to New South*, 20.

[36]The secret, or "Australian," ballot was not in common use in the United States until near the end of the nineteenth century.

[37]Diffee William Standard, *Columbus, Georgia, in the Confederacy: The Social and Industrial Life of the Chattahoochee River Port* (New York: William-Frederick Press, 1954) 20–21; Donald A. DeBats, *Elites and Masses: Political Structure, Communication, and Behavior in Ante-Bellum Georgia* (New York: Garland, 1990) 425.

[38]Hinton Rowan Helper, *The Impending Crisis of the South* (New York: Burdick Brothers, 1857) 42.

though the proportion of slaveholders in the general population was falling, their number in Southern state legislatures was on the rise. It seemed that slaveholder dominance of the South was secure and that slavery as an institution was secure as well. But even as slaveholders consolidated political control, cracks appeared at the base of the South's social pyramid. As wealth became concentrated in fewer hands and opportunities for economic advancement were increasingly closed to plain folk, those cracks began to grow.

Antislavery sentiment never completely died out among Southern whites. Some continued to view slavery as a moral evil. Others opposed it on economic grounds. Still others opposed slavery simply because they were too poor to own slaves. One source of unease was the general attitude of slaveholders, especially planters, toward plain folk. As one farmer put it, "Slaveholders always acted as if they were of a better class and there was always an unpleasant feeling between slaveholders and those working themselves." In a private letter to a friend, one planter wrote of his slaves as "baboons on two legs gifted with speech." "Of our own race," he continued, "among the low bred and uneducated class...not one in ten is in morale a whit superior to a negro."[39]

Most planters tried to keep such opinions concealed lest the hypocrisy of their "white equality" rhetoric be exposed. Occasionally, though, suggestions of planter arrogance slipped into print. In his 1854 defense of slavery, *Sociology for the South, or The Failure of Free Society*, George Fitzhugh not only insisted that slavery was "the best form of society yet devised for the masses" but also "that slavery, *black or white*, was right and necessary."[40] Could poor whites eventually be enslaved if the slave system continued indefinitely? Some were beginning to think so.

Whatever their reasons, discomfort with the slave regime was on the rise among nonslaveholding whites of the late antebellum era. Some were even willing to speak out or act. In 1849, a Georgia carpenter openly declared his opposition to slavery. Competition with slave labor, he be-

[39]Oakes, *Slavery and Freedom*, 80; Harris, *Plain Folk and Gentry*, 67.

[40]George Fitzhugh, *Sociology for the South, or The Failure of Free Society* (Richmond: A. Morris, 1854) 162–63, 225.

lieved, kept his wages low. In 1859, one poor Hancock County laborer confided to an acquaintance that if it came to a war over slavery, he was going to "black himself" and fight to end it. Without slavery, perhaps he could get better wages. That same year, a farmer in Taliaferro County was convicted of hiding a runaway slave for three months. William Allen of Troup County wrote fake passes for slaves. So did a white man in Greene County, who also taught slaves "to write and cipher."[41]

The most outspoken critic of slavery among Southern whites was Hinton Rowan Helper. Born to a nonslaveholding farm family in North Carolina, Helper wrote in his *Impending Crisis of the South* that the "lords of the lash are not only absolute masters of the blacks…but they are also the oracles and arbiters of all non-slaveholding whites, whose freedom is merely nominal, and whose unparalleled illiteracy and degradation is purposely and fiendishly perpetuated."[42] Slavery, Helper pointed out, benefitted few except slaveholders. Its very existence, funneling investment capital not into building factories but into purchasing more land and slaves, kept most white Southerners in poverty. Slavery made the South little more than a colony of the North, providing cheap raw materials and buying back more expensive manufactured goods.

Helper was hardly alone in pointing out the economic drawbacks of slavery. A British traveler, James Stirling, who passed through Georgia in the 1850s, wondered why the Southern states lagged behind in "development and prosperity." The main reason, he concluded, was slavery. "When Southern statesmen count up the gains of slavery," warned Stirling, "let them not forget also to count its cost. They may depend upon it, there is a heavy 'per contra' to the profits of niggerdom." There were Georgians as well who recognized slavery's retarding influence. Roswell King, Jr., an overseer on the Butler plantations near Darien, confided to Pierce Butler's wife Fanny: "I hate slavery with all my heart; I consider it

[41]William L. Barney, *The Road to Secession: A New Perspective on the Old South* (New York: Praeger, 1972) 48; Harris, *Plain Folk and Gentry*, 64, 91.

[42]Helper, *Impending Crisis*, 43.

an absolute curse wherever it exists. It will keep those states where it does exist fifty years behind the others in improvement and prosperity."[43]

Not only did slavery hinder economic growth, but the concentration of cotton and tobacco on its most productive lands forced the South to import foodstuffs. Georgia's comptroller-general lamented that with regard to food, the state was "every day becoming more dependent upon those 'not of us.'" Livestock production was declining. The corn crop was stagnant. In just ten years the oat crop had dropped by almost three-fourths, a decline not offset by a two-fold increase in the state's relatively meager wheat production. One newspaper editor complained about huge shipments of high-priced produce from the Midwest coming up the Chattahoochee River. He blamed planters who, fonder of growing cotton, neglected food crops. Georgia editors generally urged planters to grow more corn and less cotton. Such pleas accomplished little. By 1860 Georgia was importing at least half a million bushels of corn annually.[44]

Rising discontent within the Cotton Kingdom, of little concern to slaveholders a generation earlier, was by the 1850s causing many to panic. One planter asked, "If the poor whites realized that slavery kept them poor, would they not vote it down?" How could support for slavery continue indefinitely among plain folk if they owned no slaves and had no prospects of ever owning any? Some proslavery men suggested state laws mandating that each white family be given at least one slave. Others recommended a slave for every white person. One editor suggested re-opening the slave trade from Africa to bring the price of slaves down.[45]

---

[43]James Stirling, *Letters from the Slave States* (London: Parker and Son, 1857) 204; Kemble, *Journal*, 77.

[44]Willard Range, *A Century of Georgia Agriculture: 1850–1950* (Athens: University of Georgia Press, 1954) 28; Meyers, *Empire State*, 99; *Eufaula (AL) Express*, 1 September 1860; Joseph Paul Johnson, "Southwest Georgia: A Case Study in Confederate Agriculture" (master's thesis, University of Georgia, 1992) 57. See also George B. Crawford, "Cotton, Land, and Sustenance: Toward the Limits of Abundance in Late Antebellum Georgia," *Georgia Historical Quarterly* 72 (1988): 215–47.

[45]William L. Barney, *The Secessionist Impulse: Alabama and Mississippi in 1860* (Princeton, NJ: Princeton University Press, 1974) 42; Harris, *Plain Folk*

Slavery advocates realized that the problem of maintaining support for the institution lay not only with the expense of slaves but the lack of land as well. There was only so much fertile farmland to go around, and affluent slaveholders already had most of it. To keep nonslaveholders supporting slavery, there had to be some future expectation of slaves and cheap land. That meant expanding slavery outside the South. It also meant making slave escapes more difficult. At least one hundred thousand escaped bondage in the late antebellum era, and the rate of escape was increasing every year.[46] Clearly, the future security of slavery lay in expanding slave territory. To slaveholders, it was apparent that slavery must expand or die. The issue of slavery's expansion would dominate national politics for more than a decade and finally lead to the Civil War.

The Georgia Platform and Slavery's Expansion

The issue of slavery's expansion, though pressed with new urgency, was not new at all. Shortly after Georgia's founding in 1732, its governing Trustees excluded a number of evils from their colony, slavery included. It did not remain outlawed for long. There was too much money to be made. Pressure in favor of slavery from Savannah merchants and Carolina rice planters was constant, and slaves were smuggled into the colony despite the Trustees' ban. They finally gave in and permitted slavery in 1750. Within twenty years, nearly half of Georgia's people were enslaved.

At the same time, slavery as a viable economic institution was dying in the North. But in the South, the cotton gin gave slavery an economic vitality that grew in strength with each new slave state added to the Union. Congress reached a temporary settlement in 1820 with the Missouri Compromise. Missouri was admitted to the Union as a slave state and

---

and Gentry, 40; *Eufaula (AL) Express*, 16 December 1858. The foreign slave trade had been closed in 1808 with the backing of slaveholders, who saw it as an opportunity to inflate the value of their slaves.

[46]William H. Siebert, *The Underground Railroad from Slavery to Freedom* (New York: Macmillan, 1898) 341, 346; John Hope Franklin and Loren Schweninger, "The Quest for Freedom: Runaway Slaves and the Plantation South," in Gabor Boritt and Scott Hancock, eds., *Slavery, Resistance, Freedom* (New York: Oxford University Press, 2007) 37–38.

Maine as a free state, thus preserving the balance of free and slave states in the Senate. More significantly, a line extending from the southern border of Missouri to the Rocky Mountains (then the western limit of the United States) established a boundary between slavery and freedom. All future states created north of the line would be free. Those south of the line would be slave.

When the United States took upper Mexico in 1848 after a nearly two-year war of conquest, slavery was again thrust onto the nation's political stage. Mexico had abolished slavery almost two decades earlier. Would it now be reintroduced in the new U.S. territories? Many, like Alexander Stephens, who as a Whig congressman had opposed war with Mexico, hoped the divisive issue of slavery's expansion could be avoided. But in 1849 California requested admission to the Union as a free state and Congress was forced to act. The next year California entered the Union under the Compromise of 1850, giving the free states a two-seat advantage in the Senate. As compensation, slaveholders received a Fugitive Slave Act, which mandated the return of slaves who escaped to the North. As for the remaining former territories of old Mexico, "popular sovereignty" would prevail. Voters in the region would make the decision on slavery themselves whenever their numbers became sufficient to apply for statehood.

Reaction to the Compromise of 1850 in politically active circles was mixed throughout the South. Slaveholders liked the Fugitive Slave Act but were concerned that a loss of parity in the Senate would weaken their position in national politics. Using opposition to the Compromise as a pretext, secessionists organized movements in Mississippi, Alabama, Georgia, and South Carolina. In all but South Carolina, Union supporters quickly organized to oppose them. Georgia held a popular vote for delegates to a convention to consider the state's future in the Union, a vote that supporters of the Compromise won by a forty-six thousand to twenty-four thousand margin. Even most of those who opposed the Compromise of 1850 still supported keeping Georgia in the Union. Of the 264 delegates, 240 were Unionists.[47]

[47]Meyers and Williams, *Georgia*, 102.

When Georgia's delegates met in December 1850, all but nineteen voted to accept the Compromise. Even so, they warned that slavery took priority over the Union. In what came to be called the Georgia Platform, the convention declared Georgia ready to secede if Congress restricted the domestic slave trade, refused to admit new slave states to the Union, or interfered with slavery in the territories. The convention further insisted that Georgia's adherence to the Union depended on "faithful execution" of the Fugitive Slave Act. Alabama and Mississippi supported the Georgia Platform, and newspapers across the country credited it with having saved the Union. But given its message of slavery over union, the ambiguities of popular sovereignty, and the ambivalence of Northern law enforcement toward taking time to hunt down fugitive slaves, the Georgia Platform was little more than a formula for the Union's impending collapse.[48]

Popular sovereignty's inherent complications became clear soon after Congress passed the Kansas-Nebraska Act in 1854. In exchange for Southern congressional votes favoring organization of these territories through which Northerners hoped to build the first transcontinental railroad, both Kansas and Nebraska were opened to the possibility of slavery under popular sovereignty. It seemed to many Northern congressmen a small price to pay. They were certain that there was no real danger of either territory becoming a slave state since their geography was not suited to large-scale cotton or tobacco production.

But Kansas was just west of Missouri, a slave state, and Northern voters feared the consequences. Even so, few white Northerners called themselves abolitionists. Most were by no means opposed to slavery where it existed since it kept most blacks confined to the South. Racism played a large role in forming white attitudes in the North, as did economic fears. Laborers worried that freedom for slaves would enable them to migrate north and compete for already low-paying jobs. Northern industrialists and financiers worried that the end of slavery would mean the end of cheap cotton, which fueled textile manufacturing, the North's leading industry. What most Northerners opposed, and all they opposed,

---

[48]Ibid., 102–103; DeBats, *Elites and Masses*, 100–101.

was slavery's extension into the western territories, lands they wanted for themselves.

In the wake of Kansas-Nebraska, most Northern Whigs and many Democrats joined with Free Soilers and a smattering of abolitionists to form the Republican Party, dedicated to free land and free states in the West. They ran their first presidential candidate in 1856, John C. Frémont, calling for "free men, free land, and Frémont!" Ironically, Frémont was a Southerner, born in Savannah and raised in Charleston, who as a young man had joined the army and made a name for himself as military governor of California and one of the state's first two senators. Fear of Frémont's antislavery leanings led most Southern Whigs to join with Democrats to keep Frémont out of the White House. As a result, Pennsylvania Democrat James Buchanan, who was no threat to slavery's expansion, won the presidency that year.

Still, the Kansas question remained unsettled. Free-State activists rushed to get settlers into Kansas. Proslavery men did the same. Few slaveholders themselves made the move, but they did finance proslavery expeditions to Kansas. They provided wagons, horses, oxen, and, most importantly, land. In exchange, the new arrivals were expected to vote for a proslavery state constitution. Though most settlers were Free-Staters and should have carried the election easily, thousands of "border ruffians" crossed over from Missouri to vote illegally, giving the proslavery faction a victory. In response, Free-State Kansas men formed their own territorial government and drew up a constitution excluding both slavery and free blacks. The controversy turned violent when a proslavery raid on the town of Lawrence left one man dead. An antislavery band led by John Brown, later of Harpers Ferry fame, retaliated by killing five proslavery men along Pottawatomie Creek. By the end of 1856, more than two hundred settlers on both sides were dead.

The Supreme Court tried to settle the issue in 1857 with the *Dred Scott* case, calling enslaved blacks property that could be taken anywhere in the United States, including the territories. This decision pushed more Northerners into the Republican camp, practically insuring that the next president would be a Republican. Fearing the result, leading Southern secessionists, called Fire-Eaters for their extremist rhetoric, tried to build support for their cause by labeling all Northerners, Republicans in particular, as violent abolitionists bent on fomenting slave rebellion. The Fire-Eaters got a boost in October 1859 when John Brown led an attempt to seize the federal arsenal at Harpers Ferry, Virginia, and arm the state's slaves. His effort failed, and a state court sentenced Brown to hang for treason. But Fire-Eaters now had an incident they could use to portray Northerners as abolition-supporting, rebellion-promoting "Black Republicans."

Fire-eating Georgia papers carried news that the Harpers Ferry raiders were blacks organized and led by "blatant 'freedom shriekers.'" Some warned that it was the start of a general slave uprising designed "for the extermination of the southern whites." Several fires in November 1859 were blamed on rebellious blacks and secret abolitionists. One fire destroyed an estimated $6,000 of corn, fodder, and cotton on a Muscogee County plantation. Another fire swept through a gin house near Columbus, taking more than two dozen cotton bales with it. One Columbus editor called it "Kansas work in Georgia."[49]

The Insurrectionary Tendency of Things

This volatile atmosphere of panic and paranoia formed the backdrop of 1860's presidential campaign. The Democrats split over slavery in the territories, with Northerners holding to popular sovereignty and Southerners clinging to the *Dred Scott* decision. Most Southern delegates left the convention and formed their own party, the Southern Rights Party, and nominated John Breckinridge of Kentucky. The remaining Democrats nominated Stephen Douglas of Illinois, who selected former Georgia governor Herschel V. Johnson as his vice-presidential running mate. Southern Whigs who refused to join the Southern Rights Party formed their own Constitutional Union Party, stressing adherence to the Union, and nominated John Bell of Tennessee. Republicans, united on everything but a candidate, finally settled on a dark horse from Illinois named Abraham Lincoln.

As nearly everyone expected, Lincoln carried the November election. In Georgia, Breckinridge polled slightly more than Bell, with

[49] *Columbus Sun*, 19 and 21 October, 5, 15, and 16 November 1859.

Douglas running a distant third despite the efforts of Herschel V. Johnson and his old friend Alexander Stephens, an active supporter of the Douglas/Johnson ticket. Lincoln's name was not even on the ballot.

Nevertheless, Lincoln had strong support in Georgia and the South, albeit mostly among enslaved people who could not vote. They attended so many public campaign rallies in Columbus that whites became alarmed by their "unusual interest in politics, and the result of the Presidential election." Another Georgia editor complained that "every political speech that has been delivered in Macon has attracted a number of negroes, who, without entering the Hall, have managed to linger around and hear what the orators say."[50]

What blacks repeatedly heard was that Lincoln, despite his repeated promises to the contrary, intended to end slavery. Prompted by such talk, whatever Lincoln's intentions, blacks intended to begin the process themselves. Rebellions and rumors of rebellions pervaded Georgia and the South that summer and into the fall. Some whites blamed "black Republicans" or "abolition emissaries" for stirring up trouble. Others tried to ignore the upsurge of black resistance, uncomfortable with admitting how widespread it was. "We dislike to allude to the evidences of the insurrectionary tendency of things," wrote a Georgia newspaper in August. Nevertheless, the editor felt compelled to mention a conspiracy in Floyd County.[51]

Earlier that summer, a black man in Oglethorpe County was burned to death for murder. A Talbot County slave was hanged in July for the same crime. Fires that broke out across Georgia with unusual frequency were blamed on "negro incendiaries." "Whence come all the fires of which we read?" asked one editor. "Is it at all probable that so many in so short a time are the result of accident?"[52]

---

[50]*Columbus Sun*, 27 September 1860; *Macon Telegraph*, 8 September 1860.

[51]*Augusta Dispatch* in *The (Boston, MA) Liberator*, 24 August 1860; Clarence L. Mohr, *On the Threshold of Freedom: Masters and Slaves in Civil War Georgia* (Athens: University of Georgia Press, 1986) 28–29.

[52]Mohr, *On the Threshold of Freedom*, 31–32, 22–24.

At 2:30 in the early morning before the November election, much of Fort Gaines was consumed by fire. After town residents brought the flames under control, two blacks were shot in the act of trying to re-start the blaze. There was also an election-day slave rebellion in Crawford County, just west of Macon. More than twenty slaves, perhaps many more, went on a rampage, intending to kill their owner "and all the white folks." Well-armed whites quickly subdued the freedom fighters and prepared to mete out summary justice. "Some will be burnt," wrote a Milledgeville paper, "others hung." A few days later, Habersham County slaves conspired with a free black man to murder a local white woman and throw her body down a well. In Savannah, a free black man was caught heading a movement to have local slaves rise in rebellion on the day of Lincoln's inauguration.[53]

With Lincoln poised to enter the White House and fearing the result, secessionists pushed hard for disunion. Most slaveholders would now almost certainly support such a move. If middling folk and poor whites could be made to see Lincoln as a John Brown writ large, they too might support withdrawal from the Union. Secessionist leaders had to act quickly before Lincoln took office the next March or they might never have another chance.

The secessionists' rush was driven largely by their fear that plain folk were not behind the movement, at least not enough of them to assure its success. Hard feelings among plain folk toward slaveholders had been growing for some time. Some secessionists warned that if Southerners remained in the Union, there might soon be "an Abolition party in the South, of Southern men." One frankly admitted, "I mistrust our own people more than I fear all of the efforts of the Abolitionists." Georgia slaveholder J. Henly Smith was sure that with Republicans in control at the federal level, they would "have adherents and supporters all over the

---

[53]*Columbus Enquirer*, 13 November 1860; *Macon Telegraph*, 9 November 1860; *Milledgeville Southern Recorder* in *Augusta Chronicle and Sentinel*, 10 November 1860; Executive Committee, *Twenty-Eighth Annual Report of the American Anti-Slavery Society* (New York: American Anti-Slavery Society, 1861) 213; Mohr, *On the Threshold of Freedom*, 43.

South—in every state.... The nonslaveholders will very generally adhere to the new party, and slavery will be crushed out forever."[54]

And what of the slaves? Though slaveholders argued otherwise, they knew that slavery did not come naturally to people of African descent. They escaped, they resisted, they had to be controlled through fear and violence. They wanted to be set free and they believed, even if mistakenly, that Lincoln intended to do just that. How could they think otherwise with secessionists insisting that Lincoln's goal was to free them? One freedman remembered that slaves had "hoped and prayed he would be elected. They wanted to be free and have a chance."[55] How much more difficult would controlling slaves be with Lincoln in the White House and expectations for freedom running so high?

More than Northern abolitionists, more than Lincoln himself, slaveholders feared the South's nonslaveholding whites and enslaved blacks. Control of both groups had always been hard; by the 1850s it was getting harder. A Lincoln presidency could only make it more difficult. Most slaveholders feared that if they remained in the Union, their "peculiar institution" would sooner or later be doomed. Outside the Union, controlling plain folk and slaves might be easier and slavery might be safer. Other factors certainly helped fuel the crisis. Overestimation of abolitionist strength in the North, the issue of slavery's expansion, and personal political ambitions all played their part. But slaveholders' fear of their fellow Southerners was a primary, though publicly unacknowledged, force driving secession.

Even so, slaveholders were far from united behind the movement. Most were certainly disturbed by Lincoln's promise to keep slavery out of the territories, but wealthier and more conservative "old money" planters tended to view secession as a greater risk than remaining in the Union. With a larger stake in preserving the status quo, they tended to be more cautious than lesser slaveholders. Should withdrawal from the Union lead

[54]*Charleston (SC) Mercury*, 11 October 1860; Barney, *Secessionist Impulse*, 48–49; Harris, *Plain Folk and Gentry*, 91.

[55]Louis Meadows in Rawick, *American Slave*, supplement, series 1, vol. 1, 255.

to civil war, success would depend on widespread support from plain folk. Many planters wondered how long that support could last. Secession might hasten the end of slavery rather than preserve it.

Secession found its most enthusiastic support among the more numerous "new money" planters and lesser slaveholders. Their leaders were young up-and-coming lawyer/politicians trying to carve out a niche for themselves at the expense of the older establishment. They more readily took up secession's banner and, to the dismay of more conservative colleagues, carried it high through the late 1850s. Such divisions among Georgia's most prominent politicians set the stage for intense controversy in the days after Lincoln's election.

Nothing but Divisions among Our People

In late November 1860, the General Assembly passed, and Governor Joseph E. Brown signed, a bill calling for the election of delegates from each county to a secession convention. Though the slaveholder-dominated Assembly had forced the question, it was hardly unanimous for secession. In what one contemporary called "a large meeting of the Members of the General Assembly" at the Georgia capitol building in Milledgeville, twenty-two assemblymen were appointed to draft a resolution urging Georgia voters not to support secessionists in the upcoming election. Secession would, they insisted, lead to "nothing but divisions among our people, confusion among the slaveholding States, strife around our firesides, and ultimate defeat to every movement for the effective redress of our grievances."[56]

Benjamin Hill, a member of the committee, reminded Georgians that Lincoln was no threat to slavery where it existed. Lincoln himself had repeatedly made that point during the presidential campaign. "The wisest policy," Hill maintained, "is to demand the unconditional observance of the Constitution." Hill knew that Southerners were divided on secession, and that a divided South would likely lose should war with the North come. The South would fall and slavery with it. Alexander Stephens shared Hill's fears, saying not only that secession "puts us in the

[56] *Thomaston Upson Pilot*, 22 December 1860.

wrong" but that, should secession occur, the South would soon be at war with itself.[57]

Secessionist leaders brushed such fears aside and urged voters to fear Lincoln instead. Columbus attorney Henry Lewis Benning, a former member of the Georgia Supreme Court, warned that Lincoln's election meant not only the end of slavery but, even worse, equal rights for blacks. All who resisted, he said, would be hanged by Lincoln and his "Black Republican party." The only way to avoid the "horrors of abolition" was to withdraw from the Union immediately. "Why hesitate?" Benning asked. "The question is between life and death."[58]

Though he knew better, Governor Brown repeated the secessionist drumbeat that Lincoln intended to destroy not only slavery but also white supremacy. He encouraged plain folk to believe that both their pocketbook and their pride would suffer for it. Under a Lincoln administration, blacks would, in Brown's words, "come into competition with their labor, associate with them and their children as equals—be allowed to testify in our courts against them—sit on juries with them, march to the ballot box by their sides, and participate in the choice of their rulers—claim social equality with them—and ask the hands of their children in marriage."[59] Men such as Brown hoped that playing on racist fears would swing the popular vote their way.

Robert Toombs, one of Georgia's U.S. senators and a leading secessionist, expressed his determination to see Georgia out of the Union whether Georgia voters supported secession or not. "We demand at your hands the sword," Toombs blustered. "If you will not give it to us, we will take it." Responding to Toombs's threat, an antisecession editor in west Georgia's Upson County wrote, "Let him take it, and, by way of doing his country a great service, let him run about six inches of it into his left breast."[60]

---

[57]Freehling and Simpson, *Secession Debated*, 99, 55, 68.

[58]Ibid., 115–45.

[59]*Milledgeville Southern Recorder*, 13 November 1860.

[60]Freehling and Simpson, *Secession Debated*, 46; *Thomaston Upson Pilot*, 8 December 1860.

Among Georgians generally, it was clear that immediate secession was not a forgone conclusion. Those who opposed it, calling themselves Cooperationists, held rallies throughout the state urging calm among their fellow Georgians.[61] Citizens at a "large meeting" in Crawfordville resolved that "we do not consider the election of Lincoln... as sufficient cause for Disunion or Secession." A mass meeting in Walker County expressed the same sentiment: "We are not of the opinion that the election of any man in accordance with the prescribed forms of the Constitution is sufficient cause to disrupt the ties which binds us to the Union." Rallies in Fayette, Gordon, Chattooga, Talbot, Meriwether and other Georgia counties stated the same.[62]

Harris County's newspaper editor declared that "we are a Union loving people here, and will never forsake the old 'Star Spangled Banner.'" To stress his point, he printed the names of 175 local men, all pledging themselves to "preserve the honor and rights of the South *in the Union*." In Stewart County, a similarly "large number of citizens" attended an antisecession meeting. Union sentiment was so strong in neighboring Randolph County that secessionists were sure the tide was turning against them. In a letter to Howell Cobb, former Georgia congressman and one of the state's leading secessionists, they asked, "Where are all our speakers? We have done what little we can here but there is great need for missionaries in every part of the State." They urged Cobb to take a short tour through southwest Georgia to bolster the secession cause. By late December, it appeared that antisecessionists might win the

---

[61]Those who ran opposing secession adopted the label "Cooperationists" to indicate their insistence that any Southern response to Lincoln's election should be made in cooperation with the slave states as a whole. Their position is generally viewed as an attempt to thwart secession by garnering the undecided vote. For further discussion of the Cooperationist position in Georgia see Johnson, *Toward a Patriarchal Republic*, 26.

[62]*Augusta Chronicle and Sentinel*, 27 and 30 November 1860; *Thomaston Upson Pilot*, 10 November and 8 December 1860; *Rome Tri-Weekly Courier*, 1 January 1861; *Griffin American Union*, 14 December 1860; *Augusta Chronicle and Sentinel*, 11 December 1860.

Governor Joseph E. Brown, knowing that white Georgians were divided, appealed to racist fears in pushing for secession. Brown warned that under Lincoln's administration, blacks would "associate with them and their children as equals, be allowed to testify in our courts against them, sit on juries with them, march to the ballot box by their sides, and participate in the choice of their rulers, claim social equality with them, and ask the hands of their children in marriage."
Image from I. W. Avery, *History of the State of Georgia* (1881).

day. "All the masses of the people," wrote one Georgian from Milledgeville, "are for the Union."[63]

Although most Georgians seemed to opposed secession, some feared that their delegates might ignore the people's will. Shortly before the convention met, one furious voter accused Singleton Sisk, a Missionary Baptist preacher, of cheating Habersham County out of its vote. In an open letter to Athens's *Southern Watchman*, he told how this "janus-faced expounder of the Gospel" had declared himself a Union man to gain the nomination of Habersham's antisecessionists. With their backing, he was elected to the convention. "After the election," the writer complained, "we find that he had privately promised the Secessionists that he would, in the Convention, support Secession." Sisk indeed betrayed his constituents and voted for secession. Similar betrayals occurred among the delegates from at least twenty-eight other Georgia counties. In Campbell County, the fraud was so transparent that some who went to the polls declined to vote.[64]

A disgusted Thomaston editor also suspected fraud, complaining bitterly that Georgia voters would not have a truly representative state convention.

> We do not believe that the character of the sentiments of a majority of the Convention will reflect the wishes of a majority of the people. The delegates appear to be nominated by mass conventions assembled at the county sites; and it is plain that not half of the citizens attend these

---

[63]*Harris County Enterprise*, 29 November 1860; "Co-Operation Meeting of the Citizens of Stewart County," 18 December 1860, broadside in Stewart County folder, file 2, Georgia Department of Archives and History; Ulrich Bonnell Phillips, ed., *Correspondence of Robert Toombs, Alexander H. Stephens, and Howell Cobb* (Washington, DC: Government Printing Office, 1913) 524; *Milledgeville Southern Recorder* in *Augusta Chronicle and Sentinel*, 18 December 1860.

[64]*Athens Southern Watchman*, 16 January 1861; Michael P. Johnson, "A New Look at the Popular Vote for Delegates to the Georgia Secession Convention," *Georgia Historical Quarterly* 56 (1972): 259–75; James Eason file, Campbell County, GA, Southern Claims Commission, National Archives, Washington, DC.

> nominations. But few men living ten or fifteen miles from [the] county site go to such conventions...and as it is an admitted fact that the secession sentiment is much stronger in and around the cities than it is among the common people in the country, it is easy to see the advantage the "immediate secessionist" will have in the Convention.[65]

The day balloting took place, January 2, 1861, was cold and stormy, making it difficult for poorer folk in isolated areas to get to the polls. Alexander Stephens estimated that the foul weather cost antisecessionists at least ten thousand votes. Still the vote was very close. Historian Michael Johnson, whose detailed study of secession in Georgia remains the standard, concluded that opponents of immediate secession likely won by just over a thousand votes: 42,744 to 41,717.[66]

When the secession convention met in late January at Milledgeville, Eugenius A. Nisbet proposed a prosecession resolution to gauge the delegates' views. With several delegates voting against their constituents' wishes, the measure passed by a 166 to 130 margin. The next day, with more delegates switching sides, the convention approved a secession ordinance 208 to 89. Even Benjamin Hill and Alexander Stephens, as a show of unity, supported secession on the final ballot. It could hardly have been surprising that the convention ultimately went for secession despite the popular vote. While little more than a third of Georgia's electorate owned slaves, 87 percent of the convention delegates were slaveholders. Setting down its justifications for secession, the convention listed first and foremost "causes of complaint...in reference to the subject of African slavery."[67]

The remaining antisecession delegates urged that the ordinance be presented to Georgia's voters for ratification. Newspaper editorials throughout the state did the same. An Augusta editor reminded the del-

---

[65] *Thomaston Upson Pilot*, 22 December 1860.

[66] Johnston and Browne, *Life of Alexander H. Stephens*, 378; Johnson, *Toward a Patriarchal Republic*, 63.

[67] *Journal of the Public and Secret Proceedings of the Convention of the People of Georgia, 1861* (Milledgeville, GA: Boughton, Nisbet, and Barnes, 1861) 15–23, 31–40; *Augusta Chronicle and Sentinel*, 1 February 1861.

egates that previous conventions recommending alterations to the state constitution had sought the people's approval by ratification as a matter of course. But the convention's secessionist majority refused. Georgia left the Union without submitting the ordinance to a direct popular vote.[68]

The same was true in other Deep South states. Although nearly all the slave states held elections for delegates to secession conventions, the Upper South, comprising more than half the slave states, overwhelmingly rejected secession. Only in the Deep South did conventions issue secession ordinances, and none were presented to the electorate for an up or down vote.[69] In February, Georgia representatives, along with others from South Carolina, Florida, Alabama, Mississippi, Louisiana, and Texas, met in Montgomery, Alabama, to form the Confederate States of America.

Alexander Stephens, the Confederacy's newly appointed vice president, resolved to make the best of secession. For Stephens, as for other reluctant secessionists, that meant choosing to see the Confederacy as a means of maintaining both slavery and white supremacy. Stephens celebrated the Confederacy's formation by announcing to an excited crowd in Savannah that "its foundations are laid, its corner-stone rests upon the

[68]Allen D. Candler, comp., *The Confederate Records of Georgia*, 6 vols. (Atlanta: State Printing Office, 1909–1911) 1:349–61; *Augusta Chronicle and Sentinel*, 3 January 1861; *Columbus Sun*, 23 January 1861; *Milledgeville Southern Recorder* in *Thomasville Southern Enterprise*, 30 January 1861.

[69]In his seminal study of the secession crisis, David Potter looked at the vote on secession throughout the South and concluded, "At no time during the winter of 1860–1861 was secession desired by a majority of the people of the slave states.... Furthermore, secession was not basically desired even by a majority in the lower South, and the secessionists succeeded less because of the intrinsic popularity of their program than because of the extreme skill with which they utilized an emergency psychology, the promptness with which they invoked unilateral action by individual states, and the firmness with which they refused to submit the question of secession to popular referenda." See David Potter, *Lincoln and His Party in the Secession Crisis* (New Haven, CT: Yale University Press, 1942) 208. Potter's conclusions are supported by Paul Escott's more recent study, *After Secession: Jefferson Davis and the Failure of Confederate Nationalism* (Baton Rouge: Louisiana State University Press, 1978) 23–28, 42–44.

great truth, that the negro is not equal to the white man; that slavery—subordination to the superior race—is his natural and normal condition. This, our new government, is the first, in the history of the world, based upon this great physical, philosophical, and moral truth."[70]

News of Georgia's secession, and then the Confederacy's formation, touched off wild celebrations across the state. Savannah's Chatham Artillery fired a one hundred-gun salute. In Macon, the Jackson Artillery bested that with 119 guns. Cannons were fired in Milledgeville and Athens too. Bands played, skyrockets burst, and local militias marched out on parade. Bonfires lit Georgia's night skies and church bells pealed into the early morning hours. Joseph Clisby, editor of the *Macon Telegraph*, rejoiced that Georgia would now devote "her vast talents, influence and power, to the work of building up an independent Southern Confederacy—a white man's Republic."[71]

Not everyone saw secession as a cause for celebration. After he cast a grudging vote for Georgia's secession on the final ballot, Benjamin Hill went alone to his room and "grieved for the Union." Herschel V. Johnson later recalled that "I never felt so sad before." As bells rang out in Milledgeville during the secession "jubilee," Judge Garnett Andrews, a long-time Union man, said of the merrymakers: "Poor fools, they may ring their bells now, but they will wring their hands—yes, and their hearts, too, before they are done with it!"[72]

D. J. Brandon, observing events from south Georgia, wrote to President Jefferson Davis warning that should war come, the Confederacy would be "reduced to abject want" and that among the casualties of that war would be "the very institution of slavery for which we have been laboring." Joseph Campbell of Morgan County agreed. In a letter to Vice President Stephens, he expressed fear that "the very thing designed to be

[70]Cleveland, *Alexander H. Stephens*, 721.

[71]T. Conn Bryan, *Confederate Georgia* (Athens: University of Georgia Press, 1953) 10; Richard W. Iobst, *Civil War Macon: The History of a Confederate City* (Macon, GA: Mercer University Press, 1999) 53.

[72]Bryan, *Confederate Georgia*, 11; Eliza Frances Andrews, *The War-Time Journal of a Georgia Girl* (New York: D. Appleton, 1908) 309.

Despite initially opposing secession, Alexander Stephens, as Confederate vice president, defended the new regime as a bulwark of white supremacy. He told an enthusiastic Savannah crowd in March 1861, "Its foundations are laid, its cornerstone rests upon the great truth, that the negro is not equal to the white man; that slavery—subordination to the superior race—is his natural and normal condition. This, our new government, is the first, in the history of the world, based upon this great physical, philosophical, and moral truth." Image courtesy of the Library of Congress.

secured by cesesion will by the same be destroied, African Slavery." "And," he added, "if much evil comes upon the South, we are to blame for it."[73]

The question of whether secession would result in civil war had been on the minds of Georgians for months. One Decatur County man was so sure war would come that he referred to secessionists as "the suicides." Others were just as certain that they were nothing of the sort. The *Albany Patriot* assured its readers that Lincoln would never dare invade the South. "In all honesty we can say to our readers, be not afraid. We will insure the life of every southern man from being killed in war by the abolitionists for a postage stamp." Even if Lincoln's armies came, one Georgia editor boldly proclaimed, Southern men would drive them back "as easily as the whirlwind sweeps the chaff before it." Mary Nisbet of Macon told a friend that if war broke out, there would be "but one or two battles, and then peace we shall have on our own terms."[74]

The editor of Thomaston's *Upson Pilot* was not sure what the outcome of secession would be, but he was glad his county had gone against it. "If the demon of civil war is to ravage our fields only to fertilize them with blood—we know our Upson Delegates will be able, at the last dread account, to stand up with clean hands and pure hearts and exclaim through no chattering teeth from coward consciences:—'Thou canst not say we did it!'"[75]

Uncertainty about the result of secession reflected general ambivalence toward a military option. Common folk, North and South, were by no means eager for war. But Lincoln was under intense pressure from his financial backers and other Northern industrialists to keep the cotton states in the Union—by compromise if possible, by force if necessary. How else could they guarantee continued access to Southern markets and cheap cotton? The *Boston Herald* warned that an independent South

---

[73]O'Donovan, *Becoming Free in the Cotton South*, 64; Harris, *Plain Folk and Gentry*, 39.

[74]*Augusta Chronicle and Sentinel*, 2 October 1860; *Albany Patriot*, 15 November 1860; Harris, *Plain Folk and Gentry*, 140; Iobst, *Civil War Macon*, 52.

[75]*Thomaston Upson Pilot*, 2 February 1861.

A Savannah crowd celebrating the prospect of secession in Johnson Square. A bonfire and fireworks light the evening sky. Such scenes occurred in all of Georgia's major cities. Still, there were many who despaired at the Union's collapse. As bells rang out in the state capital of Milledgeville during a secession "jubilee," Judge Garnett Andrews said of the merrymakers, "Poor fools, they may ring their bells now, but they will wring their hands—yes, and their hearts, too, before they are done with it!" Image courtesy of the Library of Congress.

would "impose a heavy tax upon the manufactures of the North, and an export tax upon the cotton used by Northern manufacturers. In this way, she would seek to cripple the North."[76] The South might even impose a cotton embargo on the North and destroy its leading industry.

Trying to draw the Deep South back into the Union, in late February Congress passed and sent to the states for ratification a proposed thirteenth amendment to the Constitution, the Corwin Amendment, which would have guaranteed slavery to the slave states forever. In his first inaugural address on March 4, 1861, Lincoln expressed his firm support for the amendment, saying "I have no objection to its being made express and irrevocable." At the same time, he announced his intention to preserve the Union by force if secessionists ignored the offer.[77]

Even so, Lincoln had little means of carrying out his threat, so weak was support for war among Northerners. Most seemed glad to be free of their political ties to the obstinate slaveholders. They certainly had no desire to put their lives in danger trying to hold the Deep South to the Union. Many white Northerners even expressed relief when South Carolina became the first state to secede. The *Indianapolis Daily Journal* rejoiced: "We are well rid of South Carolina, if we are only wise enough to count it a riddance, and nothing worse.... If all the South follows her, let it."[78]

In January, four thousand people attended a mass meeting in Philadelphia carrying banners reading "NO CIVIL WAR." Horace Greeley,

---

[76]*Boston (MA) Herald*, 12 November 1860.

[77]Roy P. Basler, Marion Dolores Pratt, and Lloyd A. Dunlap, eds., *The Collected Works of Abraham Lincoln*, 9 vols. (New Brunswick, NJ: Rutgers University Press, 1953–55) 4:270. The amendment was presented by Thomas Corwin, a Republican congressman from Ohio. It reads, "No amendment shall be made to the Constitution which will authorize or give to Congress the power to abolish or interfere, within any State, with the domestic institutions thereof, including that of persons held to labor or service by the laws of said State." The phrases "domestic institutions" and "persons held to labor or service" were direct references to slavery and slaves. See *Congressional Globe*, 36th Congress, 2nd session (1861) 1284.

[78]*Indianapolis (IN) Daily Journal*, 22 December 1860.

editor of the *New York Tribune* and one of Lincoln's staunchest supporters in his bid for the presidency, wrote that if Southerners were "satisfied that they can do better out of the Union than in it, we insist on letting them go in peace." It seemed clear to the *New York Herald*'s editor that "the citizens of the free States are not prepared for civil war."[79]

How could Lincoln get the men he needed to make war on the South with such attitudes so prevalent in the North? A military draft was out of the question. Popular reaction might destroy the Republican Party. Lincoln considered issuing a call for troops, but that too was risky. Not only would it be likely to drive more slave states out of the Union but it would also be politically unpopular in the free states. What Lincoln needed was an incident to stir Northern patriotism and draw volunteers to the army. He needed the Confederacy to fire on the United States flag.

On April 12 , the Confederacy obliged by bombarding the federal garrison at Fort Sumter in Charleston's harbor, providing Lincoln with the incident he had sought when he threatened to resupply the facility. Georgia's Robert Toombs, now Confederate secretary of state, had advised against the attack, telling Jefferson Davis "it is suicide, murder, and will lose us every friend at the North. You will wantonly strike a hornet's nest...and legions, now quiet, will swarm out and sting us to death. It is unnecessary; it puts us in the wrong; it is fatal."[80] Davis ignored the advice and ordered Fort Sumter shelled, touching off the most devastating armed conflict in American history.

---

[79]*Philadelphia (PA) Inquirer*, 17 January 1861; Arnold M. Shankman, *The Pennsylvania Antiwar Movement, 1861–1865* (Rutherford, NJ: Fairleigh Dickinson University Press, 1980) 42; *New York Tribune*, 9 November 1860; *New York Herald*, 5 February 1861.

[80]Pleasant A. Stovall, *Robert Toombs* (New York: Cassell Publishing, 1892) 226.

Chapter 2

1861–1862: The Greatest Danger

When Confederates fired on Fort Sumter, Lincoln immediately called for volunteers to put down the rebellion. Tens of thousands responded to his call, but four more slave states—Arkansas, Tennessee, North Carolina, and Virginia—signed on with the Confederacy and sent volunteers to its service. Across the South, young men rushed to join the army in such numbers that authorities could not arm them all. Many had to provide their own weapons or secure the backing of wealthy patrons. The Miller County Wild Cats armed themselves "with every death-dealing instrument that could be procured." Each man carried a Bowie knife along with an old musket or shotgun. One elderly gentleman who had tried to talk his son out of going to war finally gave in and presented him with what was surely a prized possession—a single-barrel shotgun. "I don't want any war," the old man told his boy, "but if you will go, here's old Betsy; take her and give the Yankees hell."[1]

Ready to Shoulder Our Guns

The widespread surge of volunteering was fueled by several factors, fear of Yankee invasion among them. There was also peer pressure and a sense of adventure. Many believed that Lincoln meant to free the slaves and grant them equality. Whatever their misgivings about secession, Southern whites wanted none of that. Besides, nearly everyone was sure the war would be short and victorious. Nellie Gordon of Savannah remembered that most people "thought two or three months of soldiering would settle the matter, and that our boys would come marching home, like conquering heroes." A Troup County volunteer bragged that he was

---

[1]R. D. Chapman, *A Georgia Soldier in the Civil War, 1861–1865* (Houston, TX: n.p., 1923) 6.

One of the earliest companies to volunteer was the Clinch Rifles of Augusta. Some of its members came from slaveholding families in Richmond County. In the war's early days, it was fairly common for such men to take at least one slave with them to the front. It was also common for slaves taken so near Union lines to escape. Every slave taken with the Troup Artillery of Athens ran away. Image courtesy of the United States Army Military History Institute.

going to "whip those sons-of-bitches" and be back before breakfast. It was two years before he saw home again.[2]

Many young men sought to impress young ladies by donning a uniform. It seemed that for every soldier who left home, there was a sweetheart to see him off, showering him with kisses. Women also gave the volunteers more practical items. Throughout Georgia, they formed sewing circles, set up soldiers' aid societies, and organized farewell ceremonies. The ladies of Whitesville in Harris County presented a flag to the departing Whitesville Guards during a send-off held at the local Methodist church. Women in Randolph County did the same for the Cuthbert Rifles and said they hoped the men "would be ordered to Washington, and that they could place that flag on the Capitol first, and that Lincoln and his host could find another roost." Such scenes played out across Georgia in the weeks following Sumter. By the middle of May, Georgia had furnished more than eighteen thousand volunteers, second only to Virginia. Little wonder that the state's rail system was in chaos. According to one source, lines were clogged with trainloads of raw recruits "whose enthusiasm for the Confederate cause was equaled only by their lack of any clear conception as to the authority under which they were to serve, or of their destination."[3]

Ironically, the rush to war was heartily endorsed by leading apostles of the "Prince of Peace." Even before the state seceded, Stephen Elliot, bishop of the Episcopal Diocese of Georgia, told his clergy to delete from their prayers "President of the United States" and insert an invoca-

---

[2]Jacqueline Jones, *Saving Savannah: The City and the Civil War* (New York: Alfred A. Knopf, 2008) 129; Jerry Boykins, *Texas Narratives*, part 1, 122, in *Slave Narratives: A Folk History of Slavery in the United States from Interviews with Former Slaves*, Manuscript Division, Library of Congress, Washington, DC.

[3]Louise Calhoun Barfield, *History of Harris County, Georgia, 1827–1961* (Columbus, GA: Columbus Office Supply Co., 1961) 292; Edmund Cody Burnett, ed., "Letters of Barnett Hardeman Cody and Others, 1861–1864," *Georgia Historical Quarterly* 23 (1939): 282; *Milledgeville Southern Recorder*, 7 May 1861; Robert C. Black, "The Railroads of Georgia in the Confederate War Effort," *Journal of Southern History* 18 (1947): 517–18.

tion for the governor. In May 1861, delegates to the Southern Baptist Convention meeting in Savannah unanimously voted their support for the war. Southern Methodists, meeting in Atlanta, offered prayers to God for "brilliant victories." Georgia's Catholic clergymen urged their parishioners to pray for deliverance from the "Northern barbarians."[4]

Reverend C. W. Key of LaGrange called for the young men of his congregation to battle against the "fanatical enemy." Another Georgia cleric, in his own call to arms, declared the Confederacy to be "the last hope of Freedom and the last home of a pure Gospel." As an expression of its patriotism, Hamilton's Methodists sent thirty-three dollars to Governor Brown as a contribution to the war effort. In a reversal of the "swords into plowshares" doctrine, Methodists in LaGrange wrote Governor Brown offering to have their church bells melted down and cast into cannons.[5]

In June, Bishop Elliot concluded a sermon to Savannah's Pulaski Guards by telling the soldiers, "I send you forth with the Church's benediction.... Your cause is just.... the Lord is on your side." Church leaders were well aware that the cause was founded on slavery, and they continued to defend it just as they had before the war. Editor Samuel Boykin of the *Christian Index*, a Baptist periodical based in Macon, admitted forthrightly that "slavery is the cause of the war." And, like Elliot, Boykin was sure that slavery was a just cause. "Slavery and the South with it will live and triumph," insisted Boykin, "because it is of God." Reverend Ebenezer Warren of the First Baptist Church of Christ in Macon agreed. In January 1861, at the height of the secession crisis, Warren declared that "Christianity and Slavery are from Heaven; both are blessings to humanity; both are to be perpetuated to the end of time."[6]

---

[4]T. Conn Bryan, "The Churches in Georgia During the Civil War," *Georgia Historical Quarterly* 33 (1949): 284, 285, 287.

[5]Key to Joseph E. Brown, 23 March 1862, Governor's Incoming Correspondence, Georgia Department of Archives and History, Morrow; Bryan, "Churches in Georgia During the Civil War," 284; Charles Bedell to Brown, 19 June 1861, Governor's Incoming Correspondence.

[6]T. Conn Bryan, *Confederate Georgia* (Athens: University of Georgia Press, 1953) 231; Bruce T. Gourley, *Diverging Loyalties: Baptists in Middle Georgia*

Not all Georgians were so sure that God supported slavery or, if he did, that his support for secession necessarily followed. Even as mass volunteering and general excitement swept the state, there remained active opposition to the Confederacy. When vigilantes led by Harrison Riley threatened to seize the U.S. mint in Dahlonega and hold it for the Union, Governor Brown sent no troops to stop them. He knew sentiment in the region was largely with Riley. Union men in Pickens County flew the U.S. flag at the courthouse for weeks after secession. Randolph Mott of Columbus, a longtime Union man, was said to have kept the Stars and Stripes flying from the cupola of his home. Some called it the only place in Georgia that never left the Union.[7]

Expressing popular sentiment in northwest Georgia's Walker and Dade counties, James Aiken wrote Governor Brown in February 1861 insisting that he and his neighbors would never submit to the secession convention's decision. It had taken Georgia out of the Union not for the good of its citizens, but for "those that owns lands and Negroes!" He begged the governor to allow Georgia voters a direct referendum on secession, promising to abide by the outcome. But if Brown refused, there were 2,500 volunteers prepared to defend northwest Georgia's right to secede from the state and rejoin the Union. "If we cannot get it one way," he warned, "we know how we can get it at the point of the bayonet and the muzzle of the musket. We are just as willing as you ever seen mountain boys." Another Walker County man confirmed that there was talk of raising a company "to defend the glorious Union."[8]

---

during the Civil War (Macon, GA: Mercer University Press, 2011) 160, 19–20.

[7] *Augusta Chronicle and Sentinel*, 24 January 1861; Andrew W. Cain, *History of Lumpkin County for the First Hundred Years, 1832–1932* (Atlanta: Stein Printing, 1932) 87; I. W. Avery, *History of the State of Georgia* (New York: Brown and Derby, 1881) 186–88; Robert S. Davis, "Memoirs of a Partisan War: Sion Darnell Remembers North Georgia," *Georgia Historical Quarterly* 80 (1996): 104–105; Charles Jewett Swift, *The Last Battle of the Civil War* (Columbus, GA: Gilbert Printing, 1915) 27.

[8] Aiken to Brown, 15 February 1861, Talemon Cuyler Collection, Felix Hargrett Rare Book and Manuscript Library, University of Georgia, Athens; Constantine Wood to Brown, 11 April 1861, Governor's Incoming Corre-

From his home in the Georgia hills, John Fulton Brown wrote that "had it been left to an honest vote of the people, North Georgia, East Tennessee, and Western North Carolina, might have formed another good-sized Federal State, and without doubt, would have come to the front with a Constitution sweeping away all things looking to a parting with the stars and stripes."[9]

In north Georgia's Cass (later Bartow) County, one citizen wrote a letter to Abraham Lincoln promising that local Union men were "ready to sholder our guns" against the Confederacy. He assured Lincoln that thousands of others across Georgia were prepared to do the same. Several men in the east Georgia county of Emanuel made it clear that they were among that number, saying they "would join Lincoln's army if it came to the push." From north Georgia's Fannin County came word that "quite a number" were prepared to defend the old flag and help "whip Georgia and the South back into the Union." The correspondent left no doubt what lay behind Fannin men's Union sentiment: "They are not interested in the nigger question...this fuss was all for the benefit of the wealthy." Sion Darnell expressed a similar opinion about Unionist feeling in Pickens County.[10]

Already some of Georgia's Union men were perpetrating violence against secession's symbol if not against secessionists themselves. In the coastal town of Darien, M. B. Holland fired on the first Confederate flag

---

spondence.

[9]John Fulton Brown, *The Bushwhackers: The Story of a Reluctant Rebel During the Civil War* (Bloomington, IN: iUniverse Inc., 2009) 3. Others included northern Alabama in the list of Southern regions that might have formed a new Federal state. After a Union rally in Huntsville, one worried secessionist wrote that the possibility of a new "state of Nickajack to be formed by the counties of North Alabama and possibly by adjacent counties of Georgia and eastern Tennessee, looms large." See Wesley S. Thompson, *The Free State of Winston: A History of Winston County, Alabama* (Winfield, AL: Pariel Press, 1968) 19–20.

[10]George M. Franklin to Lincoln, 24 January 1861, in E. W. Solomons to Brown, 12 February 1861, Governor's Incoming Correspondence; Francis B. Drake to Brown, 28 May 1861, Governor's Incoming Correspondence; W. A. Campbell to Brown, 23 February 1861, Governor's Incoming Correspondence; Davis, "Memoirs of a Partisan War," 103.

raised there. So hostile were many Georgians and other Southerners to secession that an Augusta editor warned in February 1861, "Disguise it as we may, the greatest danger to the new confederacy arises not from without, not from the North, but *from our own people*."[11]

While some Georgia Unionists gave voice to their opinions, many others did not. For safety's sake, they expressed grudging support for the Confederacy when necessary. The slightest suggestion that someone might be a Unionist could have severe consequences. George Martin, a southwest Georgia man, was arrested for "uttering treasonable sentiments against the Southern Confederacy." Fearing for his life, Martin nearly killed an army lieutenant while making his escape. Authorities offered a $250 reward for Martin's capture, dead or alive.[12]

Georgians who were more reserved with their dissent still expressed doubts about secession's legitimacy. Governor Brown did not announce the results of the January vote for convention delegates until late April, and that was only at the insistence of concerned voters. Even then he lied about the figures. Brown claimed that secessionists had won by more than thirteen thousand votes when in fact they were likely defeated by a margin of slightly more than a thousand.[13]

With the Confederacy now an established fact, most people were more concerned about how the war might affect the South in general, and themselves in particular, if it did not end quickly. The consequences of an extended conflict were evident enough to those on the front lines. In August 1861, when volunteers of the 15th Alabama Regiment, many

---

[11]Alfred Prescott to P. Looney, 27 February 1865, Confederate Bible Records, United Daughters of the Confederacy, Georgia Department of Archives and History, Morrow; Frank Moore, ed., *The Rebellion Record: A Diary of American Events*, vol. 1 (New York: G. P. Putnam, 1861) part 2: "Documents and Narratives," 30.

[12]*Opelika (AL) Southern Republic*, 18 May and 1 June 1861.

[13]Brown to A. I. Whitten, T. H. Callaway, and others, 24 April 1861, Governor's Letter Book, Georgia Department of Archives and History; *Macon Telegraph*, 1 May 1861; Michael P. Johnson, *Toward a Patriarchal Republic: The Secession of Georgia* (Baton Rouge: Louisiana State University Press, 1977) 63–64.

of them from southwest Georgia, arrived in Virginia and visited Manassas a few weeks after the war's first major battle there, they found hundreds of shallow graves scattered over the fields. Rain had washed much of the dirt away and skeletal remains protruded from the ground. Hogs were feeding on the dead. It was not what the young men had expected to find.[14]

Few volunteers had allowed themselves to envision the horrors of war, but after Manassas they had no choice. Private J. W. Lokey of Muscogee County, only fifteen years old in summer 1861, later remembered that Manassas "made me realize that this war was no child's play." Little wonder that some soldiers began to reexamine their motives for volunteering. In late July, just ten days after Manassas, Joel Crawford of Quitman County wrote Governor Brown asking "if after the signing of a written instrument binding the signer to go to the present war, if any signer thereof has the legal right to withdraw his name."[15]

The soldiers had concerns beyond personal safety. Who would care for their families and work their farms if the war went on for months or years? Planters had fewer worries there. They had slaves to labor on their plantations. And taxes were going up on everything except slaves. As the fall elections approached, these issues were uppermost in the minds of common folk. In September, voters who signed themselves "Many Anxious to Hear" addressed an open letter to candidates in Floyd County.

> Please give your views concerning our present condition—about the war, and the cause of the war...and our present condition of taxation for the support of the war. Is it right that the poor man should be taxed for the support of the war, when the war was brought about on the slave question, and the slave at home accumulating for the benefit of his master, and the poor man's farm left uncultivated, and a chance for his wife to be a widow, and his children orphans? Now, in justice, would it

---

[14]Val L. McGee, *Claybank Memories: A History of Dale County, Alabama* (Ozark, AL: Dale County Historical Society, 1989) 42.

[15]J. W. Lokey, *My Experiences in the War between the States* (Tishomingo, OK: n.p., 1959) 2; Crawford to Brown, 31 July 1861, Governor's Incoming Correspondence.

> not be right to levy a direct tax on the species of property that brought about the war, to support it?

A week later, the *Rome Courier* apologized for printing the letter, saying that this kind of talk might cause class division.[16] Such expressions, in fact, reflected class divisions that were already there and that would hamper the war effort until its end. But it was still early in the war, and the Confederacy had more pressing issues. In Georgia, officials worried over the possibility of Yankee invasion along the coast and how to meet it. Weapons were in short supply. Manufacturing and stockpiling was a top priority.

The War Department quickly developed manufacturing facilities to address the need, and Georgia was central to that effort. The *Atlanta Southern Confederacy* wrote that factories were "springing up as if by magic." Iron and arms were produced in Macon and Columbus, gun powder in Augusta, and uniforms in Savannah. Smaller towns got in on the action as well. Rifled cannons came from Rome, shoes from Marietta, small arms from Athens, and knapsacks and canteens from Dalton. The penitentiary in Milledgeville became a state armory that produced 125 rifles a month. Atlanta turned out iron and munitions and became a central rail hub for the distribution of military supplies. Within a year of the war's outbreak, Georgia manufacturers, as well as those in other states across the South, were cranking out arms and supporting material at an astonishing rate. The Ordnance Bureau under Josiah Gorgas was especially efficient in producing and funneling arms and equipment from Georgia to the field. So much was manufactured and transported that no Confederate army ever lost a major battle for lack of munitions.[17]

---

[16]*Rome Tri-Weekly Courier*, 26 September 1861; *Rome Weekly Courier*, 4 October 1861.

[17]Mary DeCredico, *Patriotism for Profit: Georgia's Urban Entrepreneurs and the Confederate War Effort* (Chapel Hill: University of North Carolina Press, 1990) 25; Chad Morgan, *Planters' Progress: Modernizing Confederate Georgia* (Gainesville: University Press of Florida, 2005) 41–42; Bryan, *Confederate Georgia*, 24, 25, 27, 102–103; Richard E. Beringer, Herman Hattaway, Archer Jones, and William N. Still, *Why the South Lost the Civil War* (Athens: University of Georgia Press, 1986) 13. See also C. L. Bragg et al., *Never for Want of Powder:*

With so many men called off to war, white women took up much of the slack in Georgia's industrial labor force. Nearly all Georgia industries employed women in some way. The quartermaster depot in Columbus could not have functioned without them. At the Columbus Arsenal, fully half of the 300 employees were women. Cotton mills typically employed far more women than men. That had been largely true in the late antebellum era, but the outbreak of war called even more women into the mills. Despite the demand for their labor, wages were relatively low at eight to twelve dollars a month, about the same as a Confederate private. From those wages women had to feed, house, and cloth themselves and their children, a task that would become more difficult as the war wore on.[18]

Black folk also were drawn into the labor force, some into occupations that had previously been closed to them. Free blacks were hired as clerks and bookkeepers, most for the first time. Typically, the work was more manual. Blacks were employed at the ordnance facilities in Macon, which offered overtime pay for extra work. In Savannah, blacks found work at sawmills, saltworks, and rail facilities. Nearly a third of the Columbus Factory Company's workers were black as early as spring 1861. Slaves were employed as well. The Grant Factory of Columbus, which hired only white labor before the war, quickly began building a pool of slave labor, as did the city's giant Eagle Manufacturing Company. During the war, blacks, free and enslaved, made up half the labor force at the Rock Island paper mill just outside Columbus.[19]

The Confederate Powder Works in Augusta, Georgia (Columbia: University of South Carolina Press, 2007).

[18]Diffee William Standard, *Columbus, Georgia, in the Confederacy: The Social and Industrial Life of the Chattahoochee River Port* (New York: William-Frederick Press, 1954) 37; Edward A. Mueller, *Perilous Journeys: A History of Steamboating on the Chattahoochee, Apalachicola, and Flint Rivers, 1828–1928* (Eufaula, AL: Historic Chattahoochee Commission, 1990) 115; Bryan, *Confederate Georgia*, 104–105.

[19]Joseph P. Reidy, "States of Dependence and Independence in Civil War Georgia," in John D. Fowler and David B. Parker, eds., *Breaking the Heartland: The Civil War in Georgia* (Macon, GA: Mercer University Press, 2011) 59;

Across the state, slaves were employed to repair rail lines and build fortifications, especially around Savannah and along the coast. Free black men found new opportunities to ply their trades as carpenters, blacksmiths, bricklayers, coopers, masons, butchers, barbers, and plasterers. Black women were in demand as laundresses, nurses, and seamstresses. A number of highly skilled blacks had jobs at the Columbus Naval Iron Works. Horace King, a free black contractor, supplied more than fifteen thousand board feet of lumber for construction of the ironclad gunboat *Jackson*. Most of the five hundred employees in the shoe manufacturing division of the Columbus quartermaster depot were black. Scores of African American blacksmiths and strikers were employed at the Haiman factory in Columbus. John D. Gray also recruited carpenters and blacksmiths for his Columbus armory from the city's black community. At Griswoldville, a pistol factory employed twenty-four mechanics, twenty-two of whom were black. When the Allatoona Iron Works lost nearly all its white workers to the army, they were replaced by blacks who were, according to one witness, "expert in the business."[20]

Much of the work was dangerous, and accidents were frequent. Blacks were injured lifting heavy loads, fell from scaffolding, were hit by trains, and mangled in machinery. Still, blacks tended to see industrial work as a way to achieve some measure of economic independence and social status. Perhaps a few saw such employment as a chance to prove themselves to whites—an opportunity to destroy the racist arguments that justified oppression for all blacks and slavery for most. A major pillar of proslavery doctrine held that people of African descent were incapable of performing any but simple tasks. But such was the skill and efficiency of black bookkeepers, clerks, and mechanics that even the editor of the

---

Jones, *Saving Savannah*, 168; Standard, *Columbus in the Confederacy*, 38, 55; Clarence L. Mohr, *On the Threshold of Freedom: Masters and Slaves in Civil War Georgia* (Athens: University of Georgia Press, 1986) 150.

[20]Jones, *Saving Savannah*, 169; Standard, *Columbus in the Confederacy*, 38, 55; Thomas L. French, Jr., and Edward L. French, "The Horace King Story: Building Bridges across Rivers and between Cultures," *Columbus and the Valley Magazine* (Spring 1994): 39; Mohr, *On the Threshold of Freedom*, 150–51.

Columbus Daily Sun, once a vocal opponent of skilled black labor, called their performance "laudable."[21]

Despite such praise, there were no corresponding calls for an end to slavery or rights for free blacks. If any expected it, they were very much disappointed. The dynamics of a social system based on race simply would not allow it. Those blacks who thought hard work alone was the path to civil and social equality failed to understand that the problem was not with themselves but rather with the class-related self-image of whites and how they used blacks to bolster that image. No amount of hard work and dedication on the part of blacks could overcome that. Most black folk were probably under no illusion that it would, especially those held in slavery. Little wonder that so many began escaping soon after Union forces commenced operations along the Georgia coast.

From the war's outset, Georgia officials had been worried about the possibility of Union invasion, so much so that Governor Brown had tried to keep all firearms in Georgia from leaving the state. Some feared that Union gunboats might steam up the Chattahoochee or Flint rivers "and endeavor to lay waste...the fairest portion of Georgia with fire and sword." Others worried about spies filtering into Georgia via the rail line from Chattanooga in east Tennessee, a Unionist stronghold. Indeed, in April 1862 a team of Union saboteurs led by James Andrews captured the locomotive *General* at Big Shanty just north of Atlanta and headed for Chattanooga. They had planned to destroy rail bridges as they went but had no time to do so because railroad employees on the *Texas* were hot on their heels. The chase finally ended when the *General* ran out of fuel near Ringgold. Andrews and seven of his men were hanged as spies later that summer.[22]

---

[21]Standard, *Columbus in the Confederacy*, 56.

[22]Bryan, *Confederate Georgia*, 24, 75–76; John M. Potter to Brown, 30 June 1861, Governor's Incoming Correspondence; Wendy Hamand Venet, "From Gate City to Gotham: Sam Richards Chronicles the Civil War in Atlanta," in Fowler and Parker, *Breaking the Heartland*, 162. See also Russell S. Bonds, *Stealing the General: The Great Locomotive Chase and the First Medal of Honor* (Yardley, PA: Westholme Publishing, 2006).

The more immediate threat to Confederate Georgia was invasion from the coast. In fall 1861, Union gunboats began a campaign to drive planters from the Sea Islands and blockade Georgia's coastal towns. On November 24, several hundred Federals landed on Tybee Island at the mouth of the Savannah River. Opposite them on Cockspur Island was their main objective, Fort Pulaski, a brick and mortar bastion surrounded by a moat. The Federals set to work building emplacements for their rifled artillery, just out of range of Pulaski's smooth-bore guns. In February 1862, they removed obstructions from a man-made channel just upstream from Pulaski and moved their gunboats into the Savannah River. Pulaski was now entirely surrounded.

On April 10, General David Hunter, commanding federal forces along the southeastern coast, demanded Pulaski's surrender. Colonel Charles Olmsted, in charge of the Pulaski garrison, refused. After a two-day bombardment that breached the fort's wall, Olmsted gave up and handed Pulaski over to the Federals.[23]

Their Great Soul-Hungering Desire Was Freedom

In May 1862, Hunter delivered an even heavier blow to the Confederate cause by declaring all slaves in South Carolina, Georgia, and Florida to be free. From Hunter's standpoint, he had little choice. Beginning soon after Union troops set foot on Tybee Island, fugitives were heading for their camps in numbers too great to ignore. It was the same all along the coast. Young men among the fugitives were volunteering to serve, and Hunter needed their help. But when Lincoln learned of Hunter's freedom order, he issued a presidential proclamation making it "altogether void." Ending slavery was not yet a Union war aim, and Lincoln stressed that no field commander had authority to free slaves.[24]

---

[23]Bryan, *Confederate Georgia*, 67–72.

[24]*War of the Rebellion: A Compilation of the Official Records of the Union and Confederate Armies* (Washington, DC: Government Printing Office, 1880–1901) series 1, vol. 6, 263–64; series 1, vol. 14, 333; series 1, vol. 14, 341 (hereafter cited as *OR*); Ira Berlin, Joseph P. Reidy, and Leslie S. Rowland, eds., *Freedom: A Documentary History of Emancipation, 1861–1867*, series 2, *The Black Military*

Still, if Lincoln made clear that blacks under Hunter's command could not be free, he dodged the question of whether they could be soldiers. He left that issue to Congress, which strongly opposed the idea. It quickly passed a resolution demanding to know why Hunter had enlisted "fugitive slaves" without authority. Hunter pointed to War Department orders authorizing him to "employ all loyal persons offering their services in defence of the Union and for the suppression of this Rebellion in any manner I might see fit." Since the orders said nothing of skin color, Hunter saw his black soldiers as federally authorized recruits. Although Congress and Lincoln's War Department still refused to recognize Hunter's blacks as soldiers, he kept many of them under arms just the same.[25]

Georgia slaves escaped their owners by the thousands in what historian W. E. B. Du Bois called a general strike against the Confederacy. Every slave taken to the front by the Troup Artillery of Athens fled to Union lines. One southwest Georgia slave was hanged for organizing a mass exodus to federal vessels operating in the Gulf of Mexico. The greatest flight was to Union lines along the Georgia coast. By summer 1862 those fugitives numbered as many as twenty thousand. Among them was fourteen-year-old Susie Baker of Savannah. Along with her uncle and his family, Susie escaped to St. Catherines Island in April 1862. They were sent farther down the coast to St. Simons Island, where blacks had established a haven for themselves. Susie, who had secretly learned to read and write while enslaved, set up a school for eager black students, children and adults alike.[26]

Experience (New York: Cambridge University Press, 1982) 38 (hereafter cited as Berlin et al., *Black Military Experience*); Ira Berlin et al., eds., *Freedom: A Documentary History of Emancipation, 1861–1867*, series 1, vol. 1, *The Destruction of Slavery* (New York: Cambridge University Press, 1985) 123–25.

[25] *OR*, series 3, vol. 2, 147–48; Berlin et al., *Black Military Experience*, 50–53, 38–39.

[26] W. E. B. Du Bois, *Black Reconstruction: An Essay toward a History of the Part which Black Folk Played in the Attempt to Reconstruct Democracy in America, 1860–1880* (New York: Harcourt, Brace, and Co., 1935) 57; Bryan, *Confederate Georgia*, 127; Jones, *Saving Savannah*, 153–54, 157; Reidy, "States of Depend-

A few days after the Confederacy fired on Fort Sumter, the *Augusta Constitutionalist* had assured Georgia slaveholders that there was no need to fear their slaves: "Our negroes will remain quietly and faithfully at home, and cultivate our lands, to feed our armies." Newspapers across the South echoed the same hopeful message, but that message did little to calm slaveholder fears. Desperate to keep their slaves ignorant and in place, slaveholders told them all sorts of tales about what the Yankees intended. Some warned that Union troops were selling runaways to Caribbean slave traders. Others said that the Yankees were themselves enslaving refugees. Susie Baker recalled that "whites would tell their colored people not to go to the Yankees, for they would harness them to carts and make them pull the carts around, in place of horses." Though some pretended otherwise, blacks were hardly fooled. "I asked grandmother," Susie wrote, "if this was true. She replied, 'Certainly not!' that the white people did not want slaves to go over to the Yankees, and told them these things to frighten them."[27]

Despite efforts to conceal the war's implications from them, slaves were well aware of the stakes. Mary Gladdy of Columbus recalled "the whisperings among the slaves—their talking of the possibility of freedom." Throughout the war, slaves met in secret to hold prayer meetings for freedom. According to Gladdy, those on her plantation gathered in their cabins two or three nights a week. They placed large pots against the doors to keep their voices muffled. "Then," she said, "the slaves would sing, pray, and relate experiences all night long. Their great, soul-hungering desire was freedom." Those few slaves who could read

---

ence and Independence," 57. Baker, who became more famously known as Susie King Taylor, later served one of the Union army's first black regiments, cooking for the men, doing their laundry, and acting as nurse. She also continued to serve as a teacher. She eventually married one of the soldiers and after the war opened a school for black children in Savannah. See Susie King Taylor, *Reminiscences of My Life in Camp* (1902; rprt. with introduction by Catherine Clinton, Athens: University of Georgia Press, 2006).

[27]J. William Harris, *Plain Folk and Gentry in a Slave Society: White Liberty and Black Slavery in Augusta's Hinterlands* (Middletown, CT: Wesleyan University Press, 1985) 170; Taylor, *Reminiscences*, 7–8.

Susie Baker, more famously known as Susie King Taylor, escaped with members of her family to the Georgia Sea Islands after Union forces captured Fort Pulaski in April 1862. Susie, who had secretly learned to read and write while enslaved in Savannah, was soon teaching black soldiers recruited from slave communities along the southeastern coast. She later married one of the soldiers. After the war, she returned to Savannah and set up a school for black children. Image from Susie King Taylor, *Reminiscences of My Life in Camp* (1902).

kept up with events through pilfered newspapers and spread the word to their neighbors. Young Ella Hawkins heard the older slaves whispering among themselves, "Us is gonna be free! Jes as sho's anything. God has heard our prayers; us is gonna be free!" When a white minister preached that slavery was ordained by God and prayed aloud for Him to drive the Yankees back, Ella prayed silently to herself, "Oh, Lord, please send the Yankees on."[28]

In her reminiscences of the war years, Susie Baker wrote vividly of the excitement among her Savannah neighbors. "Oh, how those people prayed for freedom! I remember, one night, my grandmother went out into the suburbs of the city to a church meeting, and they were fervently singing this old hymn: Yes, we all shall be free, / Yes, we all shall be free, / Yes, we all shall be free, / When the Lord shall appear."[29]

Pray they did, but enslaved Georgians were not simply waiting either for the Lord or the Yankees to give them freedom. They were taking it for themselves. Though Lincoln is often credited with having freed the slaves, his Emancipation Proclamation did little more than recognize a state of affairs that blacks had already created with their "general strike" against the Confederacy. Lincoln's document, as Professor Ira Berlin points out, "heralded not the dawn of universal liberty but the compromised and piecemeal arrival of an undefined freedom. Indeed, the Proclamation's flat prose, ridiculed by the late Richard Hofstadter as having 'all the moral grandeur of a bill of lading,' suggests that the true authorship of African American freedom lies elsewhere—not at the top of American society but at its base."[30]

---

[28]Mary Gladdy, *Georgia Narratives*, part 2, 17, 26–27, in *Slave Narratives: A Folk History of Slavery in the United States from Interviews with Former Slaves*, Manuscript Division, Library of Congress, Washington, DC; Ella Hawkins in George P. Rawick et al., comp., *The American Slave: A Composite Autobiography* (Westport, CT: Greenwood Press, 1972 and 1977) supplement, series 1, vol. 3, part 1, 315.

[29]Taylor, *Reminiscences*, 8.

[30]Du Bois, *Black Reconstruction*, 57; Ira Berlin, "Who Freed the Slaves? Emancipation and Its Meaning," in David W. Blight and Brooks D. Simpson, eds., *Union and Emancipation: Essays on Politics and Race in the Civil War Era*

Georgia slaveholder Laura Comer illustrated Berlin's point when she wrote in summer 1862 that "the servants are so indolent and obstinate it is a *trial* to have anything to do with them." Slaves resisted their plight by increasingly feigning ignorance or illness, sabotaging plantation equipment, and traveling freely in defiance of the law. One disturbed white woman on a Georgia rail line was astonished to see "crowds of slaves in gayest attire" getting on and off the trains "at every country stopping place." As for forced labor, what work slaves did was done with measured effort. Some eventually refused to work for their owners at all. A plantation mistress wrote of one of her slaves, "Nancy has been very impertinent.... She said she would not be hired out by the month, neither would she go out to get work." Another mistress wrote to her husband, "We are doing as best we know, or as good as we can get the Servants to do; they learn to feel very independent."[31]

Part of that independence often involved fighting back against the physical abuse that enslaved people had suffered under for so long. In 1861, a Georgia overseer complained to his absentee employer that the slaves would not submit to traditional punishments. One slave walked away when the overseer told him he was about to be whipped. "I wish you would...come down and let the matter be settle," the overseer wrote, "as I do not feel wiling to be runover by him." Another Georgia slave drew a knife on an overseer who tried to whip him. His owner locked him up and put him on a bread and water diet, but it did little to subdue him. Such actions tended only to make slaves more rebellious. "I am satisfied that his imprisonment has only tended to harden him," one over-

(Kent, OH: Kent State University Press, 1997) 109–110. Berlin's quoted reference is from Richard Hofstadter, *The American Political Tradition and the Men Who Made It* (New York: Vintage, 1948) 132. For an in-depth look at how blacks, in various ways, brought on emancipation, see David Williams, *I Freed Myself: African American Self-Emancipation in the Civil War Era* (New York: Cambridge University Press, 2014).

[31]Laura Beecher Comer Diary, 16 August 1862, Laura Beecher Comer Papers, Southern Historical Collection, University of North Carolina at Chapel Hill; Catherine C. Hopley, *Life in the South; From the Commencement of the War*, vol. 2 (London: Chapman and Hall, 1863) 336; Bryan, *Confederate Georgia*, 125.

seer wrote soon after releasing an unruly slave. "I don't think he will ever reform."[32]

Besides being terribly painful, whipping was for slaves a key symbol of their lowly status. It is hardly surprising that resistance to whipping became one of the main ways slaves sought to achieve some measure of independence. But such resistance could be dangerous. One Troup County planter was noted for turning his dogs on slaves who refused to be whipped. A slave at the Hines Holt plantation near Columbus was shot for it. He had beaten off six men who tried to hold him down.[33]

Resistance could be collective as well as individual, up to and including armed rebellion. The danger seemed clear enough to the editor of southwest Georgia's *Albany Patriot*, who complained in May 1861 that it was no uncommon thing to see area blacks "congregate together contrary to law, *exhibit their weapons*, and no doubt devise their secret, but destructive plans."[34]

During late spring and early summer 1861, a rebellion hysteria swept across large parts of the South's plantation belt, southwest Georgia included. Panic spread through Decatur County in June when patrollers caught a slave named Israel away from his plantation without a pass. Israel's capture led officials to believe that a general slave revolt was about to break out. Rumors spread that blacks in the county seat of Bainbridge were collecting firearms and planning to "kill all of the men and old women and children and take the younger ones for their wives." No firearms were found, but two suspected insurrection leaders were imprisoned. Local whites swore that they would be killed if they were ever released.[35]

Despite such dangers, slaves continued to resist. According to former Troup County slave Celestia Avery, her owner Peter Heard allowed his slaves to be whipped "unmercifully." One day while hoeing the fields,

---

[32]Bryan, *Confederate Georgia*, 124–25.

[33]Celestia Avery in Rawick, *American Slave*, series 2, vol. 12, part 1, 24; Mary Gladdy, *Georgia Narratives*, part 2, 17.

[34]*Albany Patriot*, 23 May 1861.

[35]Mohr, *On the Threshold of Freedom*, 51; Bryan, *Confederate Georgia*, 127.

Celestia's grandmother Sylvia was told by an overseer to remove her clothes when she got to the end of a fence row. She was going to be whipped for not working fast enough. When the overseer reached for her, she grabbed a wooden rail and broke it across the man's arms.[36]

To avoid abuse, slaves often fled to nearby woods and swamps temporarily or for the war's duration. Charlie Pye of Columbus said that his mother would hide out for months at a time rather than be whipped. But she always returned "when the strain of staying away from her family became too great."[37] Celestia Avery told an especially harrowing story of her grandmother Sylvia's sadistic treatment at the hands of Peter Heard:

> Every morning my grandmother would pray, and old man Heard despised to hear anyone pray saying they were only doing so that they might become free niggers. Just as sure as the sun would rise, she would get a whipping; but this did not stop her prayers every morning before day. This particular time grandmother Sylvia was in [the] 'family way' and that morning she began to pray as usual. The master heard her and became so angry he came to her cabin, seized and pulled her clothes from her body and tied her to a young sapling. He whipped her so brutally that her body was raw all over. When darkness fell her husband cut her down from the tree. During the day he was afraid to go near her. Rather than go back to the cabin she crawled on her knees to the woods and her husband brought grease for her to grease her raw body.[38]

After his own severe beating, another Troup County slave named William escaped and dug out a large cave near the Chattahoochee River. Several nights later, under the cover of darkness, he moved his wife and two children to the cave where they lived for the rest of the war.[39]

Depriving the Confederacy of much needed labor, slaves escaping to points near or far made clear how devastating their attitudes and actions were to the Confederate war effort. So many slaves were escaping by summer 1862 that Confederate General John Pemberton, commander of

---

[36]Celestia Avery in Rawick, *American Slave*, series 2, vol. 12, part 1, 25.
[37]Charlie Pye in Rawick, *American Slave*, series 2, vol. 13, part 3, 187.
[38]Celestia Avery in Rawick, *American Slave*, series 2, vol. 12, part 1, 24–25.
[39]Ibid., 24.

the Department of South Carolina and Georgia, issued orders allowing only white men to work close to Union lines. Slaves, he knew, "could not be trusted to work so near the enemy." He also diverted troops to "prevent the escape of slaves and for protection of persons and property against insubordination of negroes."[40]

It was hardly unusual to see Confederate soldiers serving as slave patrols. Civilians too, who might otherwise have been put in the army, were paid to do patrol duty. Officials in Early County hired extra patrols for each of its districts. When men could not be hired for slave patrols, they were drafted. The city council of Cuthbert divided the town into three wards and assigned all white males between the ages of sixteen and sixty to serve on patrols.[41]

While Confederate armies were constantly outnumbered by an average of two-to-one, tens of thousands of Southern whites were kept at home to guard against escaping slaves and slave rebellion. To state and local officials, it seemed worth the cost. A grand jury in Baker County thought slave patrollers as important as soldiers. Despite their importance, patrols were often left to incompetent or apathetic men. As a result, patrol laws were often half-heartedly enforced or completely ignored. So badly was the job handled in Sumter County that slaveholders urged the local patrol commission to "appoint men to execute such duty as they know will do it in a proper manner." Slaveholders in Lowndes County, "aggrieved that the patrol law has been so much neglected," repeatedly called for stricter enforcement. "We recommend," they wrote, "that the patrol laws be strictly enforced. In fact we deem it indispensable to the protection of property in various sections of our county." Officials in Thomas County complained that slaves "under the present want of

---

[40]*OR*, series 1, vol. 14, 565, 541.

[41]Sally E. Hadden, *Slave Patrols: Law and Violence in Virginia and the Carolinas* (Cambridge, MA: Harvard University Press, 2001) 186; David Williams, *Rich Man's War: Class, Caste, and Confederate Defeat in the Lower Chattahoochee Valley* (Athens: University of Georgia Press, 1998) 158; Annette McDonald Suarez, *A Source Book on the Early History of Cuthbert and Randolph County, Georgia* (Atlanta: Cherokee Publishing, 1982) 130–31.

discipline are an absolute evil" and ordered that every plantation supply the captain of the patrol commission with a list of all slaves.[42]

Georgia's General Assembly tried to help stem the rising tide of slave resistance with several additions to the state penal code. In December 1861, it stipulated that any black person found guilty of arson would be put to death. It also forbade owners to let slaves hire themselves out and required slaves to reside on their owner's premises. In 1862, the Assembly reinforced laws forbidding slaves to travel without passes and canceled all exemptions from patrol duty.[43]

Slaveholders worried not only about resistance among blacks but also about the aid they might receive from whites. That so many had opposed secession was taken as a sign that there was cause for concern. There were more obvious signs as well. In April 1861, news reached Governor Brown from Calhoun County that "there are low white men in the county who have communicated with the negroes." The next month in Monroe County, Chappell Robinson was found "trifling with negroes." Authorities forced him to leave the state or face prosecution. In June, a citizen in Johnson County warned Brown that there was "a certain class of persons who are not disposed to enter the service of their country and whom it would not be safe to trust with the black population." One local man had been heard to say that "he and the Negroes would have fine times with the wives of the volunteers after they, the volunteers, left for the service!" Later that month, Brown received word that a man in Effingham County had tried to talk slaves into poisoning their owner.[44] The motives of whites involved with such plots were not always clear, but slaveholders kept a close watch for any expressions of dissent.

---

[42]Robert David Carlson, "Wiregrass Runners: Conscription, Desertion, and the Origins of Discontent in Civil War South Georgia" (master's thesis, Valdosta State University, 1999) 71.

[43]Bryan, *Confederate Georgia*, 126.

[44]Wm. P. Harrison to Brown, 29 April 1861, Cuyler Collection; *Augusta Chronicle and Sentinel*, 30 May 1861; James Hicks to Brown, 19 June 1861, Governor's Incoming Correspondence; William Gleeman to Brown, 20 June 1861, Governor's Incoming Correspondence.

In July, the *Columbus Sun* reported that a "vigilance committee" in southwest Georgia's Mitchell County had uncovered plans for a slave uprising to be led by several local white men. James Patillo, William McLendon, Samuel Edwards, Romulus Weeks, Stephen G. W. Wood, John C. Morgan, and Ephraim McLeod were all implicated in the scheme. According to the *Sun*, Patillo was to have supplied the slaves "with as much ammunition as he possibly could to butcher the good citizens of the county." Local law enforcement put to the lash Patillo, McLendon, Weeks, Morgan, and McLeod, then expelled them from the county. Edwards and Wood escaped a whipping, but all were ordered never to set foot in Mitchell County again "under the penalty of death."[45]

December 1861 brought word to Governor Brown from north Georgia's Gordon County of local Unionists holding secret meetings and organizing a military force to protect themselves from Confederate authorities. They swore never to serve in the Rebel army and to aid the Federals should they reach that far south. Most troubling was the writer's insistence that the Unionists "say in case of an insurrection they will help the Negroes."[46]

In spring 1862, three Calhoun County men tried to do just that. Mindful of the previous year's failed attempt in nearby Mitchell County, Harvell Scaggs, William Scaggs, and Giles Shoots, all citizens of Calhoun County, brought the Federals in on the venture. Traveling down to the Gulf Coast under pretense of making salt, the trio contacted Union blockaders. Soon they were running "superior new guns" to slaves in Calhoun County. The plot came to light in June, and the three men were sentenced "to receive a sound whipping, to be tarred all over, and then ordered to quit the State." Some thought the punishment much too light. One southwest Georgia editor asked "is it safe to the community to suffer such inhuman wretches, such dangerous animals, to go at large?" He suggested sentences of life imprisonment or death.[47]

---

[45]*Columbus Sun*, 15 July 1861.

[46]L. R. Ramsaur to Brown, 14 December 1861, Governor's Incoming Correspondence.

[47]*Early County News* in *Augusta Constitutionalist*, 24 June 1862.

Few whites were willing to go so far in helping blacks. Most never wanted secession, but they largely acquiesced to the new regime and remained committed to keeping the South a white man's country. That some whites were willing to help blacks reflected more how they felt about slaveholders than how they felt about slavery. Still, enthusiasm for the war was beginning to wane by fall 1861, especially among the soldiers. They were deserting the army in droves, promising to return once their fall harvest was in. Few remained true to that promise. Those who went home on legitimate leave often did not go back either. In December 1861, an Augusta paper acknowledged the "undisputed fact that many of our volunteers, who come home on furlough to spend a few days or weeks, although in excellent health when they arrive, are taken ill while here." The editor sarcastically quipped that perhaps "the change from the hardy habits of life in camp to the comparative ease and indolence of home, acts badly upon the system."[48]

How Are the Men to Be Got?

The volunteering boom of spring 1861 went bust by fall. In October, word reached the governor's office from Greene County that "our people don't seem to be inclined to offer their services." That same month, Captain Edward Croft of the Columbus Artillery reported that it was almost impossible to find volunteers. In February 1862, W. H. Byrd of Augusta wrote to Governor Brown that he had been trying for weeks to raise a company in what he called "this 'Yankee City,' but I regret to say every effort has failed." That failure did not result from a lack of potential recruits. The *Augusta Chronicle and Sentinel* had remarked only a week earlier that "one who walks Broad street and sees the number of young men, would come to the conclusion that no war…was now waging."[49]

---

[48]*Augusta Chronicle and Sentinel*, 31 December 1861.

[49]Green Moore to Brown, 4 October 1861, Cuyler Collection; Lynda Lasswell Crist and Mary Seaton Dix, eds., *The Papers of Jefferson Davis*, vol. 7 (Baton Rouge: Louisiana State University Press, 1992) 361; Byrd to Brown, 20 February 1862, Cuyler Collection; *Augusta Chronicle and Sentinel*, 12 February 1862.

From rural Brooks County in south Georgia, C. S. Gaulden reported that "several large families of young men in this county have not sent out soldiers." F. S. Johnson of middle Georgia's Jones County wondered "how are the men to be got?…I have within a few days heard men say they would not go to the war; they had nothing to fight for and they would not go."[50]

Those who had slaves to fight for were just as reluctant to put their lives on the line. And the more slaves they had, the more reluctant they seemed to be. A few wealthy planters did lead front line units early in the war, and several died in combat. But the great majority were content to remain safely at home, especially after Lincoln's post-Sumter call for troops made it clear that the conflict would be more than a war of words. In late April, just a week after Sumter, the *Rome Courier* published an open letter from "One of the People," who reported that there had been a rapid "withdrawing from the volunteer companies of men who have done their best to destroy this union." One Georgian who was himself a slaveholder chastised members of his class who were "doing nothing for the cause on which their *all* of earthly good depends. Surely such are slumbering over their interests or supinely hoping somebody will do their fighting for them."[51]

In spring 1862 when planters in Putnam County drew up a resolution calling on soldiers to re-enlist for the war's duration, the soldiers responded with a resolution of their own. "We are truly glad that those 'Planters' have at last waked up to the necessities of the times, and we only regret that they did not feel the same interest in their country when we were beating up for volunteers in their midst." They concluded by asking, "Can't the '*Planters*' of Putnam be induced, for their sakes, to come down and take our places for a short time while we go home to look after our *farms*?"[52]

---

[50]Gaulden to Brown, 19 February 1862, Governor's Incoming Correspondence; Johnson to Brown, 17 February 1862, Governor's Incoming Correspondence.

[51]*Rome Tri-Weekly Courier*, 23 April and 21 December 1861.

[52]*Turnwold Countryman*, 15 April 1862.

Whether men would re-enlist or volunteer was beside the point as far as Richmond was concerned. Willing or not, they had to come. In April 1862, the Confederate Congress passed its First Conscription Act, giving President Davis authority to force young men into the army with or without their consent. Under the terms of this act, commonly known as the draft, white males between the ages of eighteen and thirty-five became subject to involuntary military service. In September came the Second Conscription Act extending the age limit to forty-five. As an inducement to enlist before they were drafted, Congress offered volunteers a cash bonus of fifty dollars, more than four times a private's monthly pay of eleven dollars, and allowed them to serve in units of their choice.[53]

Knowing that they would likely be drafted in any case, thousands of reluctant men volunteered in spring 1862. One was John Joseph Kirkland of Early County. A slaveless farmer, Kirkland had a wife and five children when he enlisted as first corporal with the Early Volunteers. He was thirty-three, only two years short of exemption. His younger brother Jacob joined the Early Volunteers as well and two months later died in Virginia. John Joseph had the heartbreaking duty of escorting the body home to their mother. A year after that, having fought through the Peninsula Campaign, Second Manassas, Sharpsburg, and Fredericksburg, he was nearly killed himself when his right leg was shattered at the Battle of Chancellorsville. The leg was amputated just below the knee.[54]

---

[53]By far the most complete treatment of Civil War conscription's operation in Georgia is Robert D. Carlson, "Breach of Faith: Conscription in Confederate Georgia" (Ph.D. dissertation, Emory University, 2009).

[54]Kirkland file, Compiled Service Records of the Confederate Soldiers Who Served in Organizations from the State of Georgia, National Archives, Washington, DC; Lillian Henderson, comp., *Roster of the Confederate Soldiers of Georgia, 1861–1865*, 6 vols. (Hapeville, GA: Longina and Porter, 1959–64) 5:372; Union Missionary Baptist Church Cemetery Records, Miller County, GA. After the war Kirkland, the author's great-great-grandfather moved to neighboring Miller County and served for some years as county tax collector and treasurer. He was also a trustee of Union Missionary Baptist Church. He died in 1904 at age seventy-five and was laid to rest in the church cemetery beside his wife, Amanda Bush Kirkland.

Knowing they would likely be caught up by the recently passed draft act and lose a volunteer's fifty-dollar bonus, thousands of reluctant men enlisted in early 1862. One was John Joseph Kirkland of Early County, the author's great-great-grandfather. A slaveless farmer, Kirkland had a wife and five children when he enrolled as first corporal with the Early Volunteers. A year later, his right leg was shattered at the Battle of Chancellorsville. It was amputated just below the knee. Image courtesy of the late Martha Bush Kirkland.

Among plain folk generally, the most offensive provisions of the draft were those allowing wealthy men to avoid service. Some government officials and skilled workers could gain exemptions as well, but those with enough money could buy their way out of the draft by hiring a substitute or paying an exemption fee. Few but the most affluent could afford either option. And there was the infamous twenty-slave law, which exempted one white man of draft age for every twenty slaves owned. This meant that any planter could be excused outright from the draft. Though few seemed to realize it at the time, this law defined the nature of the war for the great mass of Southerners. From 1862 until the conflict's end, it was for them a rich man's war and a poor man's fight.

Even for loyal Confederates, national conscription in any form ran counter to white liberty and state sovereignty, the very things for which Confederates claimed to be fighting. A. W. Millican of Chattooga County's Dirt Town wrote a biting letter to Governor Brown in June 1862 asking why he was not protecting Georgians from "the centralized military despotism at Richmond." "Why," he wrote, "didn't you hang the first minion of Richmond that called himself a Conscription officer for treason against the Government [of] Georgia?" Millican insisted that if Brown were not going to defend his people from Confederate oppression, he should tell them how they might do it themselves. "You will very much oblige many men in Georgia if you will assist them in finding out whether they are *citizens* or *slaves*." Someone in the governor's office scribbled on the back of the letter "Impertinent and disrespectful. No answer." The answer seemed clear enough to one soldier, writing home that "Georgia freemen who voluntarily put their necks in the yoke in response to this country's call are to day slaves—nay, worst than slaves—bruts—chained under the yoke of military discipline and must abide their time."[55]

Compulsory military service was, in fact, nothing new in Georgia. The state had used a form of limited conscription to boost militia en-

[55]Millican to Brown, 20 June 1862, Cuyler Collection; David Carlson, "The 'Loanly Runagee': Draft Evaders in Confederate South Georgia," *Georgia Historical Quarterly* 84 (2000): 592.

rollments for decades. But until the Civil War, no centralized government had ever exercised such powers. Many in the Confederacy regarded the Conscription Acts as an ominous sign of Richmond's creeping central authority that violated the states' rights spirit of the Confederate Constitution. Herschel V. Johnson called the draft "odious." It "compelled men to fight for liberty" and "enslaved them under the pretext of making them free." Alexander Stephens viewed the draft as entirely unconstitutional.[56]

Governor Brown at first seemed undecided but soon became Georgia's leading voice against the Confederate draft. He concluded that it was "a bold and dangerous usurpation by Congress of the reserved rights of the States and a rapid stroke toward military despotism." Brown quickly expanded the state militia officer corps, using his commissioning power to help protect favorites from conscription. He informed both Jefferson Davis and Secretary of War George Randolph that any attempt by Confederate agents to conscript his militia officers would be met with the agents' arrest. Randolph replied by suggesting that he and Brown should "drive out our common enemy before we make war on each other." Brown would not relent and continued issuing militia commissions despite the lack of need for them. The *Atlanta Southern Confederacy* remarked in June 1862 that officers were being commissioned to train nonexistent militia units. Nevertheless, well-connected men swiftly gained commissions, so many that Georgians began calling them "Joe Brown's Pets."[57]

---

[56]Thomas R. R. Cobb, comp., *A Digest of the Statutes of the State of Georgia in Force Prior to Session of the General Assembly of 1851*, vol. 2 (Athens, GA: Christy, Kelsea, and Burke, 1851) 967; Bryan, *Confederate Georgia*, 85–86.

[57]*OR*, series 4, vol. 1, 1156; *Atlanta Southern Confederacy*, 20 June 1862; Bryan, *Confederate Georgia*, 86. State forces consisted at various times of the Georgia Militia, the Georgia State Line, the Georgia State Guard, the Georgia Reserve Force, and three "state armies" raised in 1861. For further details on these forces see William Harris Bragg, *Joe Brown's Army: The Georgia State Line, 1862–1865* (Macon, GA: Mercer University Press, 1987) vii–xi. Early twentieth-century historians roundly criticized Brown's opposition to the Confederate draft, focusing so much on impact that the principles behind his actions were

Mary McKinley, daughter of one of Baldwin County's wealthiest planter-merchants, berated Governor Brown's militia officers and others who claimed exemptions in an open letter to the *Macon Telegraph*. She called them "stout and healthy young men, who have refused to respond to their country's call, in the hour of her utmost need; suffering our brothers to lay down their lives for a common cause, while they barter fair fame for an inglorious,—a disgraceful safety." She insisted that "no Southern woman would willingly waste her smiles on such a man."[58]

State court judges were divided on the Confederate draft's constitutionality. Some agreed with Brown, citing the Constitution's lack of any draft reference. These judges regularly issued writs of habeas corpus to shield state officials from conscription. The practice also protected wealthy and well-to-do men, who had little difficulty finding a sympathetic judge. Other judges took an opposing view, supporting the draft on grounds that the Constitution empowered Congress to raise an army without reference to method. Implied in that power, they argued, was the authority to draft men into service. In November 1862, with its *Jeffers v. Fair* decision, the Georgia Supreme Court upheld the Confederate draft's constitutionality, ruling that the Constitution allowed for the creation of a national army while placing no restriction on how the government raised it.[59]

---

largely lost. David Carlson reminds us of Brown's commitment to "Baptist theology and Calhounian politics, both of which emphasized adherence to founding principles" in "'Remember thy Pledge!': Religious and Reformist Influences on Joseph E. Brown's Opposition to Confederate Conscription," *Georgia Historical Quarterly* 98 (2014): 26–49.

[58]Richard Iobst, *Civil War Macon* (Macon, GA: Mercer University Press, 1999) 286–87.

[59]George N. Lester, comp., *Cases in Law and Equity Argued and Determined in the Supreme Court of the State of Georgia*, vol. 33 (1870, reprint, Atlanta: Franklin-Turner, 1907) 347–71. Five Confederate state supreme courts eventually heard similar cases, all upholding the draft's constitutionality. For further information on the Confederate court system see Warren Grice, "The Confederate States Court for Georgia," *Georgia Historical Quarterly* 9 (1925): 131–58, and J. G. De Roulhac Hamilton, "The State Courts and the Confederate Constitution," *Journal of Southern History* 4 (1938): 425–48.

The ruling was a blow to states' rights advocates, but the issue was never entirely settled since there was no Confederate supreme court to settle it. Although the Constitution provided for the formation of a supreme court from a collection of district judges, Jefferson Davis, perhaps fearing how it might rule, never called the court into session. Judges throughout the South remained divided, and Governor Brown continued opposing the draft for the rest of the war.

Common folk resisted the draft as well, at first mainly by ignoring it. One newspaper reported that not a single man appeared at the April 1862 draft call in Savannah and listed 199 names of absentees. So many men dodged the draft in western Georgia's third congressional district that in August, Captain Edward Croft, district enrolling officer, threatened to have absentees treated as deserters, which meant execution. Other enrolling officers did the same. Still, thousands of draftees refused to report for duty. In Franklin County, popular disapproval made conscription efforts nearly useless. In Augusta, persons unknown set fire to the draft office. A conscript officer in Fort Gaines was nearly killed when he tried to enforce the draft. Threats to his life became so serious that he fled the state. Draft resistance was so widespread that General Howell Cobb, commanding the military district of Georgia and Florida, thought it would take the whole Confederate army to enforce conscription.[60]

Unlike most common folk, upper class Georgians tended to support both the draft and the exemptions it offered. By their reasoning, it protected the select few to whom the Confederacy looked for fiscal and political leadership. It also allowed those skilled workers who could supply the army with weapons, clothing, and transportation to remain where they could best serve. Was it not obvious that unskilled commoners should serve where best they could—on the battle front? But those commoners saw conscription in a different light. To them, elitist justifi-

[60]*Atlanta Southern Confederacy*, 10 and 16 April 1862; *Columbus Enquirer*, 2 September 1862; James A. Riley, "Desertion and Disloyalty in Georgia during the Civil War" (master's thesis, University of Georgia, 1951) 84; *Augusta Chronicle and Sentinel*, 10 December 1862; Emma J. Slade Prescott Reminiscences, Atlanta Historical Society Archives; Bryan, *Confederate Georgia*, 90.

cations aside, one thing was perfectly clear. Money and social standing protected men who wished to avoid the danger of a bloody death on the firing line.

When one Georgia farmer was drafted, he complained bitterly to a neighbor. "They've got me in this war at last. I didn't want to have any thing to do with it any how. *I* didn't vote for Secession—but them are the ones who have to go and fight now—and those who were so fast for war, stay out." An enraged Georgia soldier wrote to the *Atlanta Southern Confederacy*: "For God's sake don't tell the poor soldier who now shivers in a Northern wind while you snooze in a feather bed, that it is *just* and *right* that the men, who Congress has exempted, should enjoy ease at home, amassing untold riches, while *he* must fight, bleed, and even die."[61]

In justifying their draft exemptions, planters had promised to forgo riches, reduce their cotton crop, and focus on food production. At meetings throughout the Black Belt, planters resolved to grow no more cotton than was necessary. Terrell County planters promised to raise only enough cotton for home consumption, deeming it the best method to ally England and France with the Confederacy. Depriving foreign textile mills of Southern cotton might force recognition of the Confederacy and perhaps intervention in the war on its behalf. "Every bale of cotton made for shipment is a bonus to the Lincoln government," they proclaimed, "furnishing that infamous concern a bludgeon with which to break our own heads." A Sumter County planter suggested that only four acres of cotton per hand be allowed and that any excess be sold to benefit soldiers. Some planters promised to do even better. In an article boldly announcing that "His Majesty King Cotton was formally dethroned by his subjects of the county of Clarke," planters there pledged to produce no more than half an acre per hand.[62]

---

[61]Thomas G. Dyer, *Secret Yankees: The Union Circle in Confederate Atlanta* (Baltimore: Johns Hopkins University Press, 1999) 284; *Atlanta Southern Confederacy*, 30 October 1862.

[62]Carlson, "Wiregrass Runners," 24; *Savannah Morning News*, 12 April 1862.

Many Georgia planters were obligated by law to assist needy soldiers' families when called upon to do so. Planters became "bonded" when they agreed verbally or in writing to contribute food or sell it at a reasonable price to soldiers' families and to the army. After all, the soldiers, who came mostly from nonslaveholding households, were fighting to protect slaveholders' property. As they left their families behind, soldiers were assured that they need not worry about their loved ones back home. The planter's bond was a guarantee that they would be cared for.[63]

Menial Subjects of King Cotton

Planters' deeds rarely matched their words. Few took seriously any notion of reducing cotton production to any great extent, much less doing without it. One Georgia newspaper warned planters who continued to grow cotton, "Look out, Gentlemen, the public eye is upon you, as will soon be the public scorn unless you desist." That scorn was particularly severe among soldiers, who constantly worried about how their families were getting along. A Macon soldier wrote to his wife, "All I fear now is that the planters will plant cotton instead of corn.... There is no use for cotton—none whatever.... I do hope the planters will not be so insane as to plant *any* cotton."[64]

But there was money in cotton, as planters well knew. In April 1861, the *Columbus Times* announced that cotton was going for "the enormous price of 12½ cents per pound. It has not been so high for years." A year later it was up to 18 cents a pound. Prices continued to rise as the war went on.[65] Little wonder that Georgia planters, Robert Toombs prominent among them, kept growing cotton despite the outcry

---

[63]Peter Wallenstein, *From Slave South to New South: Public Policy in Nineteenth-Century Georgia* (Chapel Hill: University of North Carolina Press, 1987) 100.

[64]*Americus Sumter Republican*, 9 May 1862; *Macon Telegraph*, 5 April 1862.

[65]*Columbus Times* in *Milledgeville Southern Recorder*, 30 April 1861; Bryan, *Confederate Georgia*, 121. On 25 July 1862, the *Atlanta Southern Confederacy* reported that wholesale cotton was selling for fifty cents a pound in New York markets. Less than two years later, on 18 February 1864, the *Augusta Chronicle and Sentinel* listed it at nearly a dollar.

against it. According to one report, Toombs planted a full crop of cotton in spring 1862. Another called it "a larger cotton crop than usual." Committees of Public Safety condemned planters generally for such excess, but singled out Toombs.

> You are an ex-Senator, ex-Secretary of State and a Brigadier General. From *you*, *example* as well as precept was confidently expected, that would teach lessons of devoted patriotism to those who looked to you for instruction in the path of duty. How you have met these expectations, let your large *cotton crop* answer.

Condemnation could not compete with profits where Toombs was concerned. "My property," he responded, "as long as I live, shall never be subject to the orders of those cowardly miscreants, the Committees of Public Safety.... you cannot intimidate me."[66]

Ironically, just a year earlier, General Winfield Scott, a Southerner who had remained loyal to the Union, wrote Toombs asking him "to quit his rebel nonsense." Scott predicted that if the South continued on its secessionist course, it would eventually be starved into submission. In reply, Toombs sent an ear of corn by express to his old friend. Said one Georgia editor, "We consider this is one of Bob's best letters."[67] But now, unable to shake his addiction to cotton, Toombs was among the thousands of planters helping Scott's prediction come true.

In spring 1862, one indignant man from Albany wrote to Joe Brown outlining the problem of cotton production in Dougherty County and imploring the governor to do something about it. With "famine now stairing us in the face," he wrote, planters were still sowing acre upon acre in cotton.

---

[66]*Columbus Sun*, 2 May 1862; *Macon Telegraph*, 16, 17 June, and 10 July 1862; *Athens Southern Watchman*, 16 July 1862; Ulrich Bonnell Phillips, ed., *Correspondence of Robert Toombs, Alexander H. Stephens, and Howell Cobb* (Washington, DC: Government Printing Office, 1913) 595.

[67]*Atlanta Southern Confederacy* in *Rome Tri-Weekly Courier*, 4 June 1861.

Senator Robert Toombs had expressed his determination to see Georgia out of the Union whether Georgia voters supported secession or not. Still, like so many planters, he was reluctant to sacrifice for the cause. He ignored state restrictions on cotton production and used political connections to have himself protected from impressment. The *Early County News* remarked that "Toombs, because he is rich, does pretty much what he wants . . . if he were a poor man he would be hanged." Image courtesy of the Library of Congress.

> We are in great danger of *Subjugation* to the hated government that we are resisting, *not* by the army of demons invading our country, but by *avarice* and the *menial Subjects* of King cotton.... I hear of one planter who is pitching 900 acres in cotton, the overseer of another told me he is going to plant 300 acres, another...90 acres, another 300 acres, and two others full crops of cotton. And so it will be all over the state.... The country needs all the grain that can be raised, the producing forces, both in men and horses are greatly diminished, while the demand for grain is increased. I hope your Excellency will adopt some plan to stop those internal enemies of the country, for they will whip us sooner than all Lincolndom combined could do it.[68]

A Griffin man wrote to Brown warning him of planters who would "sink the Southern Confederacy for the sake of the everlasting dollar."[69]

Brown knew that support for the Confederacy among plain folk was fragile. Many already saw planters as the source of their economic woes. If they were forced to go hungry while wealthy land owners planted cotton, Brown worried about the consequences. On February 25, 1862, in a letter to his friend Linton Stephens, Brown admitted the obvious: "Our men cannot fight unless we can feed them and support their families at home." The way to do that was to "drop the cotton crop. The only question is will we do it? If we do not, in my opinion, we are ruined. If we do, our cause is triumphant. I speak plainly. There is no use in attempting to dodge the issue. We have to meet it." Brown was not sure that the issue could be met successfully. But he was sure of one thing. It was all up to the planters. "No class of our society is so wealthy and powerful as the cotton planters, and no other class has as much at stake.... I would appeal to them, therefore, by every incentive to patriotism, and by every motive of interest, to pause and reflect upon the vast responsibility which

---

[68]Frederick Burtz to Brown, 29 March 1862, Governor's Incoming Correspondence. For commentary on the Burtz letter see Lee W. Formwalt, "Planters and Cotton Production as a Cause of Confederate Defeat: Evidence from Southwest Georgia," *Georgia Historical Quarterly* 74 (1990): 269–76.

[69]Wm. L. Gordon to Brown, 29 March 1862, Governor's Incoming Correspondence.

they are about to incur." Brown released the letter for publication in newspapers throughout the state's Cotton Belt.[70]

All Brown's urging fell on deaf ears. By fall 1862, Georgia planters were growing so much cotton that the warehouses could not hold it all. In September, the Columbus firm of Dillard, Powell, and Company ran this announcement in a local paper: "TO PLANTERS: OUR Warehouse being full, Planters will please stop consignments of Cotton to our care until further notice."[71]

It was the same throughout the South's Cotton Belt. 1862 saw the second highest level of cotton produced for any year to that time, declining thereafter due in large part to rising slave resistance. Even so, labor devoted to cotton growing alone, not to mention processing and transport, amounted to 2.3 million man-years between 1861 and 1864, much more than went into defending the Confederacy.[72]

The Confederate Congress never took direct action against planters beyond a non-binding resolution requesting that they focus their efforts on food, so Joe Brown, like other cotton state governors, tried to regulate production himself. In November 1862, he asked the General Assembly to impose a tax on "each quantity of seed cotton sufficient to make a bale of four hundred pounds...produced next year...over what is actually necessary for a home supply." The assemblymen rejected Brown's suggestion of a tax on seed cotton. After all, many were planters and were not eager to place a tax on themselves. But they did make it illegal for anyone to plant more than three acres of cotton for each slave owned or farm hand employed. Violators were subject to a fine of $500 for each acre planted in cotton beyond the limit.[73]

---

[70]Brown to Stephens, 25 February 1862, Governor's Letter Book; *Savannah Morning News*, 3 March 1862; *Milledgeville Southern Federal Union*, 4 March 1862; *Macon Telegraph*, 7 March 1862; *Athens Southern Watchman*, 2 April 1862.

[71]*Columbus Enquirer*, 16 September 1862.

[72]Beringer, Hattaway, Jones, and Still, *Why the South Lost the Civil War*, 433; Stanley Lebergott, "Why the South Lost: Commercial Purpose in the Confederacy," *Journal of American History* 70 (1983): 65–66.

[73]Allen D. Candler, comp., *The Confederate Records of Georgia*, 6 vols. (At-

The act inspired little fear among planters. Godfrey Barnsley, a prominent Bartow County slaveholder, knew that state efforts to curtail cotton growing were in vain, and he knew why. "Some states have passed laws to limit the growth [of cotton]," he wrote to a friend, "but there is little doubt of a large area being planted under the stimulus of present prices." Barnsley was right. Despite public urging for planters give up cotton and grow more corn, a Commissary-General report from April 1863 noted that "not one acre in fifty" between Milledgeville and Athens was devoted to corn. A frustrated Governor Brown asked the Assembly to restrict cotton growing to only one-fourth an acre per hand and "make it highly penal" for anyone to exceed that limit. The Assembly refused and, despite continued urging from Brown, ignored the issue for the rest of the war. "If we are subdued," Brown pointedly warned, "it will be by starvation, and not by Lincoln's armies."[74]

In direct violation of state law, planters insisted on their right to grow as much cotton as they chose and to sell it to whomever they chose. And it did not matter who the buyers were. Planters and cotton merchants would sell to anyone, even the Yankees. Of the one and a half million bales that left the South during the war, two-thirds went to the North. Blockade runners carried much of it to Nassau, where they sold it to buyers from New York, Liverpool, and other textile centers. A good portion made its way to the North by more direct routes, with government officials on both sides, civil and military, paid off along the way.[75]

---

lanta: State Printing Office, 1909–1911) 2:268–69; *Acts of the General Assembly of the State of Georgia, 1862* (Milledgeville: Boughton, Nisbet, and Barnes, 1863) 20–22.

[74]Barnsley to Alfred A. Marsh, 3 January 1863, Godfrey Barnsley Papers, Felix Hargrett Rare Book and Manuscript Library, University of Georgia; *The American Annual Cyclopedia and Register of Important Events of the Year 1863* (New York: D. Appleton, 1864) 210; Candler, *Confederate Records of Georgia*, 2:367–68, 504–507, 591; Brown to T. D. Key, 11 March 1863, Governor's Letter Book.

[75]Lebergott, "Why the South Lost," 69; Stanley Lebergott, "Through the Blockade: The Profitability and Extent of Cotton Smuggling, 1861–1865," *Journal of Economic History* 41 (1981): 882–83. Figures rounded to the nearest

Much of the cotton flowed north along rail lines to Atlanta and from there to Chattanooga. In March 1862 came a report to Governor Brown that two Tennessee men were in Macon buying cotton. "It is believed they intend to let the Federals have it." Two weeks later, the *Atlanta Southern Confederacy* published a letter warning that "uncompromising adherents to the Northern Government have been, for weeks, shipping cotton to East Tennessee.... Don't sell them your cotton. They are your enemies." It was not only Tennesseans engaged in the business. The *Atlanta Southern Confederacy*'s Chattanooga correspondent reported that "a few traitorous Georgians have a finger in the pie."[76]

Georgia's rivers were also routes of illicit cotton trade. News circulated as early as December 1861 that cotton regularly made its way from Columbus down river to the Florida port of Apalachicola, "where it is clandestinely conveyed to the enemy's vessels to be carried North." The next month, a hundred bags of cotton were found on a Chattahoochee steamboat headed south to the Florida coast. In March 1862, a letter from Fort Gaines arrived on Governor Brown's desk describing the trade in considerable detail. Steamboats typically made their way up the Chattahoochee River loading cotton bales as they went, with Columbus their supposed destination. But somehow, much of the cotton seemed to find its way down to Apalachicola. There it was transferred to vessels which took "pleasure excursions" out to see the blockading Union fleet, always returning with empty cargo holds. A few days later, Brown received news of cotton smuggling out of Albany and Bainbridge along the Flint River

100,000 in Table 10 of Lebergott's "Through the Blockade" show that of the 6.8 million bales produced in the South during the war, 0.4 was used in the South, 0.5 went to the United Kingdom and Europe, 0.9 went to the North, and 3.8 was destroyed by neglect, the Union army, or Southerners themselves. The remaining 1.8 million bales were sold after the war.

[76]John Smith to Brown, 12 March 1862, Governor's Incoming Correspondence; *Atlanta Southern Confederacy*, 27 March and 9 April 1862.

Despite the Confederacy's food shortage and state restrictions on cotton growing, planters and merchants regularly produced and smuggled their product out to an eager market. The *Shamrock*, built in Columbus, Georgia, during the war, hauled cotton down river to the Gulf port of Apalachicola. There it was transferred to oceangoing vessels for transport to Europe and the North. With cotton prices at an all-time high, some planters bragged openly that the longer the war went on, the more money they made. Image courtesy of the Florida State Archives.

to the Gulf Coast. Much the same occurred along the Savannah River and the Ocmulgee-Oconee-Altamaha river system, Georgia's largest.[77]

So lucrative was the wartime cotton trade that Joe Brown eventually decided to get Georgia's state government in on the profits. The Confederate government did the same. Despite their previous insistence that planters grow more food, they encouraged the opposite by becoming some of the planters' best cotton customers. State and Confederate officials knew that much of the cotton would reach the North. But for many planters and politicians, the war had become not a crusade but a money-making enterprise. For some, that was all it had ever been.[78]

Planters' reluctance to devote themselves to food production was at the heart of an inflationary spiral that began to spin out of control soon after the war started. At first, few thought inflation would be a problem since the war was expected to end quickly. Even after First Manassas, some scoffed at the North's blockade of Southern ports and the economic threat it posed. Others were more farsighted. John B. Lamar, Howell Cobb's brother-in-law, wrote to the general in November 1861, "we can laugh at the blockade for a while if salt is $12 per sack." But he wondered what the impact would be if the blockade lasted another year. "Makes me hold my breath when I think of it." Less than a year later the blockade was tighter than ever and salt was selling for $125 a sack when it was available at all. It had been only two dollars before the war.[79]

Such dramatic price increases for even the most basic commodities were not uncommon. Butter went from twelve cents a pound in 1861 to seventy-five cents two years later. By the end of the war it was five dollars or more. Corn that was two dollars a bushel in 1863 sold for fourteen by February 1865. Bacon went from twelve cents to fifty cents a pound in

---

[77]*Augusta Chronicle and Sentinel*, 12 December 1861; *Columbus Sun*, 4 January 1862; J. H. Jones and D. Dudley to Brown, 5 March 1862, Governor's Incoming Correspondence; R. K Hines to Brown, 6 March 1862, Governor's Incoming Correspondence; *Savannah Republican*, 4 July 1863.

[78]Lebergott, "Through the Blockade," 868.

[79]R. P. Brooks, ed., "Howell Cobb Papers," *Georgia Historical Quarterly* 6 (1922): 360; Mrs. A. E. Moore to Joseph E. Brown, 7 October 1862, Cuyler Collection.

the war's first year. By the end of the war a pound of bacon was four dollars. Flour that sold for nine dollars a barrel before the war was going for four hundred by war's end. Coffee went to thirty dollars a pound shortly after the war began and from there to sixty and seventy dollars. The cost of more potent beverages was on the rise as well. Rum that was purchased for just seventeen cents a gallon in Cuba sold for twenty-five dollars after being run through the blockade.[80]

Certainly, the blockade contributed to rising prices, but profiteering and speculation by planters and merchants were even more damaging to the South's economy. In his study of Columbus during the war, historian Diffee Standard concluded that the blockade was more an excuse for than the cause of inflated prices. So did the editor of the *Albany Patriot*. In November 1861, he ran a piece titled "The Blockade no Excuse." For months, the editor had heard merchants blaming the blockade for high prices. But, he insisted, "there is dry goods alone within our southern limits sufficient to supply the wants of the people of the Confederate States for the next ten years to come. The blockade therefore is no excuse." In a private letter to a friend, one Georgia planter admitted as much. For some time, he wrote in April 1862, Southerners had been "abusing the Yankees for extortion and speculation, but [we are] quite as bad ourselves."[81]

Inflation sprang largely from inducements of the market. Merchants kept a tight grip on limited food and clothing, selling only to those who could pay top dollar or holding out for even higher prices. Planters continued to focus on increasingly profitable cotton, leaving inadequate land for the food production Georgia and the South needed. Both groups took the same self-interested path that had served them so well before

[80]Parthenia A. Hague, *A Blockaded Family: Life in Southern Alabama during the Civil War* (1888; repr., Freeport, NY: Books for Libraries Press, 1971) 101; Bryan, *Confederate Georgia*, 61; Standard, *Columbus in the Confederacy*, 47; John F. Reiger, "Deprivation, Disaffection, and Desertion in Confederate Florida," *Florida Historical Quarterly* 48 (1969–70): 280.

[81]Standard, *Columbus in the Confederacy*, 46; *Albany Patriot*, 28 November 1861; Godfrey Barnsley to Thomas C. Gilmour, 8 April 1862, Barnsley Papers.

the war, following the dollar wherever it led. In so doing, they left the interests of plain folk, and ultimately the Confederacy, far behind.

The Money Thieves, Those Speculators

Even as delegates were birthing the Confederacy in Montgomery, speculators were trying to corner local markets. "Is there no boundary to their desire to accumulate money?" asked the *Athens Southern Watchman* in February 1861. "Will not the cries of widowhood and orphanage pierce their dull, cold ears?" The disgusted editor was sure that had Southern speculators lived in "the days of Judas [they] would have taken the contract to betray the Savior for *fifteen* instead of *thirty* pieces of silver."[82]

Later that year, a Georgia man complained to Vice President Alexander Stephens that "common farmers" were finding it difficult "to keep our heads above the flood of destruction" brought on by "the money thieves, those Speculators." If small farmers were ruined by speculation, the Confederacy would be ruined as well. The *Savannah Republican* warned in December that "one speculator can do the Southern cause more injury in one week than a dozen Yankees could in a month." But, wrote the editor of Thomaston's *Upson Pilot*, speculators cared little for the cause. "They love Dollars and Cents, and nothing else. Money is their God—their country—their all!"[83]

In spring 1862, a woman from Griffin wrote an open letter titled "A Word to the Wise is Sufficient." She urged speculators to stop hoarding products for higher prices and taking advantage of the disadvantaged. Fearing her letter would be taken as too outspoken she wrote, "I am a woman, and am perhaps out of my proper sphere, if an interest in her suffering country can be out of a woman's sphere. I would keep silent, if the men were active, but many who remain at home, are so deeply immersed in the various schemes for money making that they seemingly pay little heed to the emergency of the times." The letter was signed, "A DAUGHTER OF GEORGIA."[84]

---

[82]*Athens Southern Watchman*, 19 February 1861.
[83]Bryan, *Confederate Georgia*, 60; *Thomaston Upson Pilot*, 19 October 1861.
[84]*Augusta Chronicle and Sentinel*, 23 March 1862.

Such letters poured into the governor's office as well. Wrote one Athens man early in the war, "there is a good deal here held by speculators who will not even sell for present prices.... The poor are actually suffering." An Atlanta woman wrote of extortionists and the poor: "Even here in Atlanta, where there is an abundance of provisions, there is a great deal of suffering among the poor class in consequence of the high price of provisions and the low price of labor." She continued, "When the war first began I thought there was a great deal of patriotism among us, but, alas, where is it? Avariciousness has almost conquered it!" In fall 1862, a Fort Valley widow reported on grossly inflated prices. "In the name of humanity," she asked Governor Brown, "must poor widows and helpless orphans be brought to suffering even for bread?"[85]

An open letter to the Georgia Assembly predicted that the country would soon have "swarms of speculators who prey upon the Government and upon the people." That prediction was quickly coming true. The superintendent of Georgia's Southwestern Railroad was inundated with so much cargo from speculators that he had problems completing government shipments.[86]

It was not long before inflation and speculation began to take their toll on Confederate currency. With prices going up every day, government notes became increasingly worthless. Many Georgians abandoned the use of paper money altogether in favor of a barter system. Most were already accustomed to some degree of barter. According to one rural Georgian, "cattle, cow hides, peas, pork, 'possum and potatoes were legal tender" even before the war.[87] But so serious did inflation become by the war's second year that livestock, farm equipment, corn, and cotton all became regular media of exchange.

Gadwell Pearce, president of LaGrange Female College, advised a Troup County woman to "get all the thread you can. It is an article of

---

[85]R. S. Taylor to Brown, 26 June 1862, Cuyler Collection; Mrs. Dr. Wellborn to Brown, 16 November 1862, Governor's Incoming Correspondence; A. E. Moore to Brown, 7 October 1862, Cuyler Collection.

[86]Carlson, "Wiregrass Runners," 30.

[87]Chapman, *Georgia Soldier*, 5.

necessity and good currency, vastly better than Confederate." Pearce knew what he was talking about. Newspapers throughout Georgia advertised items for barter, and yarn was one of the most common. Prices were running so high for yarn by late 1862 that a group of Bartow County women urged Governor Brown to seize control of Georgia's cotton and wool factories.[88]

Thomaston's *Upson Pilot* got in on the barter system when its editor began trading subscriptions for nearly any commodity of value. An entry labeled "Anything for Pay" promised just that. "We will take in exchange for our paper, or in payment of old accounts: Fire-wood, Pork, Bacon, Beef, Mutton, Wheat, Flour, Corn, Meal, Potatoes, Butter, Chickens, Eggs, Peas, Oats, Fodder, Good Hay, Wheat Bran, Cotton Seed, Coffee, Salt, or '*Goobers*.'"[89]

The torrent of pleas from anguished citizens, along with the impact of inflation and speculation on the currency, could not be ignored for long. In November 1861, the General Assembly called on the judiciary committees of the House and Senate to jointly establish a plan to restrain speculation by "the most effectual means of accomplishing such suppression." A few weeks later, the Assembly outlawed speculation in all sorts of basic commodities including "clothing, shoes, leather, cloth of any kind, provisions, wheat, flour, corn, cornmeal, meat, bacon, hogs, cattle, salt, bagging, rope, and twine." Those who ignored the law could be fined up to $5,000 and imprisoned for up to three years.[90]

Even so, in spite of all efforts to curb it, profiteering continued to sap the South's economy and morale. Governor Brown was sure that speculators and profiteers were among the Confederacy's greatest threats, but admitted that anti-speculation laws were a "dead letter."[91] Merchants simply ignored such laws and continued their price gouging.

---

[88]William H. Davidson, *Brooks of Honey and Butter: Plantations and People of Meriwether County, Georgia*, 2 vols. (Alexander City, AL: Outlook, 1971) 1:203; *Rome Tri-Weekly Courier*, 14 October 1862.

[89]*Thomaston Upson Pilot*, 14 December 1861.

[90]*Acts of the General Assembly of the State of Georgia, 1861* (Milledgeville: Boughton, Nisbet, and Barnes, 1862) 132, 66–67.

[91]Brown to Zebulon B. Vance, 26 September 1862, Brown Papers, Library

Several Georgia newspapers reprinted an entry about one particularly callous speculator in the Confederate capital. Titled "A Heartless Wretch," the story charged that "a creature in the good city of Richmond told a poor woman, whose despair at his asking her seventy-five dollars for flour caused her to inquire of him what she was to do to live. 'I recon, madam, you will have to eat your children!' What a monster!" Though perhaps apocryphal, this article reflected the attitude of many a speculator, and the attitude of many a citizen in return. When an Atlanta woman accidently ran over a pedestrian with her buggy, she was mortified, thinking she had hit a soldier. After a closer look, she recognized the man as a well-known speculator. She left him in the street "regretting that her buggy wheels had not run over his neck."[92]

Despite their socially paternalistic self-image, planters were just as eager to reap huge profits. Like their urban counterparts, planters commonly stockpiled foodstuffs to force higher prices. Initial market projections in 1861 set corn at one dollar per bushel, but few would sell at that price. Jeremiah Wilson, who owned a plantation two miles outside Albany, had two thousand bushels that he would not sell for less than two dollars each. Neither would John Jones of Dougherty County, who had ten thousand bushels. Captain Stow, a commissary agent sent to purchase food, had contracted with Dougherty County planters for up to 170,000 bushels of corn, but most was never delivered. Planters held fast to their corn, anticipating that prices would soon rise from one dollar a bushel to perhaps five or six. Wrote Stow to his superiors, "You have no idea the number of corn-buyers in southwestern Georgia, mostly on speculation. They must be stopped in some way or our Army will suffer."[93]

The crisis in corn prices was made even worse by those who could afford it still clamoring for whiskey. R. R. Hunt of Ellijay wrote in February 1862 that "the distilleries have bought up all the corn and [are] making it into Liquor[.] [O]ur families must suffer for bread if it is not

---

of Congress.

[92]*Rome Tri-Weekly Courier*, 12 November and 19 December 1863.

[93]*OR*, series 1, vol. 14, 682–83.

Kate Cumming, a Scottish-born Confederate nurse from Mobile who served in Georgia during the war, criticized speculators for "making *piles* of money out of the misfortunes of their country." She expressed the feeling of many Southerners when she wrote that speculators were destined to burn in hellfire. "If they only suffer one half the pangs of which they have been the cause, their case will be sad indeed." Image from Kate Cumming, *Gleanings from Southland* (1895).

amediately stoped[.] [It is] a worse scourage than Lincoln's army." Later that year, the General Assembly prohibited distillation of corn, wheat, rye, into "spirituous liquors" except for medicinal, hospital, chemical, or mechanical purposes. Anyone found guilty of illegal distillation could be severely fined. Half the money went to the informer. The other half was entrusted to the justices of local inferior courts for support of soldiers' wives, widows and children. But the law was easy to dodge, and some law officers found great profit in overlooking unlicensed distillers for a portion of their profits.[94]

Corn needed for starving families was continuously siphoned away by distillers who could pay more because their customers could. R. R. Hunt insisted that such men were a tremendous asset to the Union cause: "If they were acting as Lencolns agents the[y] could not fall on a better plan to favour him." A soldier from Morgantown complained of the many stills in his area and the men who were buying up all the corn and rye. The state of affairs was hampering enrollment since potential recruits were reluctant to leave their families "to the mercy of a drunken set of men and extortioners." He and other volunteers threatened to destroy the stills if the governor took no action, writing, "If there is not something done, I am fully convinced that many of the soldiers' wives and families of the soldiers will suffer for bread to eat."[95]

Some planters organized "corn combinations" to set local prices. The move was purportedly a defense against speculators, but functioned to defend planters' own inflated prices. If speculators were holding out for more, so the argument went, planters had to do the same. Critics called the combinations unpatriotic cabals that helped undermine the Confederate cause. But one combination defender insisted that although "the wives and children, widows and orphans of the soldiers will suffer

---

[94]Hunt to Brown, 19 February 1862, Adjutant and Inspector General's Incoming Correspondence, Georgia Department of Archives and History; *Acts of the General Assembly of the State of Georgia, 1862*, 25–28, 141–42.

[95]Hunt to Brown, 19 February 1862, Adjutant and Inspector General's Incoming Correspondence; M. Greenwood to Brown, 19 February 1862, Adjutant and Inspector General's Incoming Correspondence.

mostly by this arrangement...it is their misfortune to be poor and they must suffer the consequences."[96]

Nelson Tift of Albany, a chief proponent of the combinations, was in a unique position to profit from the war. By the 1860s, his financial and political interests extended throughout southwest Georgia. He had spearheaded attempts to draw the railroad to Dougherty County and sponsored legislation to clear obstructions in the Flint River for steamboat travel. He was one of the largest land owners in Dougherty County, and his Albany Bridge Company controlled the town's only crossing over the Flint River. He was also in negotiations with the Confederate navy for a lucrative commissary contract.

If the local corn combination had accepted government pricing, Tift's hands would have been tied and the rapid growth of his real estate and infrastructure holdings would never have occurred. Instead, the combination's "average" pricing scheme allowed him to charge at or near his usual levels, enabling Tift to build a complex of warehouses along the Flint River.

At the center of this complex, and predating it by a decade, was Tift's bridge house, a two-storied brick warehouse that served as the bridge entrance. The ground floor contained Tift's private office and the bridge keeper's quarters, separated from one another by an arched passageway. It was through this arch that anyone entering Albany from the east side of the Flint River had to pass after paying whatever toll Tift chose to impose.

To pay for his wartime projects, Tift increased both the tolls on his bridge and his prices on corn and other supplies. He charged tolls twice on wagons loaded for market, once when entering town and again when leaving. And he began charging pedestrians to cross, who had paid no toll before the war.

Popular opinion soon turned against Tift, and the Dougherty County Inferior Court declared him in violation of his charter. It ordered him to lower rates to those fixed in the charter and to post those rates at the bridge house. Tift refused. The court, finding him in contempt, pub-

[96]Carlson, "Wiregrass Runners," 32.

lished their own rates. Tift ignored the court order and continued charging his increased rates.[97]

Nelson Tift was but one example of the planters and merchants who preyed on their neighbors all over Georgia and the South. They provided daily evidence that the struggle was little more than a rich man's war. And as the rich became richer, the more reluctant they became to support those who were fighting their war. In February 1862, the *Milledgeville Confederate Union* called on wealthy men in Baldwin County to "COME UP WITH YOUR MONEY!" Soldiers' families were suffering, and the editor reminded planters of their obligation to help: "It is for you and your property that tens of thousands of poor men are now fighting.... What are the rich men of Baldwin doing? Nothing. Wake up from your slumber."[98] But they did not awake, neither in Baldwin County nor in all of Georgia.

---

[97]Ibid., 33–36.

[98]*Milledgeville Confederate Union* in *Savannah Morning News*, 19 February 1862.

Chapter 3

1862–1863: Harrowing Beyond Description

In early 1862, the *Milledgeville Confederate Union* chastised wealthy men of Baldwin County for doing so little to aid soldiers' families while profiting at their expense. Such criticism did little good. A year later the *Union* editor wrote, "There are many men, in every county in the state, who have fallen short of their duty.... When called on to make subscriptions to aid a poor disabled soldier, or help a soldier's suffering family, they have turned the back of their hands." The editor doubted that these "miserable abortions of humanity, who have been a living lie for more than two years" would ever change their ways. A writer to the *Athens Southern Watchman* suggested that Lincoln should give such men officers' commissions in the Union army "as they can accomplish far more than many of his Federal appointments."[1] Certainly they were doing as much to undermine Confederate morale as any Union soldier ever had. Though they were not shooting Confederates, they were starving soldiers and their families.

The Leeches and Sharks of Our Own People

Speculating planters and merchants were a major force driving what became a spiraling inflationary trap. Planters fed a lucrative market in cotton, devoting not nearly enough acreage to food production. Scarcity forced food prices up, and speculation drove them even higher. Rampant inflation inevitably followed, making planters and smaller farmers even less willing to exchange what food they had for increasingly worthless Confederate currency.

---

[1] *Milledgeville Confederate Union*, 19 February 1862, 12 May 1863; *Athens Southern Watchman*, 25 June 1862.

By winter 1862–1863, the Richmond government determined that what it could not procure with paper, it would take by force. Congress passed, and Davis signed into law, a series of taxes, the most significant of which was a 10 percent levy on such farm items as livestock, wheat, corn, oats, rye, hay, fodder, buckwheat, sweet potatoes, Irish potatoes, sugar, cotton, wool, tobacco, peas, beans, and peanuts. Even this tax-in-kind did not provide enough food to meet military needs. So Confederate officials began "impressing" these items, and anything else they wanted, far beyond the 10 percent level.

Some farmers resisted impressment, making government agents' and army quartermasters' jobs increasingly dangerous. They were beaten, shot at, and sometimes killed. Joe Brown, an avid opponent of Confederate impressment, warned that the practice and its "baneful operations" could only encourage opposition to the central government by producing an "evil spirit, bordering already in many cases upon open disloyalty."[2]

Brown was foremost among Southern governors in his hostility to Confederate impressment. As early as 1861 when the Davis administration tried to seize engines and cars on the state-owned Western and Atlantic Railroad, Brown threatened to call out the Georgia militia. Davis thought it wiser to fight one war at a time and canceled the order. When the Confederacy began general impressment, Georgia's Assembly passed a resolution declaring it unconstitutional.[3]

As hostile as Brown and the Assembly were toward Confederate impressment, they did not hesitate to impose their own. Georgia was among the first Confederate states to begin impressing supplies. One citizen, pointing to numerous seizures by the state, wrote to a Georgia newspaper complaining of Brown's hypocrisy: "And yet this same Governor had made more noise about the legal and constitutional rights of

---

[2] *War of the Rebellion: A Compilation of the Official Records of the Union and Confederate Armies* (Washington, DC: Government Printing Office, 1880–1901) series 4, vol. 2, 944 (hereafter cited as *OR*).

[3] Allen D. Candler, comp., *The Confederate Records of Georgia*, 6 vols. (Atlanta: State Printing Office, 1909–1911) 3:132, 134; James A. Riley, "Desertion and Disloyalty in Georgia during the Civil War" (master's thesis, University of Georgia, 1951) 27.

Impressment was often accompanied by depredations of all sorts. A seventy-year-old Bibb County man was threatened with a beating if he did not hand over his horse. An impressment officer shot and killed a man in Social Circle who refused to give up his cattle. Though intended for the army, agents often sold confiscated goods and pocketed the funds. One citizens' committee warned that impressment officials would "ultimately alienate the affections of the people from the government." Image from Daniel Ellis, *Thrilling Adventures* (1867).

the people than all the men in the Confederacy." Editor William Scruggs of the *Columbus Sun* sarcastically observed that impressment "originated in this state with Governor Brown, who, of course, does everything according to the 'Constitutional' square and compass." Robert Toombs, who often joined the governor in opposing Confederate policy, wrote of his friend, "I see Brown has got him an impressment law too. How catching is thieving."[4]

Whether impressment was done by Georgia or the Confederacy, compensation was nearly always a point of argument. In October 1862, Secretary of War George Randolph asked Attorney General Thomas Watts for an opinion on the legality of impressment. Watts concluded that impressment was indeed legal as long as the government paid "just compensation." The problem was that impressment agents and property owners rarely agreed on what "just compensation" meant. Davis tried to address the problem by establishing impressment committees to set prices, but inflation was so severe and committees met so infrequently that the government's fixed prices were almost always far below market value. Within months after impressment began, the official price allowed for flour was half that available on the open market. Government corn prices were only a third.

In most cases, farmers were lucky to get even a small payment for their impressed produce. Corruption was so rampant among impressment officers that it was not unusual for them to pocket a portion of funds reserved for paying farmers. One Georgia farmer complained bitterly when he discovered that the government had authorized fifty cents a pound for bacon. Confederate agents had given him only thirty-five. Sometimes farmers received promissory notes instead of cash. Very often they did not even get that. It was just as well. The notes were nearly impossible to redeem. When one Georgia man tried to collect on a note

[4]*Milledgeville Southern Recorder*, 17 March 1863; *Columbus Sun*, 28 November 1862; Ulrich Bonnell Phillips, ed., *Correspondence of Robert Toombs, Alexander H. Stephens, and Howell Cobb* (Washington, DC: Government Printing Office, 1913) 660.

that was ten months past due, he was met by a sign "placed up conspicuously in large letters, 'No funds.'"[5]

In south Georgia's Thomas and Brooks counties, impressment agents took cattle "without paying at all." The same was happening in north Georgia. John Cain of Whitfield County wrote Governor Brown complaining that agents were "taking our produces, our horses, cattle, sheep and hogs and very seldom pay anything." From Calhoun County, J. H. B. Shackleford wrote the governor that a great many agents "take the liberty to help themselves without money." William C. Humphreys of Clinch County told the governor that there was "a general system of stealing going on under the impressment act."[6]

Some agents sold confiscated produce on the open market and kept the money for themselves. In late 1862, scandal rocked the War Department when quartermaster officers were discovered selling army food supplies to speculators and embezzling the proceeds. An Augusta man told Governor Brown that local quartermasters were "involved and complicated" with speculators. The *Columbus Sun* noted that "a Quartermaster is looked upon with a feeling of distrust in almost every community."[7]

Those presenting themselves as government agents were not always what they appeared to be. Farmers often tried to redeem promissory notes only to find that they had been swindled by imposters. The problem became so bad that the General Assembly mandated ten years' imprisonment for anyone engaged in confiscation without authority to do so. Governor Brown favored an additional punishment of "thirty-nine

---

[5]Rebecca Christian, "Georgia and the Confederate Policy of Impressing Supplies," *Georgia Historical Quarterly* 28 (1944): 13, 16; *OR*, series 4, vol. 3, 968.

[6]*Savannah Morning News*, 14 June 1862; Cain to Joseph E. Brown, 28 September 1863, Governor's Incoming Correspondence, Georgia Department of Archives and History, Morrow; Shackleford to Brown, 27 September 1863, Governor's Incoming Correspondence; Humphreys to Brown, 27 November 1863, Governor's Incoming Correspondence.

[7]G. W. Lamar to Brown, 16 December 1862, Governor's Incoming Correspondence; *Columbus Sun*, 10 September 1863.

lashes on the bare back," but the legislature thought imprisonment sufficient.[8]

Even when impressment was done by legally sanctioned officials, it was often accompanied by depredations of all sorts. Soldiers' wives or widows were the most frequent targets since their husbands were either dead or hundreds of miles away. Agents occasionally used their impressment power to victimize political or personal enemies as well. Sometimes abuse involved more than threats of violence. An impressment officer shot and killed a man in Social Circle who refused give up his cattle. "Let these outrages be stopped," demanded the editor of Atlanta's *Southern Confederacy*.[9]

Distrust of government agents, state and Confederate, had been widespread for some time. As early as fall 1861, a farmer wrote to the *Athens Southern Watchman*, "I have never entertained the shadow of a doubt as to our success—our whipping out all the Yankees that can be produced—but God knows how we shall escape the *corruptions* of our own Government, and the *leeches and sharks* of our own people." Another exasperated Georgian was sure that there was only one route of escape and begged Governor Brown to take it. "Do for God's sake put an end to this unrighteous war. We shall be eaten up by Confederate Office holders and Speculators."[10]

I Don't Think I Will Last Much Longer

When confiscated food products made it to government depots without being sold off by corrupt impressment agents or quartermasters, it frequently went to waste through incompetence or neglect. In March 1863, the *Columbus Times* reported that while thousands faced starvation, more than half a million bushels of corn languished in government depots throughout southwest Georgia. Albany had a hundred thousand bushels

---

[8]Christian, "Georgia and the Confederate Policy of Impressing Supplies," 20.

[9]*Atlanta Southern Confederacy*, 27 February 1863.

[10]*Athens Southern Watchman*, 23 October 1861; Anonymous to Brown, n.d., Governor's Incoming Correspondence.

rotting in its warehouses while trains loaded with cotton were daily pulling out of town. "Is the Southwestern Railroad leaning to *favorites*," asked the outraged *Albany Patriot*, "or speculating in the article themselves?"[11]

To soldiers who were suffering on account of corruption and neglect, it was just as outrageous that men of property, especially those with twenty slaves or more, could so easily avoid the draft. One enraged Georgia trooper wrote to the *Atlanta Southern Confederacy*, "For God's sake don't tell the poor soldier who now shivers in a Northern wind while you snooze in a feather bed, that it is *just* and *right* that the men, who Congress has exempted, should enjoy ease at home, amassing untold riches, while *he* must fight, bleed, and even die."[12] Another Georgia soldier called planters

> the most contemptible of all our public enemies.... These fellows talk loudly about *their* constitutional rights—that no body has a right to say how much cotton they shall plant and intend to put at defiance the law and the authorities. But listen again and you will hear them loud for the enforcement of the Conscript Law. Oh, yes! Their negroes must make cotton and whilst doing it the poor men must be taken from their families and put in the Army to protect their negroes. Was ever a greater wrong, or a more damning sin, perpetrated by men or devils?[13]

Some soldiers felt that planters who used the twenty-slave law to shield themselves from military service "ought to be made to fight for their property or ought to be deprived of it."[14]

[11]Christian, "Georgia and the Confederate Policy of Impressing Supplies," 14–15; Robert David Carlson, "Wiregrass Runners: Conscription, Desertion, and the Origins of Discontent in Civil War South Georgia" (master's thesis, Valdosta State University, 1999) 26.

[12]*Atlanta Southern Confederacy*, 30 October 1862.

[13]*Milledgeville Confederate Union*, 31 March 1863.

[14]*Macon Telegraph*, 14 July 1863.

Shielded from the draft in various ways, planters who wished to avoid military service had little trouble doing so. "Their negroes must make cotton," complained one Georgia soldier, and "the poor men must be taken from their families and put in the Army to protect their negroes. Was ever a greater wrong, or a more damning sin, perpetrated by men or devils?" Image from *Harper's Weekly* (1862).

Of most concern to soldiers was the condition of their families. Letters described the struggles of destitute wives and mothers. Mary Brooks was left with three young children, a baby not yet weaned, and a farm to run near Greenville. She wrote to her husband, Rhodam, "I never get any rest night or day, and I don't think I will last much longer." She was running low on bacon and salt as well as money with which to purchase them. "It is money for everything," she said, "so you may know it is getting low with me." Most soldiers had little or no money to send since enlisted men went without pay for months at a time. One Georgia soldier wrote home about officers in his regiment receiving their pay while the enlisted men got none. In protest, they laid down their arms until the payroll arrived.[15]

Money was usually a secondary concern for soldiers' wives. What they most wanted was for their men to come home. Mary Jane Curry of Decatur County wrote to her husband, "I had such a pleasant dream last night. I thought you was at home and expected to remain."[16] Writing from Troup County, Sallie Lovett spoke in moving terms of how the days dragged by as she waited for her Billie's return.

> My dearest husband:
>
> It is with a sad and heavy heart I take my pen in hand to write you a few lines. I received your very welcome letter last evening, glad indeed to hear from you and hear you was getting along so well. For it is more than I am. Billie, I am in so much trouble this evening. I have looked for you so hard today. I thought you would be sure to come.... Every time I hear a train I go to the door. I say, well, I do hope Billie [will] come down on that train. I wait and look until dinner. Then I say, well, I do hope he will come this evening. I wait until dark. No Billie yet. Then I bring a long sigh, perhaps a tear and say, well, I don't know why

---

[15]Mary Frances Brooks to Rhodam Maxie Brooks, 3 September 1862, Confederate Letters Collection, United Daughters of the Confederacy, Georgia Department of Archives and History; J. Boyd to his brother, 16 February 1862, Boyd Letters, Columbus State University Archives, Columbus, GA.

[16]Mary Jane Love Curry to Duncan Curry, 9 December 1862, Curry Hill Plantation Records, Georgia Department of Archives and History.

> he don't come. Every time I hear a noise towards the gate I run to the door, but what do I see: nothing but trees and bushes. I strain my eyes almost out of their sockets but no Billie can I see. I turn 'round with a sigh. To think he has forgotten me! ...I am not living any now, only breathing. It is true I am well in body but not at heart. My heart is grieved, the worst of all diseases. Honey, why don't you come home?

Like so many other women, Sallie cared much more for her family than anything else. "I would give a world of Confederacies," she later wrote Billie, "just to be with you."[17]

Soldiers wanted to come home just as badly as their wives wanted them to, but it was difficult for enlisted men to get furloughs. William Asbell wrote home that none of the men in his company were getting furloughs and there was no telling when they would. A month later furloughs were still unavailable. Eli Hurst received word from his wife in Thomas County that the fence around his land had been destroyed by fire, leaving crops exposed to the livestock. He requested an eight-day leave to mend the fence or make arrangements for someone else to do so. G. W. Huguley asked for leave after receiving word that his child was ill, possibly dying. His wife was in a "wreched and desolate condition."[18] Such pleas occasionally brought furloughs, but they were few and far between.

If furloughs were hard to get, discharges were nearly impossible to come by. One Georgia private said of his commander, "This damned general won't give you a furlough or a discharge till you are dead ten days, and *then* you have to prove it." But letters from home were filled with such gloom that tens of thousands of men left the ranks without permission. Knowing the possible impact of such letters, one Georgia

---

[17]Mills Lane, ed., *Times That Prove People's Principles: Civil War in Georgia—A Documentary History* (Savannah: Beehive Press, 1993) 97, 105.

[18]Lewis N. Wynne and Guy Porcher Harrison, eds., "'Plain Folk' Coping in the Confederacy: The Garrett-Asbell Letters," *Georgia Historical Quarterly* 72 (1988): 114, 116–17; Hurst to C. H. May, 1 April 1862, Talemon Cuyler Collection, Felix Hargrett Rare Book and Manuscript Library, University of Georgia, Athens; Huguley to commander, 3rd Brigade, 9 April 1862, Cuyler Collection.

editor warned soldiers' families, "If you feel sad, don't write at all, rather than write in a sad strain."[19]

In early 1863, one soldier received a letter from his wife, who told of her suffering and begged him to come home. After several days of reading and re-reading the letter, he abandoned his post. Soon after, he was captured, tried, convicted of desertion, and executed by firing squad. One unsympathetic commentator insisted that the man's wife was to blame, writing in an Atlanta paper that "she inconsiderately brought her husband to a dishonorable death." He chastised women generally for writing sad letters. "Wives! mothers! beware what you write to your sons and husbands in the army. A thoughtless and imprudent letter may lead to discontent, desertion and death."[20]

Absence from their families was for many men the greatest struggle they faced during the war. Letters from soldiers to their families were filled with painful regret at being so far from home. That was clearly evident in one of George Fowler's letters.

> Dear Wife, I would like to bee thare with you in youre sickness to waite on you[,] as it is I cant. I want you to take care of yourself as I want to see [you] more in this life and if we are note permited to meete nomore in this life I doo hope that we will bee prepared to meete in thate uper and beter world where there, there will bee no more parting of wives A[nd] husbands And children fathers And mothers.[21]

Soldiers frequently offered advice on what to do until their return. In November 1863, William Asbell wrote to his wife Sarah: "I have received both of your letters and was glad to hear Through them that you are all alive but sorry to know that the children are sick on your hands when I cannot be there to assist you with Them." William told Sarah to feed their hogs corn once a day and potatoes the rest of the time. "If the children are not able to dig the potatoes," he said, "fence of a portion of

---

[19]Geoffrey C. Ward, *The Civil War* (New York: Alfred A. Knopf, 1992) 201; *Augusta Chronicle and Sentinel*, 8 August 1861.

[20]*Atlanta Southern Confederacy*, 11 February 1863.

[21]Fowler to Tabetha C. Fowler, 7 October 1863, Civil War Miscellany, Georgia Department of Archives and History.

the patch for [the hogs]." As the weather grew colder and food ran low, William told Sarah, "You had better try and sell one or other of the horses…as you are scarce of Provisions. You will have to do the best you can."[22]

For many women laboring under the burdens of inflation, impressment, sick children, and absent husbands, their best was simply not good enough. A flood of despairing letters poured into Governor Brown's office telling of illness at home, sons being taken away, husbands needed to take in crops or mend fences. There were tales of children having no bread or meat and widows trying to provide for infants. In February 1862, a Georgia woman wrote to Brown, "I hope before many days we will have better times than we have now. For, if we don't, what will become of us all? We have the war to support and nothing to support with, for the provisions is so high and no money that people can't get it if they don't make it at home. And when the men all leaves, who will make support for the soldiers and the rest?"[23]

Very often, Georgia's many illiterate women got others to write for them. Two women from Whitfield County dictated a letter to Governor Brown about their desperate condition and signed an "X" in place of their names. Both their husbands were serving in the army. "We are willing to bear all that is possible," they said, "but when our poor children calls to us for bread and we have none to give them the case is harrowing beyond description."[24]

In October 1862, the *Augusta Chronicle and Sentinel* published a letter describing conditions in the governor's home county of Cherokee. "There are hundreds of families without salt, or leather, or thread to cloth[e] themselves and their children, without wheat and but half crops of corn." The writer stressed that most of the sufferers were women and children whose menfolk had gone to war—a great many of them now

---

[22]Wynne and Harrison, "'Plain Folk' Coping in the Confederacy," 115, 117.

[23]Mary Malory to Brown, 23 February 1862, Cuyler Collection.

[24]J. Clements and Isabella [illegible] to Brown, 8 October 1863, Cuyler Collection.

dead or maimed for life. As conditions grew worse, editors increasingly called on affluent citizens to support the poor. The *Columbus Sun* frequently reminded west Georgia planters of their obligation to care for soldiers' families. Athens's *Southern Watchman* did the same. "Give to the Poor!" read the heading for an article in the *Macon Telegraph*.[25]

Meat was among the greatest needs. As one editor wrote in January 1863, there was a huge demand for pork, but much of it was being hoarded for higher prices. Citing an earlier selling price of thirty cents a pound, the *Southern Watchman* chastised speculators for hoarding it to force prices up. "We suppose those who have it expect to get *a dollar per pound for bacon* next summer. God help the poor!"[26]

Leather goods were also scarce. "The article of leather for making shoes has reached enormous prices," wrote W. C. Cale of Lumpkin County in September 1862. He had tried to purchase leather to make shoes for soldiers' families, but found that raw leather had jumped from thirteen cents a pound to two dollars or more. Cale insisted that there was leather enough available and that such price gouging was unnecessary. He suggested that inferior courts be empowered to purchase shoes or leather at reasonable prices for soldiers' widows and wives or they would suffer terribly in the coming winter months. Writing on the outside fold of Cale's letter, Brown responded by saying that he had no authority over county courts regarding price control, but that "the legislature may do something when it meets."[27]

Even firewood for cooking, curing meat, and warming the household became a scarce commodity, hoarded like any other item of value. By early 1862, the shortage was so great in Atlanta that, on his own, Georgia's state railroad superintendent began procuring wood for soldiers' families and the indigent. In November, Augusta's *Chronicle and*

---

[25]*Augusta Chronicle and Sentinel*, 21 October 1862; *Columbus Sun*, 29 October 1861; *Athens Southern Watchman*, 1 May 1861; *Macon Telegraph*, 23 May 1861.

[26]*Athens Southern Watchman*, 21 January 1863.

[27]Cale to Brown, 9 September 1862, Governor's Incoming Correspondence.

Sentinel urged the city to organize wood distribution to Richmond County's poor before winter. The *Milledgeville Confederate Union* lamented that "the present prices of wood foreshadows great suffering among the poor for wood during the coming winter." It suggested that inferior courts impose a tax to supply wood for indigents and called on the wealthy not to forget their poor neighbors. "Will not those in authority attend to this business before they hear of families freezing to death in our midst?" Some counties had already levied relief taxes, but as a letter in the *Atlanta Southern Confederacy* pointed out, there was rarely a systematic method for dispersing supplies to needy families. The writer suggested appointing committees to organize relief efforts. "Let them visit every family, and relieve the wants of those who are entitled to it."[28]

An equally pressing need was for thread to make clothing. Both rich and poor felt that need, but there were wide degrees of difference. Planters' wives and daughters, accustomed to silks and other finery, had to settle for homespun dresses. With most of the vital ports blockaded, fashionable silk dresses and hoop skirts were becoming more expensive. Milledgeville's *Confederate Union* reported that President Davis, during a trip through Jackson, Mississippi, tipped his hat to a lady wearing homespun. He expressed pride at seeing an upper-class woman doing her part for the cause by wearing anything but imported fine silk. The editor expressed hope that wealthier ladies would wear more homespun and "thus prove to the world that the Southern woman's principle and patriotism are not subordinate to the pride of the eye."[29]

To some debutantes of the day, the war was no excuse to ignore fashion. One young lady calling herself "Jennie Freedom" responded to an editorial discouraging imported hoop skirts. The editors had suggested that young ladies, "old maids," and children not wear hoops, citing a shortage of material to make the undergarment wiring. "Miss Jennie" would hear none of it. "Wouldn't my new silk look a *fright*, all *tucked up*

---

[28] *Atlanta Southern Confederacy*, 23 March 1862; *Augusta Chronicle and Sentinel*, 1 November 1862; *Milledgeville Confederate Union*, 27 October 1863; *Atlanta Southern Confederacy*, 1 September 1861.

[29] *Milledgeville Confederate Union*, 13 January 1863.

to keep it out of the mud! And then, if it were not for hoops, how could I and my two dear class mates fill up a whole pew at church and keep out all common folks from jamming down by us?" She feared what they might overhear if the girls happened to "whisper a little." She declared that she would wear her hoops as long as they were fashionable and if "awkward pedestrians" did not like it, they could step out of the way.[30] Aside from fashion, her reasons for wearing hoops were clear—to keep "common folks" at a distance.

The great difficulty common people had when it came to clothes was obtaining the money to buy them or the cloth to make them. T. M. Furlow of Americus wrote to Governor Brown of manufacturers charging outrageous prices for cotton and wool cloth, and of speculating merchants making the problem even worse. Furlow suggested ways Brown could stop such speculation and warned that "if you do not do it, I would not be surprised to see the people rise in mobs and put it down themselves." Bartow County women told Brown about their husbands, brothers, fathers, and friends suffering on the battle front, and that they wanted to make uniforms and blankets for them. "We suffer when we know they suffer," wrote the women. "We are unable to relieve them as the stony hearted owners of factories have placed the materials of clothing beyond our reach."[31]

Troup County women were suffering as well. One letter told of a local factory's unwillingness to sell cloth or cotton cards at reasonable prices. The writer asked, "How is a poor soldiers wife to clothe her children when she has no cards?" The letter further complained of factories employing able-bodied men who should have been in the army, and suggested that they be sent to the front so that women could be hired in their places. That way the women's families would have some means of support.[32]

---

[30] *Atlanta Southern Confederacy*, 3 November 1861.

[31] Furlow to Brown, 15 February 1862, Governor's Incoming Correspondence; Petition from Bartow County to Brown, 10 October 1862, Cuyler Collection.

[32] Anonymous to Brown, 7 August 1863, Cuyler Collection. Cotton cards

Even those women fortunate enough to find work were in dire straits since their wages came in the form of increasingly worthless Confederate currency. Worse yet was receiving no pay at all. Martha Russell of Augusta, who had three children working at the state arsenal, was upset because they had not received their wages. "I am poore and desolate and I stand in neede of money and I cant get a sent and I wish you would try and get it for me," she wrote to Governor Brown.[33]

Factory owners holding government contracts to employ "needle women" had ample opportunity to skim wages. Some paid their workers barely half the wages due, keeping the rest for themselves. Such schemes, taking advantage of the government and the poor, drew the attention of the *Columbus Sun* in spring 1863.

> Only think of it. A sleek speculator growing rich by the labor of the poor half-famished needle woman, who gave up her husband as a sacrifice on the altar of our country! A man who forcibly wrests from the hands of starving children that which is to make him rich! A man who will deliberately rob the widow and orphan of their daily bread, that he may add to his opulence. A man who professes not only to be a patriot, but also a christian, who would deliberately drive the poor sewing woman to choose between a life of shame or an ignominous death by starvation! How dare such a monster look his fellow man in the face without cowering in very shame? The milder forms of villiany [sic], such as treachery, and counterfeiting sinks into insignificance when compared with such enormities.[34]

Despite increased profits flowing into the pockets of Southern industrialists, wages were generally low from the war's outset. In October 1861, a "poor mechanic" wrote the *Athens Southern Watchman* complaining that he could not find work that paid nearly what he got before the

---

were small hand-held paddles with approximately one-eighth-inch wire bristles embedded in one side. A pair was used to line up cotton fibers in preparation for spinning.

[33]Russell to Brown, 13 March 1863, Governor's Incoming Correspondence.

[34]*Columbus Sun* in *Milledgeville Confederate Union*, 14 April 1863.

war. With prices on the rise, he wondered how he was going to support his family. He was not alone. The paper's editor knew that many local workers faced similar hardships. The only thing he could add to the man's "words of truth and soberness" was "God help the poor day-laborers."[35]

Working conditions were just as appalling as wages. In some cases, they were deadly. With labor readily available, few industrialists saw much point in spending money on worker safety. The result was that throughout the war, Georgia's urban newspapers were filled with reports of fatal industrial accidents. One of the worst occurred at Augusta's Confederate States Laboratory when several tons of gunpowder exploded, killing nine employees. The concussion stripped all the leaves from neighborhood trees and broke window panes in all the surrounding buildings. According to one report, the victims were "blown to atoms. Hardly a vestige of them remaining. Portions of the bodies were found hanging on the trees—a most shocking spectacle."[36]

Children in the labor force were even more imperiled. Because they were usually unskilled and economically less valuable, they often performed the most hazardous jobs. Martin Reilly, who worked at a Savannah foundry to support his widowed mother, was blinded in one eye when molten lead splattered his face. A falling timber killed John Henry, a boy of fifteen, at Oglesby's Mill near Augusta. His father had already died working at the same mill. Jack McElrath and John Madden, aged twelve and fifteen respectively, were horribly mangled when an artillery shell they were working on exploded at the Columbus Naval Iron Works. Both suffered through more than an hour of agony before they died.[37]

Facing dangerous conditions and low wages, one group of working women chose to strike for higher pay. Late in the war, after years of

---

[35] *Athens Southern Watchman*, 30 October 1861.

[36] *Augusta Chronicle and Sentinel*, 28 August 1864.

[37] *Savannah Republican*, 18 August 1862; *Augusta Chronicle and Sentinel*, 24 March 1863; David Williams, *Rich Man's War: Class, Caste, and Confederate Defeat in the Lower Chattahoochee Valley* (Athens: University of Georgia Press, 1998) 73.

struggle, the "female operatives" of Augusta's gunpowder works finally walked out when they were refused a salary increase. The owners opted to advertise for new workers but offered barely a living wage. A local paper complained that "it is rather a criminal sort of economy which arranges a schedule of pay upon a calculation of the minimum amount of food it requires to sustain a human life."[38]

Along with other sources of working-class anger, high food prices among them, a controversy over trade unions sparked unrest in cities throughout Georgia. When the General Assembly considered a bill outlawing trade unions and strikes in April 1863, workers throughout the state howled in protest. In an open letter to their legislators, one group of enraged mechanics wrote, "We feel sirs, that you would rob our children's mouth of their last crust. We feel that you would grind us down to porridge and rags. We feel that you would have us gravel [sic] in the dust beneath your aristocratic tread." They spoke for many common folk when they charged that the Confederacy had been "formed solely for the benefit (socially and pecuniarily) of the aristocrats."[39] Such conflicts further entrenched an already common "rich man's war" attitude among working folk.

Refuse Me and I Die

Inequities of the free market, cotton overproduction, rising food prices, general inflation, and lack of effective regulation all contributed to the rising poverty and hunger that plagued common folk from near the war's beginning. By the war's second year there were increasingly desperate calls for organized poor relief. The editor of the *Savannah Republican* wrote, "The poor have been fed and clothed in other cities, and it can, and *should* be done in ours." Some called on Savannah's city council to impose a tax for poor relief. Voluntary contributions were hardly enough. One local newspaper noted that collected funds under the voluntary system were not evenly distributed and that it was an "uncertain charity" at

---

[38]*Augusta Chronicle and Sentinel*, 27 October 1864.

[39]Clarence L. Mohr, "Slavery and Class Tensions in Confederate Georgia," *Gulf Coast Historical Review* 4 (1989): 65.

best. In fact, wrote the editor, it was not charity at all to support families sacrificing their men to the war. It was simply their "just dues."[40]

A movement to establish stores for the poor began in 1863 in Atlanta and soon spread to Columbus and Milledgeville. The *Macon Telegraph*, hoping to spark a reaction, asked its readers, "Why should other cities and towns of Georgia be ahead of Macon in this provision for the more indigent classes of the community?" Unfortunately, many well-intentioned plans never materialized, especially in the war's latter phase. Savannah's effort to establish a cost-free market for soldiers' families elicited only a "feeble response" from contributors and was subsequently abandoned.[41]

Like their urban counterparts, Georgia's rural counties also faced problems with voluntary contributions. It quickly became obvious that there were not enough volunteers to meet the need. When Clarke County's inferior court issued $5,000 in bonds for relief of soldiers' families, a local editor wrote, "This was a move in the right direction," but "the idea of raising funds by voluntary contributions was not a good one." Too many wealthy men were "closefisted," so much so that relief had to come from the county's general tax fund.[42]

Other counties adopted similar plans to help the poor. Sumter County's superior court minutes from 1863 reported that 279 soldiers' families received relief funds from which monthly payments totaled nearly $28,000. Six dollars went to each soldier's wife and two dollars to each child less than ten years of age. Parents of soldiers having no means of support received two dollars. Muscogee County's grand jury appropriated $60,000 for poor relief.[43]

---

[40]*Savannah Republican*, 13 December 1862; *Savannah Morning News*, 4 March 1862.

[41]Wendy Hamand Venet, *A Changing Wind: Commerce and Conflict in Civil War Atlanta* (New Haven, CT: Yale University Press, 2014) 140; *Macon Telegraph*, 2 April 1863; *Savannah Republican*, 14 April 1862.

[42]*Athens Southern Watchman*, 12 June 1861.

[43]Presentments of the Grand Jury, 15 October 1863, Sumter County Superior Court Records, Georgia Department of Archives and History; Ella Lonn, *Desertion During the Civil War* (New York: Century Co., 1928) 115.

In Savannah, the city council purchased provisions for the needy and asked a "committee of ladies" to help distribute the goods. The pride that ran deep in most families made them reluctant to ask for assistance and made it difficult to determine who required help. The council felt that women could more readily reach out to destitute families and ascertain their needs in confidence.[44]

Issues other than pride contributed to confusion in the poor relief process. Frequently, when men joined companies from counties other than their own, a question arose as to which county was responsible for aid to their families. The *Macon Telegraph* discussed such a predicament in 1863. B. Blair of Taylor County joined a company in neighboring Bibb County since none were forming in his own at the time. His wife and children applied for aid in Taylor, but were denied because the company was organized in Bibb. They were turned down in Bibb as well because they resided outside the county. An enraged citizen wrote that Taylor County "takes care of the families of those who join its company, scattered perhaps all over the State, and none other" while Bibb County "assumes charge of all resident families, regardless of the company in which they serve, and none other; so that between them, many needy families are left entirely destitute, of whom the Blair family is but an example." If all counties were as inflexible as Taylor and Bibb, suffering was inevitable for soldiers' families.[45]

The outcry for indigent aid became so persistent that it forced Milledgeville to take increasing notice. Governor Brown called for taxation and distribution not only by local governments but by the state as well. The General Assembly responded by making poor families exempt from property and poll taxes while increasing taxes on the wealthy. By 1864, disbursements from Georgia's state treasury focused mainly on welfare. More than half the state's budget that year went toward indigent relief. But inflation took its toll on the public as well as private sector and seriously hampered relief efforts. As early as December 1862, the whole-

[44]*Savannah Republican*, 13 June 1863.
[45]*Macon Telegraph*, 3 January 1863.

sale price index was already seven times what it had been before the war.[46]

Other difficulties plagued the relief system. Once a state or county agent procured items for poor relief, there was no guarantee that they could be delivered in a timely fashion. Two men in north Georgia's Dawson County wrote in 1863 about such a problem. Their court agent received $11,000 for indigent families from the state and went to middle Georgia to buy corn but could not obtain transportation. Three months went by and still no corn. It was a mystery because adjoining counties had bought and received corn since the Dawson agent purchased his supply. The two believed that Dawson's agent had done "his duty" but there were women in the county in desperate need of relief, "and if they are going to get any help it is time they had it." Whether or not embezzlement was involved, such episodes eroded trust in court officials.[47]

Very often, problems with relief arose from miscommunication. In May 1862, the state relief agent in Miller County wrote to Governor Brown asking for clarification on how he should distribute salt rations. "The salt which by your order was sent to Miller County has come to hand," the agent wrote, "and there is great need of it." But, he continued, there was "some difference of opinion" over who should receive it. Was it for the families of all soldiers then in service or only those in service when the order was issued? And did the order include both Confederate and state troops?[48]

Salt procurement was no small concern. Without salt, meat could not be cured and preserved, and hides could not be tanned for use in leatherwork. Salt had been imported before the war, but Lincoln's

---

[46]Peter Wallenstein, "Rich Man's War, Rich Man's Fight: Civil War and the Transformation of Public Finance in Georgia," *Journal of Southern History* 50 (1984): 25; Peter Wallenstein, *From Slave South to New South: Public Policy in Nineteenth-Century Georgia* (Chapel Hill: University of North Carolina Press, 1987) 114.

[47]J. Heard and J. Leadbetter to Brown, 8 July 1863, Governor's Incoming Correspondence.

[48]J. B. Guest to Brown, 20 May 1862, Governor's Incoming Correspondence.

blockade had nearly cut off outside supplies. To meet the crisis, Governor Brown began contacting various city officials and militia officers across the state about gathering the salt supplies on hand. One dispatch to Colonel Robert May of Augusta, who was also the city's mayor, read, "Take in custody for State from dealors having Stocks two thousand sacks of salt for the State and see that none goes out of the State." To the mayor of Columbus, Brown wrote, "See to it that not another sack of salt is shipped out of the State from your City."[49]

Private citizens and government agents began producing salt along the Gulf Coast early in the war, much of which was shipped up the Chattahoochee River to Columbus. But the supply was never adequate, and costs increased dramatically. In some Georgia towns, prices soared from fifty cents to ten dollars a sack. As early as December 1861, M. H. Sandwich wrote Brown of poor people in Upson County being unable to pay such high prices for salt. The county agent had traveled to Savannah looking for salt, but "returned without any as he could not procure it [for] less than $10 per sack." One citizen from Macon warned the governor to increase salt distribution from state warehouses or farmers might act for themselves. "They say they will take it by force as they must have salt to save their pork."[50]

It was no small task for Governor Brown to obtain salt and arrange for its distribution. In December 1862, he instructed officials to supply one bushel each at a cost of five dollars to families in several isolated Georgia counties. Brown chose those counties because they were far removed from rail lines, making salt transportation costlier. But there was no guarantee that once orders were issued they would be followed. Though the governor set prices for state salt, local agents found it easy to inflate those prices and keep a portion for themselves. In Valdosta, two

---

[49]Brown to May and others, 27 November 1861, Governor's Letter Book; Paul D. Escott, "Joseph E. Brown, Jefferson Davis, and the Problem of Poverty in the Confederacy," *Georgia Historical Quarterly* 61 (1977): 61.

[50]Sandwich to Brown, 16 December 1861, Governor's Incoming Correspondence; W. R. Singleton to Brown, 16 December 1861, Governor's Incoming Correspondence.

men assigned to distribute government salt sold it at more than twice what the state allowed and pocketed the difference.[51]

Just as state agents could not always be relied upon, county officials also frequently mismanaged poor relief. One man wrote to Governor Brown with news that Irwin County's indigent rolls were not "just and true." He listed the names of needy women, and the number of children in their households, that county agents had ignored. John Cain of Whitfield County complained that his local agent was denying aid to a number of destitute women and wondered why their names did not appear on his schedule. Was he keeping part of the fund for himself?[52]

Tales of corruption, incompetence, and even cruelty among state and county agents flooded Governor Brown's office. H. W. Blake of Hog Mountain in Hall County told of local justices who refused to distribute funds to soldiers' families, insisting "that they should only be allowed Bread to eat and no meat.... I sincerely hope that the decision of the Inferior Court may never reach our Brave Men from this County that there wives and children should be compelled to live on bread alone." Alfred Harris, an elderly Dahlonega man with sons in the army, wrote that Lumpkin County's inferior court refused him "any of the Benefits of publick Corne so liberally apropriated by the State to this County."[53]

Whether mismanaged or not, relief efforts were hampered mainly by rising prices and diminishing food stocks, brought on largely by cotton over-production. There was hardly enough food to supply soldiers in the field, much less their families back home. Abandoned and hungry, many women became beggars just to keep their families alive. Leaving children at home for days or weeks at a time, they roamed the countryside pleading for money and food. Sympathetic railroad and steamboat men occasionally provided transportation, but most often the women made their

---

[51]Brown to J. L. Whitaker, 16 December 1862, Governor's Letter Book; Guest to Brown, 20 May 1862, Governor's Incoming Correspondence; James C. Cothern to Brown, 15 January 1862, Governor's Incoming Correspondence.

[52]John Henderson to Brown, 8 July 1863, Governor's Incoming Correspondence; Cain to Brown, 5 May 1863, Governor's Incoming Correspondence.

[53]Blake to Brown, 6 May 1863, Governor's Incoming Correspondence; Harris to Brown, 3 April 1864, Cuyler Collection.

This widely circulated engraving contrasts the condition of soldiers' families in one frame with that of wealthy men in the other. There were state and local relief efforts, but food was too scarce and corruption too rampant to meet most needs. One Columbus resident wrote to a local newspaper that many women in dire circumstances could get help only if "offered assistance at the sacrifice of their honor, and that by men who occupy high places both in church and State." Image from *Leslie's Illustrated* (1862).

way on foot. Some better-off people gave what they could. Others gave nothing at all. Even the more generous viewed these unfortunates with contempt. One planter called the starving women "perfect nuisances."[54]

Some desperate women turned to prostitution. It was not uncommon for men of wealth and power to demand sexual favors in return for money, clothing, or food. One Columbus resident wrote to a local newspaper that women in dire circumstances were "offered assistance at the sacrifice of their honor, and that by men who occupy high places both in church and State."[55]

Public expressions of home-front hardships sometimes took a poetic turn. In spring 1863, Georgia newspapers circulated this heart-wrenching verse. It was a reminder of sacrifices made by soldiers' families as well as a general cry for help.

The Widow's Appeal

Stranger, have you corn?
Can you my wants supply?
My infant, early born,
Needs succor, else 'twill die.

At Crampton,[56] where the skies
With bullets were o'ercast—
There my loved Charlie lies,
And sadly breathed his last.

---

[54]Wayne Flynt, *Poor but Proud: Alabama's Poor Whites* (Tuscaloosa: University of Alabama Press, 1989) 41.

[55]*Columbus Sun*, 13 October 1863.

[56]The Battle of Crampton's Gap near Burkittsville, Maryland, occurred on 14 September 1862. It was part of a larger engagement known as South Mountain during the Maryland Campaign of 1862. That campaign reached its climax three days later at the Battle of Sharpsburg, or Antietam.

I cannot, will not steal,
Me loved one to supply.
Will you my sorrows heal?
Refuse me and I die.

The days are sad and drear,
Since Charlie left me alone,
I'm a stranger, pilgrim here,
To Heaven I make my moan.[57]

Although the poem reflected women's reluctance to steal, they nevertheless did whatever they had to do to feed their children. By the time this poem saw print in early 1863, they had long since begun taking matters into their own hands. As early as June 1862, a group of soldiers' wives in Bartow County descended on Cass Depot and demanded cotton. They needed only a small amount and intended to pay, but the agent refused to deal with them. That would not be the end of it. Returning later that day, the women "called for the Agent as a witness of their doings, and cut the rope from one bale, took what they needed, and marched very quietly home with it." In November, a "party of Ladies…driven by necessity" raided a Cartersville store and "appropriated a small stock of goods."[58] With desperate times calling for desperate measures, others soon followed their example.

The Women Rising

Cities throughout the South saw women rioting for food and other goods in early 1863: Salisbury, North Carolina, on March 18; Mobile, Alabama, on March 25; and Richmond, Virginia, on April 2. Other riots took place in Lafayette, Alabama; Abingdon, Virginia; Archer, Florida; and Sherman, Texas.[59] Georgia too saw robberies and riots that spring. They would continue with some regularity for the rest of the war.

---

[57]*Americus Sumter Republican* in *Athens Southern Watchman*, 3 April 1863.
[58]*Atlanta Southern Confederacy*, 17 June and 7 November 1862.
[59]Harriet E. Amos, "'All Absorbing Topics': Food and Clothing in Con-

Widespread outbreaks of looting hit the state's northern and central urban centers first, where deprivation was most concentrated and keenly felt. Raids later spread south, occurring mainly along rail lines where food was stockpiled. Most took place in the spring after winter supplies had been exhausted. Speculators were rioters' prime targets in the larger cities such as Atlanta, Columbus, and Savannah. Government warehouses and depots frequently bore the brunt of attacks in smaller towns like Valdosta and Colquitt. In the rural counties of Early, Miller, and Pierce, planters felt the women's wrath. Near the towns of Marietta, Thomasville, and Forsyth, women attacked wagons loaded with food or other goods.[60]

On March 16, 1863, about a dozen women raided a store on Whitehall Street in Atlanta. Their leader, "a tall lady on whose countenance rested care and determination," asked about the price of bacon. When she heard it was a dollar a pound, she protested that her companions were soldiers' wives and daughters and could not afford such prices. She then "proceeded to draw from her bosom a long navy repeater, and at the same time ordered the others in the crowd to help themselves to

federate Mobile," *Atlanta Historical Journal* 22 (1978): 17–28; Michael B. Chesson, "Harlots or Heroines? A New Look at the Richmond Bread Riot," *Virginia Magazine of History and Biography* 92 (1984): 131–75; Paul D. Escott, *Many Excellent People: Power and Privilege in North Carolina, 1850–1900* (Chapel Hill: University of North Carolina Press, 1985) 65; Christopher A. Graham, "Women's Revolt in Rowan County," *Columbiad* 3 (1999): 131–47; E. Merton Coulter, *Confederate States of America, 1861–1865* (Baton Rouge: Louisiana State University Press, 1950) 423; Tracy J. Revels, *Grander in Her Daughters: Florida's Women During the Civil War* (Columbia: University of South Carolina Press, 2004) 74. The most complete overview of Southern riots can be found in David Williams, *Bitterly Divided: The South's Inner Civil War* (New York: The New Press, 2008) 90–101.

[60]For a concise overview of women's riots in Georgia and the factors contributing to them see Teresa Crisp Williams and David Williams, "'The Women Rising': Cotton, Class, and Confederate Georgia's Rioting Women," *Georgia Historical Quarterly* 86 (2002): 49–83. See also Teresa Crisp Williams, "'The Women Rising': Class and Gender in Civil War Georgia" (master's thesis, Valdosta State University, 1999).

Women in Miller County wrote to Jefferson Davis warning that God would "send down his fury and judgment" if the Confederacy continued to allow soldiers' families to suffer. But they were not waiting for God or Davis. With a fury of their own, women in all of Georgia's major cities and many smaller towns—including Colquitt, the seat of Miller County—rioted for food. Image from *Leslie's Illustrated* (1863).

what they liked." They ransacked the store and made off with nearly $200 in bacon. A few weeks later, just north of Atlanta in Cobb County, a "gang of women" robbed several bales of yarn from a wagon headed for Marietta.[61]

April found women entering a store near Augusta's upper market and asking about prices for shoes and calico. The proprietor sensed mischief and hurriedly closed his store due to "pressing business" elsewhere. The women moved on to other stores, but took nothing and dispersed after authorities came on the scene. They arrested one man for "telling the women they did perfectly right." An Augusta paper labeled the women "Amazonian warriors" even though the group never turned violent.[62]

When asked why she had participated in the Augusta disturbance, one woman said, "We heard that they had raised the red flag all over the country, and people only had to go and take what they wanted." Women throughout the state, driven by the same red flag of hunger and deprivation, imposed what some called "mobocracy" as they took up knives and pistols, raiding depots, warehouses, and stores.[63]

On April 11, Columbus women numbering about sixty-five rallied at the north end of Broad Street and marched southward on a mission to raid "the stores of speculators." Armed with knives and pistols, the rioters shouted curses as they went. They first struck George A. Norris's dry goods store and "commenced helping themselves to whatever they wanted." Police arrived in time to disperse the crowd before it could reach other stores. Seven months later, Columbus women warned Governor Brown that they were prepared to again mount a raid if they could get no assistance. Brown forwarded their letter to Muscogee County's inferior

[61]*Atlanta Intelligencer* in *Americus Sumter Republican*, 27 March 1863; *Atlanta Southern Confederacy*, 24 April 1863.

[62]*Augusta Chronicle and Sentinel*, 4 and 11 April 1863; *Augusta Constitutionalist*, 11 April 1863.

[63]*Augusta Constitutionalist*, 11 April 1863; *Athens Southern Watchman*, 23 July 1862.

court justices, "requesting them to take such action in the premises as the court might think proper."[64]

Macon saw its women rioting that same month. In what one editor called "The Women Rising," a crowd armed with pistols and knives attacked Rosenwald's store on Second Street to seize calico and other supplies. The proprietor grabbed one of his assailants, wrestled a Bowie knife from her, and retrieved two bolts of calico. Others escaped with their loot.[65]

The morning of April 14 found Milledgeville women robbing a dry goods store, apparently intent on robbing others. They dispersed only after Judge L. Harris promised immediate relief if they would end their march and return the goods. The women did as Harris asked and received funds from the city treasury.[66]

April also saw a band of twenty-eight women, most of them armed with pistols and knives, robbing a freight wagon from Butts County on its way to the rail depot at Forsyth. Macon's *Telegraph* called on "the good old county of Monroe to nip this dangerous business in the bud." Sensing class animosities reflected in that spring's rising tide of riots and robberies, the editor emphasized that protecting property for both elites and commoners was at stake. "The rich can better afford to be robbed than the poor, and when that game is set afoot the poor will be the greatest sufferers." But from the perspective of common folk, the rich had already robbed them through speculation and impressment. They saw themselves as taking back only what was, in a general sense, theirs by right.[67]

Most newspaper editors did not share that view, at least not at rioting's onset. An *Athens* editor warned of dire consequences should women continue their miscreant ways. "Every body and every thing we hold

---

[64]*Columbus Sun*, 11 April 1863; *Augusta Chronicle and Sentinel*, 23 November 1863. A brief account of the Columbus riot can also be found in *Official Records of the Union and Confederate Navies in the War of the Rebellion* (Washington, DC: Government Printing Office, 1894–1927) series 1, vol. 17, 432.

[65]*Savannah Morning News*, 3 April 1863; *Macon Telegraph*, 2 April 1863.

[66]*Augusta Chronicle* in *Columbus Sun*, 14 April 1863.

[67]*Macon Telegraph*, 22 April 1863.

dear," he feared, "would be involved in one common ruin." A few weeks later, he refused to publish a letter defending women's riots, suggesting that those who supported such action were "in favor of an abrogation of all government.... Why, Hell itself, with all its horrors, has never descended to the degradation of mob violence." A Milledgeville editor, calling the women "of the baser sort," suggested that rioters receive an "application of the Hydropathic principle from the noozle of a Fire Engine."[68]

Editors generally were quick to suggest that no respectable woman would participate in lawlessness, dismissing hunger as a motive for the riots. Said one editor, "The class composing the mobs are of the lowest—prostitutes, plug uglies...and those who have always been a nuisance to the community, and who are not in a perishing, or even suffering condition, for want of food." Another editor wrote that the raiding parties were made up of loafers, vagrants, prostitutes, professional thieves, and jail birds instigating riots under the pretense of "stern necessity." Others accused rioters of working with the Yankees to throw loyal citizens into "a state of confusion, consternation and terror."[69]

Joseph Addison Turner, who published a weekly newspaper called the *Countryman* on his Turnwold Plantation in Putnam County, most clearly reflected the patriarchal prejudices of his day in criticizing the rioters: "Women do not transgress the bounds of decorum so often as men, but, when they do, they go [to] greater lengths.... for with reason somewhat weaker, they have to contend with passions somewhat stronger. Besides, a female by *one* transgression forfeits her place in society forever." In Turner's view, a woman's modesty was her greatest asset. If she engaged in stealing and rioting, she forfeited her heavenly "ornament." "If an angel falls," he insisted, "the transition must be to a demon."[70]

---

[68]*Athens Southern Watchman*, 2 and 23 July 1862; *Milledgeville Confederate Union*, 28 April 1863.

[69]*Troy (AL) Southern Advertiser*, 22 April 1863; *Columbus Sun*, 8 April 1863.

[70]*Turnwold Countryman*, 7 April 1863.

The editor of Atlanta's *Southern Confederacy* wrote that female rioters must be "under the control of cowardly, villainous men, and by them instigated to the commission of these robberies." Some thought that men might be more directly involved. One editor likened Georgia's riots to those of the French Revolution, "inaugurated by women and men dressed in women's clothes." Another editor, blindly insisting that food supplies were adequate and no family was in real want, urged authorities to crack down on "the worthless beings."[71]

At least one editor took a more sympathetic view. In April 1863, with riots breaking out all over the South, the *Athens Southern Watchman*'s editor looked for the root cause of the disturbances. He concluded that ultimate blame lay not with the rioters but with self-interested elites, especially speculators, who cared more for profit than patriotism. In a passionately worded editorial, he begged the well-off to change their ways: "In the name of our beloved country—in the name of outraged humanity—in the name of that religion they profess to reverence—in the name of the God they pretend to fear—we call upon these men to change their policy before it shall be too late! Our sun may yet set in anarchy and blood."[72]

At the height of rioting that spring, Congress passed a joint resolution urging, but not requiring, that planters, "instead of planting cotton and tobacco, shall direct their agricultural labor mainly to the production of such crops as will insure a sufficiency of food for all classes, and for every emergency, thereby with true patriotism subordinating the hope of gain to the certain good of the country." But planters ignored the resolution and continued, as one Georgia editor later put it, to "carry their patriotism in the *pocketbook*."[73]

Efforts to guarantee employment for soldiers' families helped ward off further riots in some towns. There were stepped-up charity efforts as well. In Atlanta, the city council increased funding for "pauper relief."

[71] *Atlanta Southern Confederacy*, 24 April 1863; *Athens Southern Watchman*, 8 April 1863; *Troy (AL) Southern Advertiser*, 22 April 1863.

[72] *Athens Southern Watchman*, 8 April 1863.

[73] *OR*, series 4, vol. 2, 468; *Early County News*, 27 April 1864.

Some Atlanta merchants donated food outright, fearing that it might be taken in any case. Savannah's city council issued emergency funds to the Board of Health, Widow's Society, and at least two orphanages. It also opened a non-profit city store that sold basic provisions at cost. Augusta and other cities did the same. Such help was certainly welcomed, but with most planters and speculators unwilling to change their ways, hunger and destitution remained serious problems.[74]

In summer 1863, a band of Pickens County women, said to be anti-Confederate Unionists, stormed a tanyard at Talking Rock. According to one report, they "helped themselves to as much leather as they could well carry off" and threatened to raid other businesses. One local merchant wrote to Governor Brown begging him to stop the riots and to protect the community from those "who have not our cause at heart."[75] But prices were too high and necessities, especially food, were too scarce. Rioting continued in Georgia for the rest of the war.

I Had No Idea How I Loved You All at Home

Food scarcity was common in the army as well. Though the South was renowned for its agricultural productivity, its troops were constantly hungry. It was no secret that the main reason was planter insistence on growing cotton. By 1863, angry citizens were setting cotton fields afire, sending a clear message to planters that their focus on cotton was unappreciated.[76]

Governor Brown had long since warned that the army must be fed or the Confederacy would come to ruin. No one knew that better than Columbus native Raphael Jacob Moses, chief commissary officer for

---

[74]LeeAnn Whites, *The Civil War as a Crisis in Gender: Augusta, Georgia, 1860–1890* (Athens: University of Georgia Press, 1995) 78, 81; Wendy Hamand Venet, "From Gate City to Gotham: Sam Richards Chronicles the Civil War in Atlanta," in John D. Fowler and David B. Parker, eds., *Breaking the Heartland: The Civil War in Georgia* (Macon, GA: Mercer University Press, 2011) 161; Jacqueline Jones, *Saving Savannah: The City and the Civil War* (New York: Alfred A. Knopf, 2008) 172.

[75]A. J. Glen to Joseph E. Brown, 7 August 1863, Cuyler Collection.

[76]*Rome Courier*, 14 April 1863.

General James Longstreet's Corps, Army of Northern Virginia. Thousands of troops looked to him for provisions, but he had little to give. In a desperate attempt to supply his men, Moses journeyed home to Columbus begging for food. "It occurred to me," he later wrote, "that if I could go to Georgia and speak to the people who had sons, brothers, relatives, and friends who were suffering for supplies, I could get supplies." It would not be that simple. When Moses called a meeting at Temperance Hall, only thirty people came.

> I thanked them for their presence and stated when I last spoke in this hall it was to urge the people to send their sons and brothers to confront the hazards of war and to redress their country's wrongs, the house was full from pit to gallery with patriotic citizens ready for the sacrifices asked. Now I come from those near and dear to the people here, to appeal to them for bread for the starving army, and I am confronted with empty benches.[77]

When the army could not supply food, soldiers foraged for it. John Hagan of southwest Georgia, in a letter to his wife, wrote of how common foraging was and how devastating was its effect. "I beleave our troops are doing as much harm in this country as the yankees...and in fact wheare this army goes the people is ruined." Sometimes soldiers' theft extended to their own comrades. Louis Merz of West Point wrote in his diary of a soldier stealing fifteen pounds of sugar, coffee, bacon, butter, and beef from the company mess tent.[78]

Keeping food in their bellies was a constant challenge. Daniel Snell of Hamilton wrote from distant Virginia that he caught a catfish and an eel one Saturday and cooked them for breakfast the next morning. He wished he had caught more, but "there's not much fish in this country."

---

[77]Jacob Raphael Moses, "A Southern Romantic," in Jacob Rader Marcus, comp., *Memoirs of American Jews, 1775–1865*, vol. 1 (Philadelphia: Jewish Publication Society of America, 1955) 185–86.

[78]Bell Irvin Wiley, ed., "The Confederate Letters of John W. Hagan," *Georgia Historical Quarterly* 38 (1954): 196; "Diary of Private Louis Merz, C.S.A., of the West Point Guards, 1862," *Chattahoochee Valley Historical Society Bulletin* 4 (1959): 19.

When the soldiers could catch no fish, there were always rats. It seemed that they infested every camp. When food ran low, the rats became the rations. William Andrews of Clay County wrote that each morning "rat details" would form, armed with sticks and shovels prepared to do battle with the rodents. "The rats burrow under a row of cedars near the camps and the boys will dig them out and then let them run for their lives. They don't get far before they are knocked on the head. After the boys kill about 50, they turn too and dress them, each man cooking to suit his taste. Some fry, some stew, while others bake them, and the boys say they eat as well as a cat squirrel."[79]

Hard as it was to keep themselves fed, it was equally difficult to keep themselves well. Doctors of the time had little knowledge of what caused diseases like dysentery, typhoid, and malaria. Ill fed, ill clothed, and living in crowded and unsanitary conditions, soldiers were susceptible to all kinds of sickness. Twice as many died of disease during the war as were killed from combat-related injuries. Not surprisingly, the men were more afraid of illness than the enemy. After a severe attack of "bowel disease," one soldier wrote to his wife, "I had much rather take the risk and fight than [have] the sickness I fell in."[80]

Hardly a letter was written home that did not contain some mention of the soldier's health. William Clarke wrote to his family in Cuthbert that "my health is very bad; I weigh just 95 lbs.... I have had chills more or less ever since I started. I want to get stout and sometimes think I am better. I have a very severe cough which I fear this cold mountainous country will not help." Such misery served only to make the soldiers miss their loved ones and the comforts of home more than they already did. Private William Turner of Troup County, after a week of chills and high

---

[79]Louise Calhoun Barfield, *History of Harris County, Georgia, 1827–1961* (Columbus, GA: Columbus Office Supply Co., 1961) 758; William H. Andrews, *Footprints of a Regiment: A Recollection of the First Georgia Regulars, 1861–1865*, annotated and introduction by Richard M. McMurry (Atlanta: Longstreet Press, 1992) 151.

[80]Fred S. Watson, *Winds of Sorrow: Hardships of the Civil War, Early Crimes and Hangings, and War Casualties of the Wiregrass Area* (Dothan, AL: Hopkins Printing, 1986) 18–19.

fever, wrote home, "O! mother how I did wish you or sister was here to bathe my aching brow. Dear mother I had no idea how I loved you all at home."[81]

As if hunger and disease were not enough for the soldiers to endure, there was also the humiliation of excessive military discipline. Most higher-ranking officers came from the slaveholding class and habitually treated those under their command much as they did their slaves. Thomas Lightfoot complained in a letter to his cousin, "A soldier is worse than any negro on [the] Chtahooche[e] river. He has no privileges whatever. He is under worse task-masters than any negro. He is not treated with any respect whatever. His officers may insult him and he has no right to open his mouth and dare not do it." William Clarke cared just as little for army discipline. "Military rule," he said, "is perfectly despotic."[82]

Soldiers also resented the special privileges officers received. Private Cyrus Jenkins of Troup County complained bitterly that those of his rank, like slaves away from their plantations, had to carry a pass whenever they left their units for any reason. There was no such requirement for officers. Jenkins found the practice insulting. "Why should a private soldier carry a pass when an officer can go at will," he asked, "for what is an officer but a man!"[83]

The soldiers were especially annoyed with the privileges of rank when it came to more serious issues like medical treatment. Early in the war, William Andrews described the impact of disease on the men and how the officers received exceptional care. "There has been a great deal of sickness in camps and many deaths, especially among the rank and file.... The officers always manage to get home or to a hospital. Have never

---

[81]Edmund Cody Burnett, ed., "Letters of Barnett Hardeman Cody and Others, 1861–1864," *Georgia Historical Quarterly* 23 (1939): 289; Turner to his mother, 17 August 1861, William Weaver Turner Letters, Troup County Archives, LaGrange, GA.

[82]Edmund Cody Burnett, ed., "Letters of Three Lightfoot Brothers, 1861–1864," *Georgia Historical Quarterly* 25 (1941) 389; Burnett, "Letters of Barnett Hardeman Cody and Others," 290.

[83]Cyrus F. Jenkins Diary, Troup County Archives.

known one to die in camps." But, as one Confederate private observed, "the officers have all the glory. Glory is not for the private soldier, such as die...eaten up with the deadly gangrene, and being imperfectly waited on." It was too much for some soldiers. Soon after he recovered from wounds received in the September 1862 Maryland Campaign, James Glass of the Miller Guards was listed on the company roll as absent without leave.[84]

Their own difficulties were hard enough to endure, but despondent letters from home were more than many of the men could stand. A young soldier from Columbus wrote home to a friend, "If it is the best our government can do, I am willing to live on dry bread for our cause; but I don't want mother to suffer for anything as long as I live. I am willing for her to work and I know she will do it; but when I hear she is in want of provisions and can't get them, I am going home.... The last two letters I received from her don't suit me." R. H. Brooks of the 51st Georgia Regiment wrote to his wife, "tell Charles Sirmons if he ever gets home to stay there...if ever I get home I will stay as long as I can."[85]

Getting leave was near impossible, but that hardly mattered to men whose families were in dire straits. In January 1862, Private James Atkins of Calhoun County wrote in his diary that "all my efforts to get a furlough are unavailing—What shall I do?" In April, he deserted. So did John Sheffield of Miller County later that year. According to his friend Milo Grow, Sheffield "cursed the government and everything connected with it." Grow was himself "fully sick of the manner in which the government is administered." When it came to begging for a furlough, Lee Dupont insisted that he "did not belong to that breed of dogs who could

---

[84]Andrews, *Footprints of a Regiment*, 26; Sam R. Watkins, *"Co. Aytch"* (1882; repr., Wilmington, NC: Broadfoot Publishing, 1987) 194; Lillian Henderson, comp., *Roster of the Confederate Soldiers of Georgia, 1861–1865*, 6 vols. (Hapeville, GA: Longina and Porter, 1959–64) 5:396.

[85]*Columbus Sun*, 18 November 1863; Brooks to his wife, 25 July 1863, William Brooks, Civil War Letter, AC 00–268, Georgia Department of Archives and History.

so humble themselves, that if it became an imperative duty to visit my family I should do it without leave and risk the consequences."[86]

Patriotic principles also compelled Georgia soldiers to desert. Some felt that serving the Confederate States made them traitors to the United States, which they still considered their true country. John Fulton Brown had joined the Confederate army in late 1862 under threat of conscription. In August 1863, still in his teens, he deserted. His reasoning reflected the views of his hill-country neighbors, "nearly the whole," as Brown later wrote, "dyed in the wool Unionist."

> First, I was Union to the bottom and opposed all things pointing to a division of the States. Second, I was helping to establish a cause I did not want established. My heart was not in it and neither did I think my interest there. I had no such belief or feeling as that of deserting my country, but on the other hand, my desertion would tend much toward my country's welfare.

Like so many other deserters, Brown, who was stationed near Savannah, had various reasons for leaving. Aside from his Unionist leanings, he was homesick and hungry, realized that the Confederacy was dying, and feared that he might die with it. He wrote, "I longed for my mountain home. Those low, stenchy districts, vibrating with reptiles and insects, were not to my liking and I was well satisfied that victory would show up against us.... I was half-starved all the time and really, the prospects of perishing grew more real every day."[87]

Whatever soldiers' motives for desertion, their risk was the same. Unauthorized absence could and often did result in execution. Brown himself had seen a man killed by firing squad for deserting. William An-

---

[86]James Atkins Diary, 22 January 1862, Civil War Miscellany, Personal Papers, Georgia Department of Archives and History; Atkins file, Compiled Service Records; Milo W. Grow to Kate Baughn Grow, 26 June 1862, *Confederate Reminiscences and Letters*, 7 vols. (Atlanta: United Daughters of the Confederacy, 1997) 5:156; David Carlson, "The 'Loanly Runagee': Draft Evaders in Confederate South Georgia," *Georgia Historical Quarterly* 84 (2000): 592.

[87]John Fulton Brown, *The Bushwhackers: The Story of a Reluctant Rebel During the Civil War* (Bloomington, IN: iUniverse Inc., 2009) 3, 7–8.

drews, serving with Lee's Army of Northern Virginia, wrote that it was "an everyday occurrence for men to get letters from home stating that their families are on the point of starvation. Many a poor soldier has deserted and gone home in answer to that appeal, to be brought back and shot for desertion."[88]

Some were never returned for execution but simply shot on sight. Samuel Henderson Frier of Irwin County, like the rest of his family, had opposed secession. Too poor to hire a substitute, he joined the army under threat of conscription in May 1862. Frier deserted later that year in Virginia and made his way back home. The next year, a conscript force gunned him down. Frier's widow, two young children, and other family and friends laid him to rest in the Brushy Creek Primitive Baptist cemetery. Despite such risks, soldiers abandoned their ranks by the thousands and headed home. According to one report, if challenged along the way to show their furlough, they simply patted their rifles and replied, "This is my furlough."[89]

Increasing sympathy from friends and neighbors encouraged more and more men to desert. By summer 1862, newspapers across Georgia were filled with lists of deserters' names and offers of rewards for their capture. A thirty-dollar bounty was on the table for Fulton County native Thomas Miller. Similar bounties were offered for E. J. Lewis of Hancock County, J. L. Morris of Wilkinson County, and John Burns of Augusta.[90] In July, an Augusta newspaper ran this notice.

> DESERTED
>
> $30 REWARD offered for the apprehension of each of the following. Wm. A Daniel, age 20, Co. A, Banks County Guards. Jere Martin, age 20, Co. D; A. S. King, age 24, Co. F; F. P. Williams, age 20, Co. F;

---

[88]Ibid., 8; Andrews, *Footprints of a Regiment*, 39.

[89]"Samuel Henderson Frier, 1833–1863: AWOL from the Confederate Army," *Huxford Genealogical Society Magazine* 26 (1999): 81; *OR*, series 4, vol. 2, 721.

[90]*Augusta Constitutionalist*, 24 June and 24 July 1862; *Milledgeville Southern Federal Union*, 29 July 1862.

> John Huchins, age 26, Co. F. All from the 2nd Regiment of Georgia Volunteers. Reward will be paid on delivery to the jail at Augusta.[91]

Such lists soon took up so much print space that some papers refused to publish them.

By fall 1862, more than half the soldiers from northeast Georgia had "skedaddled" and were hiding in the mountains. At least a third of Lumpkin County's "Blue Ridge Rifles" deserted. Nearly half the county's "Boyd Guards" did the same. The next year, War Department officials reported to Secretary James Seddon that "the condition of things in the mountain districts of North Carolina, South Carolina, Georgia, and Alabama menaces the existence of the Confederacy as fatally as…the armies of the United States."[92]

As their ranks grew, many deserters formed armed guerrilla bands. They raided plantations, attacked army supply depots, and drove off impressment and conscript officers. Some areas were so hostile to the Confederacy that army patrols dared not enter them. The pine barrens region of southeast Georgia was a favorite hideout for those trying to avoid Confederate entanglements. Soldier Camp Island in the Okefenokee Swamp was home to a thousand deserters or more. Deserter gangs also roamed the Chattahoochee River bottomlands.

Summer 1862 found half a dozen men in Marion County organizing "armed resistance" to the conscript law and swearing vengeance against anyone who tried to arrest them. In August, a Confederate officer reported that forty men in Coffee County had "secured and provisioned a house and arranged it in the manner of a military castle, with a determination to resist to the last extremity their capture."[93]

From north Georgia's Gilmer County came news in July 1862 of "Tories and traitors who have taken up their abode in the mountains."

---

[91]*Augusta Constitutionalist*, 26 July 1862.

[92]*The American Annual Cyclopedia and Register of Important Events of the Year 1862* (New York: D. Appleton, 1863) 16; Andrew W. Cain, *History of Lumpkin County for the First Hundred Years, 1832–1932* (Atlanta: Stein Printing, 1932) 158–64, 165–68; *OR*, series 4, vol. 2, 786.

[93]*Macon Telegraph*, 19 September 1862.

That same month, a letter arrived on the governor's desk from Fannin County, just north of Gilmer, warning that "a very large majority of the people now here perhaps two thirds are disloyal." That fall, anti-Confederate violence became so frequent in Fannin that one resident called it a "general uprising among our Torys of this County." Most of northeast Georgia's Tory bands wanted nothing more than to sit out the war. Others, especially those with no family ties in the region, were more prone to violence. September 1862 saw Lumpkin County being overrun by Tories and deserters, robbing pro-Confederates of guns, money, clothes, and provisions. One Confederate sympathizer wrote that "the Union men—Tories—are very abusive indeed and says they will do as they please." The *Dahlonega Signal* estimated that one of Lumpkin County's Tory bands, led by "the notorious Jeff Anderson," numbered up to two hundred.[94]

One of the earliest formed and most active bands of Union men in northeast Georgia was led by Horatio Hennion. A Northerner by birth, Hennion had moved to White County's Mossy Creek community in his early twenties and married a local girl. The other men in his band of at least two dozen were from Georgia and the Carolinas. All were non-slaveholders, some of them tenants or day laborers who owned no land. Those who did own land held no more than a few hundred dollars' worth of real estate and personal property.

Hennion worked as a wagon maker in Gainesville during the secession crisis, and made his support for the Union clear. Even after war broke out, Hennion remained openly anti-Confederate even as other local Unionists were falling silent. Threats to his life forced him and his family back to Mossy Creek, where he hoped to live in peace. Within weeks, local pro-Confederates tried to kill him. In August 1861, he fled to North Carolina but returned a year later and organized a band of an-

[94]W. W. Findley to Brown, 26 July 1862, Governor's Incoming Correspondence; W. A. Campbell to Brown, 12 July 1862, and 28 February 1863, Governor's Incoming Correspondence; Josiah A. Woody to Brown, 6 September 1862, Governor's Incoming Correspondence; *Dahlonega Signal* in *Augusta Chronicle and Sentinel*, 30 January 1863.

ti-Confederates that included men from White County and neighboring Hall County. They fought running battles with Confederate conscript companies, rescuing one of their comrades from the White County jail after his arrest. Hennion's band became even more effective when he and his men signed "an agreement of mutual protection" with deserters hiding out in the region.[95]

Soon after receiving news of events in the mountains, Governor Brown issued a proclamation aimed at the "very considerable number of deserters and stragglers" and those who aided them. Brown knew "that numbers of these deserters, encouraged by disloyal citizens in the mountains of Northeastern Georgia, have associated themselves together with arms in their hands and are now in rebellion against the authority of this State and the Confederate States." He issued a proclamation "commanding all persons…to return to their respective commands immediately." Brown also warned "all disloyal citizens to cease to harbor deserters or encourage desertion…as the law against treason will be strictly enforced against all who subject themselves to its penalties."[96]

Brown's warning had little effect. In late January 1863, he acted. Brown sent a mounted force under Colonel George Washington Lee, commandant of Atlanta, and Captain E. M. Galt to Dahlonega with orders to "secure the arrest of deserters and restore the public tranquility." By early February, six hundred deserters had been rounded up and marched back to the army. Fifty-three civilian Unionists had been arrested and sent to Atlanta, among them the Tory leader Jeff Anderson. Despite their apparent success, only a month later Confederate loyalists in Lumpkin County were begging Governor Brown for more troops.[97]

---

[95]Keith S. Bohannon, "They Had Determined to Root Us Out: Dual Memoirs by a Unionist Couple in Blue Ridge, Georgia," in John C. Inscoe and Robert C. Kenzer, eds., *Enemies of the Country: New Perspectives on Unionists in the Civil War South* (Athens: University of Georgia Press, 2001) 98–106.

[96]*OR*, series 4, vol. 2, 360–61.

[97]Henry C. Wayne to E. M. Galt, 17 January 1863, Adjutant General's Letter Books, Georgia Department of Archives and History; *Atlanta Southern Confederacy*, 4 February 1863; G. W. Lee to Brown, 5 February 1863, Governor's Incoming Correspondence; Citizens of Dahlonega to Brown, 4 March

In June, the *Athens Southern Watchman* reported that "some of those who were forced into the army by the cavalry last winter have returned with Government arms and ammunition in their hands and are creating serious apprehensions of future troubles." Already, anti-Confederates led by a Hall County man calling himself Major Finger had attacked a small iron works in White County. They burned the coal, stole the tools, and broke the forge hammer. In Fannin County, Tories attacked a group of Confederates sent to arrest deserters, killing one man and wounding several others.[98]

Fannin County was hit again in August when Tories led by Soloman Bryan disarmed Confederate loyalists. According to one pro-Confederate, they "robbed our people of every single gun and all the ammunition." Similar confrontations took place across northeast Georgia. A Union County man informed Governor Brown that the "mountains are filling with deserters and disloyal men," and begged him to send arms and ammunition. Brown sought help from Richmond, telling Jefferson Davis that "tories and deserters in North Eastern Georgia are now disarming the loyal people and committing many outrages." Brown got no response, and the outrages continued. He finally sent another expedition to northeast Georgia in October 1863. It arrested "quite a number of deserters, stragglers, marauders," but so many remained that it had little effect on the general state of affairs.[99]

For Our Rights and Liberty

Black folk too were becoming more difficult to control. From the war's early days, resistance that had been ubiquitous in the prewar years become even more so—and it became more obvious. Sabotage was more

---

1863, Cuyler Collection.

[98]*Athens Southern Watchman*, 17 June 1863.

[99]W. A. Campbell to Brown, 4 August 1863, Governor's Incoming Correspondence; T. J. Haralson and others to Brown, 7 August 1863, Governor's Petitions, Georgia Department of Archives and History; Brown to Davis, 25 August 1863, Governor's Letter Book; G. W. Lee to Brown, 6 October 1863, Cuyler Collection.

frequent. So was feigning illness. Raids on plantation smokehouses, root cellars, and corn cribs became more common. Cattle, sheep, chickens, and hogs mysteriously vanished, their disappearance blamed by the slaves on panthers, foxes, and "strange dogs." There were also work slow-downs and outright refusals to work. In March 1863, the *Atlanta Southern Confederacy* reported that a group of slaveholding women was in town to buy food. There was none available on their plantations since they were "unable to control the negroes and make them work."[100]

If slaves increasingly refused to work for their owners, they were perfectly willing to work for themselves. Unable to manage large numbers of slaves at home, some owners agreed to hire them out for a portion of their wages. Some slaves tried to keep all their wages by escaping to urban areas looking for jobs. With so many whites called off to war, it was not difficult for blacks to find employment, no questions asked. One newspaper reported that Georgia's towns and cities were filled with slaves acting "as if they were free people." The *Columbus Sun* wrote that "farm negroes frequently run away and come to the city, where they remain for months." A slaveholder visiting Columbus found one of his slaves working in a machine shop. A southwest Georgia man noted with alarm that slaves in Fort Gaines were "doing as they please, hiring out their time which the law of Georgia forbids." Blacks impressed to work on fortifications around Savannah regularly escaped to the city, where they might be paid for their labor.[101] To seek work for wages had always been a hallmark of freedom. Black Georgians were taking that freedom eagerly for themselves.

Blacks also sought income from Union forces operating along the coast. On Georgia's Sea Islands such as Cockspur, St. Catherines, Ossa-

---

[100]Susan E. O'Donovan, *Becoming Free in the Cotton South* (Cambridge, MA: Harvard University Press, 2007) 95, 105; T. Conn Bryan, *Confederate Georgia* (Athens: University of Georgia Press, 1953) 125.

[101] Chad Morgan, *Planters' Progress: Modernizing Confederate Georgia* (Gainesville: University Press of Florida, 2005) 90, 91; Bryan, *Confederate Georgia*, 132; *Columbus Enquirer*, 9 April 1862; Mary Grist Whitehead, ed., *Collections of Early County Historical Society*, vol. 2 (Tallahassee, FL: Rose Printing, 1979) 160; Jones, *Saving Savannah*, 175.

baw, Sapelo, and St. Simons, fugitives established their own villages, where they planted crops, raised livestock, and sold much of their produce to soldiers and seamen. Women took in laundry and sewing to earn cash. Some blacks hired themselves to the Federals as scouts and guides, supplying valuable intelligence and leading their allies though uncharted marshes.[102]

As quickly as they settled in, Sea Island blacks armed themselves for defense against Confederate marauders. They went on the offense as well, traveling many miles inland to raid plantations and bring friends and family out of slavery. One of the most active raiders was a fugitive named Nat, who escaped from Glynn County in 1860. By summer 1862 he was using St. Simons as a base from which he launched a number of inland ventures. During one of his most daring raids, Nat led six men thirty miles up the Altamaha River to rescue their wives and children. The party twice fended off white attackers and traded gunfire with a Confederate river patrol. Such dangerous exploits finally caught up with Nat two years later when a Confederate shotgun blast ended his life. By that time, Nat was credited with having led a hundred slaves or more to freedom.[103]

Another active emancipator was March Haynes, who before the war worked as a stevedore and pilot on the Savannah River. Soon after Fort Pulaski fell in April 1862, Haynes began smuggling refugees to Union lines. When Haynes sensed that the whites with whom he worked were becoming suspicious, he escaped with his wife and continued rescue operations from his base on the Sea Islands. He repeatedly slipped into Savannah and beyond, leading dozens of fugitives past Confederate outposts and through the marshes to safety. The Federals aided Haynes, supplying him with a "staunch, swift boat" and any supplies he needed

[102]Clarence L. Mohr, *On the Threshold of Freedom: Masters and Slaves in Civil War Georgia* (Athens: University of Georgia Press, 1986) 82; Joseph P. Reidy, "States of Dependence and Independence in Civil War Georgia," in John D. Fowler and David B. Parker, eds., *Breaking the Heartland: The Civil War in Georgia* (Macon, GA: Mercer University Press, 2011) 57.

[103]Mohr, *On the Threshold of Freedom*, 78.

for his trips. In exchange, Haynes brought back "exact and valuable" intelligence on Confederate defenses.[104]

From early in the war, some blacks had tried to serve the Union as soldiers but had been turned away. Abraham Lincoln made it clear in the war's first months that his objective was not to free the slaves but to preserve the Union. The *New York Tribune*, a staunchly pro-Lincoln newspaper, was quick to remind its readers that this was "a War for the preservation of the Union, not for the destruction of Slavery.... Slavery shall receive no damage from a Union triumph." Lincoln had said much the same in his inaugural address, and Congress agreed. In a near unanimous vote, it passed the Crittenden-Johnson resolution assuring Americans that the government's aim was not to overthrow or interfere "with the rights or established institutions" of the slave states but only "to defend and maintain the supremacy of the Constitution and to preserve the Union."[105]

Things began to change in 1862. Like their Southern counterparts, Northern recruiting officers found it increasingly difficult to get volunteers. And like Confederate armies, Federal forces began to experience problems with desertion. Homesickness, hardship, and disease all took their toll on Union ranks. During the war's first year, nearly every man in the Union army suffered at one time or another from diarrhea and dysentery. By late 1862 almost one in four Union soldiers were absent without leave.[106]

Something had to be done to get more men into the army, even if those men were black. But would large numbers of blacks fight for a cause that promised no end to slavery? Probably not. On the other hand, making the war a crusade against slavery might lead more white soldiers to desert. It might even result in more states leaving the Union. Besides,

---

[104]Ibid., 77.

[105]*New York Tribune*, 14 May 1861; *Journal of the House of Representatives of the United States*, 37th Congress, 1st session (Washington, DC: Government Printing Office, 1861) 58: 123; *Journal of the Senate of the United States*, 37th Congress, 1st session (Washington, DC: Government Printing Office, 1861) 53: 91.

[106]Ward, *The Civil War*, 184.

Enslaved Georgians escaping to Union lines, such as those pictured here in 1863 on Cockspur Island, established settlements on the Sea Islands and traded with the Federals. Some joined Union armed forces, serving as soldiers, seamen, spies, and guides. Others formed unofficial militias for protection against Confederate raiders. They went on the offense as well, traveling many miles inland to raid plantations and bring friends and family out of slavery. Image courtesy of the Library of Congress.

most white Northerners doubted that blacks would make good soldiers in any case. General William T. Sherman bluntly remarked that blacks were "not the equal of the white man."[107] But with few whites volunteering and desertion on the rise, Lincoln had little choice.

On September 22, 1862, only days after Lee's army was turned back in Maryland, Lincoln announced the Emancipation Proclamation. It was a tentative document that freed only those slaves held behind Confederate lines, but it did introduce emancipation as, at least in part, a Union war aim. Just as significantly, it gave blacks a cause for which to fight.

Blacks had, in a sense, been fighting for freedom all their lives. The war only intensified that struggle. By escaping in their tens of thousands, fugitives proclaimed their own emancipation and helped forced Lincoln to follow suit. In so doing, they made the war their own—a war for freedom, not a war simply for the Union. They had been fighting that war in their own way long before Lincoln requested their services, and they continued to make clear that when they fought, they fought for their own cause. "We will fight for our rights and liberty," insisted one former slave. "We care nothing about the Union. We have been in it slaves for over two hundred and fifty years."[108]

When blacks volunteered, their reasons tended to be more personal than patriotic. At a "war meeting" of former slaves on St. Simons Island, a Northern correspondent witnessed several speakers, including one black man, trying to draw new recruits.

> They were asked to enlist for pay, rations and uniform, to fight for their country, for freedom and so forth, but not a man stirred. But when it was asked them to fight for themselves, to enlist to protect their wives and children from being sold away from them, and told of the little homes which they might secure to themselves and their families in after

[107]Ira Berlin, Joseph P. Reidy, and Leslie S. Rowland, eds., *Freedom: A Documentary History of Emancipation, 1861–1867*, series 2, *The Black Military Experience* (New York: Cambridge University Press, 1982) 110–111.

[108]Ibid., 154–55.

years, they all rose to their feet, the men came forward and said "I'll go," and the women shouted, and the old men said "Amen."[109]

As early as summer 1862, Union forces recruited Sea Island blacks. Within weeks, they were conducting amphibious operations along the coast, disrupting Confederate communications and seizing or destroying contraband property. Plantations were special targets, particularly those from which the soldiers had escaped. One planter, William Brailsford, was captain of the Savannah Mounted Rifles, a unit that he sometimes used to capture Sea Island refugees. During a raid up the Sapelo River, black soldiers drove off a small force of Confederates and burned Brailsford's plantation, including the mansion itself. After the attack, one soldier who had earlier belonged to Brailsford said he felt as if he had "grown three inches." Sam Miller, whom Brailsford had once badly whipped for refusing to betray an escapee, felt that he was now "a heap more of a man."[110]

In August 1862, Union General David Hunter received word of a Confederate raid on St. Simons Island and sent a company of blacks to beat back the Rebels. When they arrived, they found that the island's self-emancipated former slaves, led by a man named John Brown, had already been at the task for nearly two weeks. They had chased their quarry all over the island, finally cornering them in a swamp. There the Rebels laid an ambush in which Brown was killed and several others wounded. After an exchange of gunfire both sides withdrew. Hunter's men took up the search, but the Confederates managed to escape in a small boat, arriving on the mainland "tattered and dirty from head to foot." Their leader later wrote to a friend, "If you wish to know hell before your time, go to St. Simons and be hunted ten days by niggers."[111]

As their operations on the southeastern tidewater continued through late 1862 and into 1863, Union commanders found the service

---

[109]*Boston (MA) Commonwealth*, 21 February 1863.

[110]Reidy, "States of Dependence and Independence," 54; Mohr, *On the Threshold of Freedom*, 79.

[111]Thomas Wentworth Higginson, *Army Life in a Black Regiment* (Boston: Fields, Osgood, and Co., 1870) 274–75.

of their black volunteers to be indispensable. "They know the country, while white troops do not," wrote Colonel T. W. Higginson in February 1863 after a successful raid along the Georgia-Florida coast.

> Instead of leaving their homes and families to fight they are fighting for their homes and families, and they show the resolution and the sagacity which a personal purpose gives. It would have been madness to attempt, with the bravest white troops, what I have successfully accomplished with black ones. Everything, even to the piloting of the vessels and the selection of the proper points for cannonading, was done by my own soldiers. Indeed, the real conductor of the whole expedition up the Saint Mary's was Corporal Robert Sutton of Company G, formerly a slave upon the Saint Mary's River, a man of extraordinary qualities, who needs nothing but a knowledge of the alphabet to entitle him to the most signal promotion. In every instance when I followed his advice the predicted result followed, and I never departed from it, however slightly, without finding reason for subsequent regret.

The men's performance was such that "no officer in this regiment now doubts that the key to the successful prosecution of this war lies in the unlimited employment of black troops." Roughly two hundred thousand blacks did ultimately serve in the Union armed forces. More than 3,500 were Georgians, not counting the many thousands more who worked as cooks, laundresses, teachers, spies, scouts, guides, pilots, stevedores, and other laborers.[112]

Into the spring and through summer 1863, black soldiers native to the region conducted numerous raids up Georgia's coastal rivers. They harassed rebel patrols, captured food supplies, and destroyed anything that could be of use to Confederates. They set fire to lumber mills, laid waste to salt works, and tore up rail lines.[113]

In June 1863, in one of the most controversial acts of the war, black regiments under Colonel James Montgomery headed up the Altamaha River, raided the town of Darien, and burned it to the ground. Hardly a

---

[112]*OR*, series 1, vol. 14, 195–98; *OR*, series 3, vol. 5, 138.

[113]Jacqueline Jones, "Georgia Lowcountry Battlegrounds during the Civil War," in Fowler and Parker, *Breaking the Heartland*, 84–85.

building was left standing by the time they left. Colonel Robert Gould Shaw, commanding one of the regiments, objected to Montgomery's destruction order and refused to take any responsibility for it. Shaw called it "a dirty piece of business," writing, "Not a shot had been fired at us from this place.... All the inhabitants (principally women and children) had fled on our approach." Montgomery justified himself by insisting that "Southerners must be made to feel that this was a real war...that they were to be swept away by the hand of God, like the Jews of old." Shaw retorted, "When it comes to being made the instrument of the Lord's vengeance, I myself don't like it."[114]

As the townspeople returned, they found little more than smoldering wreckage. One witness called Darien a "plain of ashes and of blackened chimneys." Only the Methodist church and three small houses remained. "I feel this calamity severely," exclaimed a Darien resident. "I have lost heavily since the war commenced, but I had still a good home left. This is now also gone."[115] And the war was barely half over. Much more would be gone before its end.

---

[114]Spencer B. King, Jr., *Darien: The Death and Rebirth of a Southern Town* (Macon, GA: Mercer University Press, 1981) 3–4, 67–71; Peter Burchard, *One Gallant Rush: Robert Gould Shaw and His Brave Black Regiment* (New York: St. Martin's Press, 1965) 106–111; Russell Duncan, ed., *Blue-Eyed Child of Fortune: The Civil War Letters of Colonel Robert Gould Shaw* (Athens: University of Georgia Press, 1992) 342–43.

[115]King, *Darien*, 71.

Chapter 4

1863–1864: The Price of Blood

Summer 1863 found Confederate fortunes in sharp decline. Federal forces held large swaths of the southeastern tidewater, including the Georgia Sea Islands. Farther afield, northern Virginia, southern Louisiana, much of Arkansas, and most of Tennessee were in Union hands. On July 3, Robert E. Lee's effort to defeat Northern troops on their home ground and sue for peace met a dismal end at Gettysburg. The next day, Vicksburg fell to Union forces under Ulysses S. Grant, putting the entire Mississippi River under Federal control and splitting the Confederacy in two.

Of most concern militarily to Georgians were events just to the north around Chattanooga, Tennessee. In August, General William Rosecrans, commanding the Union's Army of the Cumberland, shelled the city as a diversion while the bulk of his forces moved to the southwest. This flanking maneuver, which threatened to cut off the Confederate Army of Tennessee from its supply lines, forced General Braxton Bragg to order Chattanooga abandoned. In late September, as Rosecrans moved his army into northwestern Georgia, Bragg struck him hard at Chickamauga Creek and sent the Federals flying back to Chattanooga. The Battle of Chickamauga was the Confederacy's only major victory outside of Virginia.

Bragg occupied the heights overlooking Chattanooga on Missionary Ridge and Lookout Mountain, then laid siege to the city. That siege was broken in November when Federals under Grant stormed the heights and drove Bragg's army south to Dalton, Georgia. Now all of Tennessee—along with Chattanooga, the "gateway to the lower South"—was firmly under Union control.[1] It would soon become the staging ground for a Union advance into Georgia.

Voting by Classes

The Confederacy was collapsing from internal pressures as well. Inflation had made Confederate currency nearly worthless. The only paper bills circulating in the South that had any real value were Yankee greenbacks, and they were few and far between. Slaves were escaping by the hundreds of thousands. Those who remained were taking unprecedented liberties and doing whatever else they could to undermine the Confederacy. Hunger plagued soldiers and civilians alike, which lead to food riots, rising desertion, and declining support for the war. In July 1863, after little success in drumming-up recruits for two home guard companies, Linton Stephens wrote to his brother Alexander, "There is a *fearful* giving way among our people. The spirit of volunteering is dead, dead, *dead*."[2]

That so few Georgians were willing to enlist either for state or Confederate service reflected deep fractures in Southern society that ran largely along class lines. From its beginnings, many plain folk had seen the conflict as a rich man's war. That view became more widely held as the months dragged by. In a September 1863 letter to the *Savannah Morning News*, one outraged Georgian asked, "What class has most interest in the war and has made the most money by it, *and sacrificed the least to maintain it*? ...It is the class known as the planters."[3]

Slaveholders had been responsible for bringing the Confederacy into existence but would not grow enough food to feed its soldiers or their

---

[1]For excellent treatments for these engagements see Steven E. Woodworth, *Six Armies in Tennessee: The Chickamauga and Chattanooga Campaigns* (Lincoln: University of Nebraska Press, 1998); Peter Cozzens, *This Terrible Sound: The Battle of Chickamauga* (Champaign: University of Illinois Press, 1992); Peter Cozzens, *The Shipwreck of Their Hopes: The Battles for Chattanooga* (Champaign: University of Illinois Press, 1998).

[2]J. William Harris, *Plain Folk and Gentry in a Slave Society: White Liberty and Black Slavery in Augusta's Hinterlands* (Middletown, CT: Wesleyan University Press, 1985) 178.

[3]*Savannah Morning News*, 10 September 1863.

families. Speculators were driving prices of necessities far beyond the reach of most people. The burdens of taxation and impressment fell heaviest on small farmers, and it was they and other plain folk who bore the brunt of conscription. For those who could afford to, it was easy enough to avoid the draft. An anonymous letter to Governor Brown from Catoosa County expressed that familiar complaint. The writer pointed to class inequity between two men named Stuart and Lee. "Old Mr. Stuart has five sons in the army, one sent home dead. Stuart is a poor man. Lee is rich and his sons are all at home. And it is so with other familiys. They want other people [to] do all the fighting."[4]

Such attitudes produced a class-based political consciousness that made itself felt in the fall 1863 elections. As campaigning heated up that summer, loyal Confederates worried about how the result might affect the war effort. Augusta's *Chronicle and Sentinel* noted that the South contained "a large number of persons who not only sympathize with the Federals, but who are doing all in their power to injure us in every possible manner." That summer found some Georgia citizens publically calling for an end to the war and a reconstruction of the old Union. D. H. Johnson, editor of Griffin's *Southern Union*, did just that. In north Georgia, several candidates for the General Assembly ran on the "Union" ticket.[5]

Not all those who opposed incumbents were anti-Confederate, nor did they all do so for class related reasons. But for many plain folk, class resentment certainly swayed their votes. Citizens in southeast Georgia made that clear when, in an open letter to the *Savannah Morning News*, they called on two members of the General Assembly to make public their position on a recent state tax. "There was a tax act passed at the last session for the support of indigent widows and orphans of deceased soldiers, *from which the planters were specially exempted*. Did you, or either of

---

[4]Anonymous to Joseph E. Brown, n.d., Governor's Incoming Correspondence, Georgia Department of Archives and History, Morrow.

[5]*Americus Sumter Republican*, 21 August 1863; *Milledgeville Confederate Union*, 25 August, 8 and 22 September 1863; *Augusta Chronicle and Sentinel*, 6 June 1863.

you, vote *for that exemption*, or oppose it? And how did you manifest your opposition to that gross and palpable injustice?" They signed themselves "Many Voters Who are not Planters."[6]

Planters and their allies became so worried that their political control might be slipping away that there were efforts to restrict voting rights along class lines. Some advocated raising the poll tax. Others supported property qualifications for voting and office holding. In May 1863, the Reverend H. W. Hilliard, a former member of Congress, spoke out publically for restricted suffrage. When word of Hilliard's remarks reached Athens, the *Southern Watchman* raved that "the most unfeeling, unjust and cruel wrong we have ever witnessed is this effort of designing politicians and juggling priests who are lying about home doing nothing, and worse than nothing, to disfranchise the brave and noble poor men who are fighting the battles of the country."[7]

Some elites were more discreet than Hilliard, expressing their opinions only to members of their own class. In a private letter to a friend, Godfrey Barnsley accused Governor Joe Brown, because of his opposition to Confederate conscription, of trying to "make himself popular among the lower classes to get re-elected." Barnsley held England's restricted franchise to be an example that the Confederacy should follow.[8]

Brown's opposition to Confederate conscription and impressment, but firm support for secession, positioned him at the political center that year. Opposing him were Joshua Hill, former member of the U.S. Congress and anti-secessionist in 1861, and political newcomer Timothy Furlow, a wealthy southwest Georgia planter who strongly supported the Davis administration. The public's perception of Hill was somewhat ill-defined. He denounced any notion of reunion with the North by force of arms, but his earlier anti-secession stance and his continued support

---

[6] *Savannah Morning News*, 1 October 1863.

[7] *Turnwold Countryman*, 26 May 1863; *Athens Southern Watchman*, 29 April, 2 May, 3 June 1863.

[8] Barnsley to Thomas C. Gilmour, 31 December 1862, Godfrey Barnsley Papers, Felix Hargrett Rare Book and Manuscript Library, University of Georgia.

among Union men marked him as perhaps open to some type of compromise with Lincoln. Furlow, on the other hand, made clear not only that he was an ardent, uncompromising secessionist, but that he was a nearly unquestioning supporter of centralized Confederate authority. "My official support should upon every call be given to the Government, when not clearly unconstitutional," Furlow insisted. "This is no time for factious opposition or grudging support to the Administration." Although not entirely explicit about his positions during the campaign, Brown had already effectively staked out a middle ground between his two opponents, establishing an image as white Georgians' protector from both the "Black Republican" Lincoln and the "tyrant" Davis.[9]

Brown's strategy worked. Of the 64,804 votes cast, more than 56 percent went to Brown. Hill garnered 28 percent, and 15 percent went to Furlow. Voter turnout, even counting the soldier vote, was considerably less than it had been in previous elections—20 percent less than the 1861 gubernatorial race and 40 percent less than the 1860 presidential campaign. Still, Brown's victory gave him an unprecedented fourth term. No previous governor had ever held office for more than two.[10]

Most other state and Confederate officeholders were less fortunate than Brown. Milledgeville's *Confederate Union* reported that in the General Assembly, "but few of the old members have been returned." The news was even worse for Georgia's congressional incumbents. Voters sent nine new representatives to Congress, eight of whom were elected on platforms opposing the Davis administration. Julian Hartridge of southeast Georgia's First District was the only member of the state's ten-member House delegation to retain his seat. This 90 percent freshman rate was the highest in the Confederacy. Little wonder that new members were much more attuned to the concerns of plain folk than

---

[9]T. Conn Bryan, *Confederate Georgia* (Athens: University of Georgia Press, 1953) 42–44; *Atlanta Intelligencer*, 6 October 1863; Joseph Howard Parks, *Joseph E. Brown of Georgia* (Baton Rouge: Louisiana State University Press, 1977) 251–52.

[10]Bryan, *Confederate Georgia*, 45, 36; Parks, *Joseph E. Brown*, 252; Christopher C. Meyers and David Williams, *Georgia: A Brief History* (Macon, GA: Mercer University Press, 2012) 249–51.

their predecessors. Most Georgia representatives in the First Confederate Congress had supported both conscription and impressment. In the Second Congress, only three backed conscription. A single congressman, Julian Hartridge, continued to support impressment.[11]

At the local level, men frequently sought elected office as a means of avoiding military service. When the Confederacy made county officials exempt, such positions became the focus of heated campaigns. Thirty-one Washington County candidates ran for the inferior court. In Early County, thirty-seven candidates did the same. "But there was no politics in the race," wrote one resident. "The candidate just wanted the office to keep him out of the war." M. W. Johnson of Oglethorpe County, a soldier of the 6th Georgia Regiment, went home on furlough and had himself elected justice of the peace.[12]

A Sumter County man noted with disgust that many local officeholders were younger men who could be replaced by older ones, exempt by age from military service. Sarcastically, this "Reformer," as he signed himself, wrote that "young men, burning with a patriotic desire to serve their country, should not be kept at home away from the field of honor and usefulness, to fill these *petty* offices. Turn them loose, to go where glory and fame await them." It was no use. In early 1864, General Howell Cobb wrote to Governor Brown of able-bodied young men elected "to the exclusion of old men competent to fill the places.... This class I fear is large." Later that year, the head of Georgia's Confederate enrollment

---

[11]*Milledgeville Confederate Union*, 3 November 1863; Kenneth C. Martis, *The Atlas of the Congresses of the Confederate States of America, 1861–1865* (New York: Simon and Schuster, 1994) 87, 110–13. See also William Alexander Percy, "Localizing the Context of Confederate Politics: The Congressional Election of 1863 in Georgia's First District," *Georgia Historical Quarterly* 79 (1995): 192–209.

[12]*Milledgeville Southern Recorder*, 15 November 1864; Mary Grist Whitehead, ed., *Collections of Early County Historical Society*, vol. 1 (Colquitt, GA: Automat Printers, 1971) 134; James A. Riley, "Desertion and Disloyalty in Georgia during the Civil War" (master's thesis, University of Georgia, 1951) 64.

service reported at least eight thousand military age officials claiming exemption on account of the posts they held.[13]

Not all city governments held elections that year, but in those that did, laborers could more easily organize and class issues tended to be prominent. In Columbus, common folk offered their own slate of candidates for city office on the "Mechanics' and Working Men's Ticket." According to the *Columbus Enquirer*, the new party "prevailed by a very large majority." Its success sent shock waves through the ranks of the city's political establishment.[14]

The *Enquirer* voiced upper class fears just two days after the vote when he chastised plain folk for their "antagonistic" attitude and condemned the "causeless divisions of our citizens into classes." The editor conceded that, because of their numbers, the city's commoners could control any election in which they were united. But, he insisted, this fact alone was among the strongest reasons why they should not unite. "Nothing can be more mischievous in any society," he warned, "than antagonistic organizations of its classes. Such divisions are more bitter in their alienations than any other political parties, and are far more apt to produce hurtful collisions."[15]

Reaction to the *Enquirer*'s criticism was swift and direct. A competing city paper, the *Columbus Sun*, under the title "Voting by Classes," ran a letter it received from a local man signing himself "Mechanic." The writer argued that mischief had already been done by men of wealth and property. Common folk were trying only to protect themselves from further harm.

---

[13]*Americus Sumter Republican*, 12 December 1862; *Milledgeville Southern Recorder*, 5 January 1864; Cobb to Brown, 21 April 1864, Joseph E. Brown Papers, Felix Hargrett Rare Book and Manuscript Library, University of Georgia; *War of the Rebellion: A Compilation of the Official Records of the Union and Confederate Armies* (Washington, DC: Government Printing Office, 1880–1901) series 4, vol. 3, 868–70 (hereafter cited as *OR*).

[14]*Columbus Enquirer*, 9 October 1863; *Columbus Sun*, 13 October 1863.

[15]*Columbus Enquirer*, 9 October 1863.

Editor Daily Sun: I notice in the Enquirer, of Friday evining [sic] an article complaining bitterly of the people voting by classes, in which both classes are accused of clannishness, but the burden of his complaint seems to rest on mechanics and working men. He says, "there is certainly no ground for any antagonism in the city." In this the Enquirer is mistaken; for any man, woman or child can see that the people are dividing into two classes, just as fast as the pressure of the times can force them on. As for example: class No. 1, in their thirst for gain, in their worship of Mammon, and in their mighty efforts to appropriate every dollar on earth to their own account, have lost sight of every principle of humanity, patriotism, and virtue itself, and seem to have forgotten that the very treasures they are now heaping up are the price of blood, and unless this mania ceases, will be the price of liberty itself; for we know something of the feeling which now exists in the army, as well as in our work-shops at home. The men know well enough that their helpless families are not cared for, as they were promised at the beginning of the war.... They know, too, that every day they remain from home, reduces them more and more in circumstances, and that by the close of the war a large majority of the soldiery will be unable to live; in fact, many of them are ruined now, as many of their homes and other effects are passing into the hands of speculators and extortioners, for subsistence to their families. Thus you see, that all the capital, both in money and property, in the South, is passing into the hands of class No. 1, while class No. 2 are traveling down, soon to take their station among the descendants of Ham. You can easily see who are class No. 2. The soldiery, the mechanics, and the workingmen, not only of Columbus, but of all the Confederate States. In view of these things, is it not time that our class should awake to a sense of their danger, and in the mildest possible manner begin the work of self-defense, and endeavor to escape a bondage more servile than that imposed by the aristocracy of England on their poor peasantry? Then we claim the right, as the first alternative, to try and avert the great calamity, by electing such men to the councils of the nation as we think will best represent our interests. If this should fail, we must then try more potent remedies.[16]

[16] *Columbus Sun*, 13 October 1863.

Fighting Each Other Harder than We Have Ever Fought the Enemy

Efforts to find "more potent remedies" had already given rise to the South's most widespread antiwar organization, the Peace Society, generally dedicated to ending the conflict with or without Southern independence. The Peace Society was one of several widespread secret or semi-secret organizations, along with many smaller and often affiliated groups, that sprang up across the South to oppose the war. Little is known of the Society's early days. It probably formed in north Alabama or east Tennessee during spring 1862 and later spread to Georgia. Some Free Masons may have been involved, based on the similarity of its features to Masonic recitations and rituals. The Peace Society was composed mostly of Unionists who wanted nothing more than an end to the fighting, and those Unionists remained its principal advocates throughout the war.

Though its associates and sympathizers numbered in the thousands, the Peace Society was loosely organized. One contemporary wrote that it had "no regular times or places of meeting, and has no organized 'lodges' or 'communities.' Men who have studied the obligations, signs, &c., and who can communicate them well are styled 'eminent,' and pass through the country giving the 'degree' to all whom they regard as fit subjects." Those inducted into the society promised always to aid other members and their families. They also promised never to "cut, carve, mark, scratch, show, &c., upon anything, movable or immovable, under the whole canopy of heaven, whereby any of the secrets of this order might become legible or intelligible." Finally, the inductee concluded with this statement: "I bind myself under no less penalty than that of having my head cut open, my brains taken from thence and strewn over the ground, my body cast to the beasts of the field or to the vultures of the air should I be so vile as to reveal any of the secrets of this order."[17]

Members recognized each other by a variety of complicated signs. One of the most complex was the society's handshake. It was, according to one report, "given by taking hold of the hand as usual in shaking

[17] *OR*, series 4, vol. 3, 393–95.

hands, only the thumb is turned with the side instead of the ball to the back of the hand." The following dialogue, which each member committed to memory, would then commence.

> What is that?
> A grip.
> A grip of what?
> A constitutional peace grip.
> Has it a name?
> It has.
> Will you give it to me?
> I did not so receive it, neither can I so impart it.
> How will you impart it?
> I will letter it to you.
> Letter it and begin.
> Begin you.
> No, you begin.
> Begin you.

Then, starting with any letter but the first, they spelled the word "peace" by calling out letters alternately to each other.[18]

Signs of recognition included a salute with the right hand closed and the thumb pointed backward over the shoulder, throwing a stick to the right using both hands, or tapping on the toe of the right foot three times with a stick or switch, then waving it to the right. In a crowd, a society member made himself known by three slaps on the right leg. One might also use the phrase "I dreamed that the boys are all coming home." A distress signal was given by using the expression "Oh! Washington!" or "by extending the right hand horizontally and then bringing it down by three distinct motions." Repeating the word "Washington" four times might get a member of the Peace Society released from jail if his guard happened to be a fellow member.[19]

---

[18]Ibid., 397.
[19]*OR*, series 1, vol. 32, part 3, 682–83; *OR*, series 4, vol. 3, 397.

The Society's activities included spreading dissent among soldiers as well as civilians. Apparently, the organization met with considerable success. General James Longstreet, Lee's senior corps commander, wrote that "the large and increasing number of desertions, particularly amongst the Georgia troops, induces me to believe that some such outside influence must be operating upon our men." In October 1863, perhaps encouraged by Society members, troops in southeast Georgia demanded peace and threatened to mutiny or desert if they did not get it. Shortly after, an insurrection plot was discovered among soldiers at the Rose Dew Island batteries south of Savannah. Supported by local citizens connected with the Peace Society, the soldiers took an oath to refuse to fight, to desert at the earliest opportunity, and to urge others to do the same. The Peace Society even claimed credit for Confederate defeats at Vicksburg and Missionary Ridge.[20]

Other resistance movements included Atlanta's "Union Circle," whose members worked to undermine Confederate authority and sometimes aided federal prisoners of war. Emily Farnsworth, Cyrena Stone, and other women of the city's anti-Confederate underground slipped prisoners cash and other contraband to ease their escape.[21]

From the war's outset, Southern Unionists were much more numerous than later generations would readily admit. Many went so far as to take up arms against the Confederacy. About three hundred thousand Southern whites served in Union armies, not counting those in irregular units, who numbered many more. Thomas A. Watson of Fannin County, William Fife of Harris County, Cornelius Dawson of Clinch County, and Andrew T. Harris of Murray County were among more than twenty-five hundred white Georgians known to have served in federal units. When Union armies under General William T. Sherman pushed south

[20]James Longstreet, *From Manassas to Appomattox: Memoirs of the Civil War in America* (Philadelphia: J. B. Lippincott, 1896) 651; *OR*, series 1, vol. 28, part 2, 411; *OR*, series 1, vol. 35, part 1, 529–32; Georgia Lee Tatum, *Disloyalty in the Confederacy* (1934; repr. with new introduction by David Williams, Lincoln: University of Nebraska Press, 2000) 68–69.

[21]Thomas G. Dyer, *Secret Yankees: The Union Circle in Confederate Atlanta* (Baltimore: Johns Hopkins University Press, 1999) 163.

from Chattanooga in spring 1864, hundreds of Georgia men enlisted in their ranks. One gang of Georgia ex-Confederates led by Alonzo Rogers and Porter Southworth formed a battalion calling itself the "Volunteer Force of the United States Army from Georgia."[22]

Unionism and more general antiwar sentiment was so strong by 1863 that state and Confederate officials could do little against it. Popular support and innumerable hiding places made it difficult to track down deserters and draft dodgers, much less recruit volunteers for the job. The Bureau of Conscription's superintendent admitted that public opinion attached no disgrace to desertion or draft evasion. One band of deserters quietly set up camp on an island in the Chattahoochee River. Family and friends kept them supplied with food and other necessities until the war was over. Some deserters were more defiant. In Stewart County, several men of the 3rd Georgia Regiment openly declared that they had no intention of returning to the army.[23]

Even when deserters and draft dodgers were caught, there was no guarantee of punishment. When a conscript company in Franklin County captured several deserters, the local jailor refused to lodge them. In

---

[22]Watson photo, Small Print Collection, box 18, no. 79, Georgia Department of Archives and History; Fife file, Compiled Service Records; *Pioneers of Wiregrass Georgia*, vol. 8 (Homerville, GA: Huxford Genealogical Society, 1988) 82; Harris file, Murray County GA, Archives 004 143B, Southern Claims Commission; Robert S. Davis, "Forgotten Union Guerrilla Fighters from the North Georgia Mountains," *North Georgia Journal* 5 (Summer 1988): 32; Robert S. Davis, "Memoirs of a Partisan War: Sion Darnell Remembers North Georgia," *Georgia Historical Quarterly* 80 (1996): 113; Richard N. Current, *Lincoln's Loyalists: Union Soldiers from the Confederacy* (New York: Oxford University Press, 1994) 217; Jonathan Dean Sarris, *A Separate Civil War: Communities in Conflict in the Mountain South* (Charlottesville: University of Virginia Press, 2006) 104; Robert S. Davis, "White and Black in Blue: The Recruitment of Federal Units in Civil War North Georgia," *Georgia Historical Quarterly* 85 (2001): 348, 357.

[23]*OR*, series 4, vol. 3, 1119–20; *Milledgeville Southern Recorder*, 17 November 1863; W. R. Houghton and M. B. Houghton, *Two Boys in the Civil War and After* (Montgomery, AL: Paragon Press, 1912) 237–41; John W. Riley to Brown, 22 July (no year), Governor's Incoming Correspondence.

White County, a mob of perhaps forty men broke into the jail and released a draft dodger. Disaffection prevailed to such an extent in some counties that judges could not hold court on anti-Confederates without a military escort. Even when trials were held, convictions were uncertain. Juries regularly refused to issue guilty verdicts against those who opposed the war. Howell Cobb conceded in August 1863 that to drag antiwar men into court was "simply to provide for a farcical trial." He was right. Later that year, two Lumpkin County men, John Woody and John A. Wimpy, were tried on charges of treason. In the face of strong evidence against them, and after Woody's own brother testified against him, both men were acquitted. A short time later, Woody left for Tennessee and joined the Union army.[24]

Antiwar feeling could be found in the state militia itself. Indeed, many militiamen had joined home-based units to avoid the war. When Joe Brown reorganized the state militia in December 1863, John Oliver of Effingham County declared himself a Unionist and ran on that platform for captain of his company. "He lives in a section of the County," wrote one local man to Brown, "that is generally poor people and where it has been with great difficulty to inforce the Conscript act."[25]

From Richmond County, Colonel A. C. Walker informed Brown that "most of the militia officers in the counties around here are young and robust men, and without exception obtained these offices from the

---

[24]Riley, "Desertion and Disloyalty," 69; Keith S. Bohannon, "They Had Determined to Root Us Out: Dual Memoirs by a Unionist Couple in Blue Ridge, Georgia," in John C. Inscoe and Robert C. Kenzer, eds., *Enemies of the Country: New Perspectives on Unionists in the Civil War South* (Athens: University of Georgia Press, 2001) 105; *Athens Southern Watchman*, 12 November 1862; *OR*, series 1, vol. 28, part 2, 273; Jonathan Dean Sarris, "An Execution in Lumpkin County: Local Loyalties in North Georgia's Civil War," in Kenneth W. Noe and Shannon H. Wilson, eds., *The Civil War in Appalachia: Collected Essays* (Knoxville: University of Tennessee Press, 1997) 141–42; William S. Kinsland, "The Civil War Comes to Lumpkin County," *North Georgia Journal* 1 (Summer 1984): 23–24; Sarris, *A Separate Civil War*, 95–96, 100.

[25]M. E. Mills to Brown, 29 January 1864, Governor's Incoming Correspondence.

The war divided families and communities as well as the nation. In 1863, John Woody (above) was tried for treason after attempting to free two of his sons jailed in Dahlonega for desertion. Woody's own brother Josiah (below), a staunch Confederate, testified against him, saying that John had insisted "secession was wrong and had brought the war upon us." John himself confessed his sentiments. Still, the jury refused to convict him. After his acquittal, John left for Tennessee and joined the Union army. Images courtesy of the Georgia Department of Archives and History.

most sordid motives. As far as I know them I heartly believe they would take the oath of alligence to Lincoln tomorrow." A month later, Samuel Knight wrote from southwest Georgia warning Brown that there was among "the common people…a strong Union feeling existing…the same feeling exists among the soldiers in the field to an alarming extent."[26]

J. F. Morton summed up soldier dissatisfaction in a December 1863 letter to Brown. Morton had often heard the question asked, "What is the Confederacy worth to a man when it has taken all he has, brought himself and family to poverty and want, his posterity together with himself burdened with a debt that will enslave them for generations to come?" Throughout the war, concern for their families remained the dominant influence in a soldier's decision to desert the ranks or in a conscript's decision to evade the draft. Enlistments had left many women home with small children and little or no help to tend the fields. That concern was evident in a Thomas County soldier's letter to his wife: "Write mee how my crops did turn out. I want to know what prospect you have for something to eat. I want to know how my hogs done. They was so little that I was doubtful that they would not make meat anuff for my famaly. I want to know how you are fairing about sault to save your meat."[27]

For soldiers who received no satisfactory reply to such letters, it was a common thing to desert. By late 1863, little more than half the men were present for duty out of nearly five hundred thousand on the rolls. Close to half the Confederate army was absent without leave. Promising amnesty for those who returned voluntarily, Jefferson Davis assured his reluctant countrymen in an August 1863 open letter that if all those subject to military service would simply do their duty, the war could quickly be won. "Victory is within your reach. You need but stretch forth your

[26]Walker to Brown, 18 January 1864, Governor's Incoming Correspondence; Knight to Brown, 22 February 1864, Governor's Incoming Correspondence.

[27]Morton to Brown, 24 December 1863, Governor's Incoming Correspondence; David Carlson, "The 'Loanly Runagee': Draft Evaders in Confederate South Georgia," *Georgia Historical Quarterly* 84 (2000): 596.

hands and grasp it." Davis's plea did little to draw dispirited men away from their families. The next month, in a letter to the *Savannah Republican*, one citizen pointed out what by then was obvious. "A large portion of our army are sick and tired of war, and those who have been for months hiding from…the conscription officers had as soon become gally slaves as to be mustered into our army."[28]

The Confederacy's enrollment difficulties only worsened over the following months. In February 1864, General Howell Cobb wrote that "there are men enough at home able to be in the field to make another army." Later that year, President Davis publically admitted that nearly two-thirds of Confederate soldiers had deserted.[29]

Despite their growing numbers and empathy from local residents, life for deserters could be precarious. They were harassed by state patrols, and sympathizers often had little food to give them. Some sought refuge with the Federals. In early 1864, word reached the governor's office from Dawsonville of "a grate many citizens or unionists moving to the enemy." And there were local residents who aided them on their way. Austin Mason of Union County helped organized a chain of safe houses to shelter prisoners, deserters, and draft evaders as they fled north through the Georgia mountains.[30]

Men like Mason were not unusual in the region. The Union movement in north Georgia established an extensive network of safe houses, guides, and secret signals to aid refugees in making their way to Union lines. Those requiring the services of Georgia's mountain Unionists were most grateful. A Wisconsin colonel trying to reach Sherman's army in Chattanooga later wrote that they were "generous, hospitable, brave, and

---

[28]Paul Escott, *After Secession: Jefferson Davis and the Failure of Confederate Nationalism* (Baton Rouge: Louisiana State University Press, 1978) 127; *Columbus Enquirer*, 11 August 1863; *Savannah Republican*, 15 September 1863.

[29]Cobb to his wife, 4 February 1864, Howell Cobb Papers, Felix Hargrett Rare Book and Manuscript Library, University of Georgia; *Macon Telegraph*, 24 September 1864.

[30]D. J. Burt to Brown, 26 February 1864, Governor's Incoming Correspondence; Mason file, Union County, GA, Archives 0044 24C, Southern Claims Commission.

Union men to the core; men who would suffer privations, and death itself, rather than array themselves in strife against the Stars and Stripes, the emblem of the country they loved.... [U]nder their homespun jackets beat hearts pure as gold, and stout as oaks."[31]

Such men frequently joined with deserters and draft dodgers who had been resisting Confederate authority for some time. All across Georgia, from the mountains to the Piedmont to the Pine Barrens and Wiregrass, there raged an inner civil war so violent that in late 1863 the editor of Milledgeville's *Confederate Union* wrote, "We are fighting each other harder than we have ever fought the enemy."[32]

In early November, White County Confederates went after local Tories. They hid along a wooded roadside, posted a sentinel, and waited for his signal. When it came, the men sprang from the woods and ordered their adversaries to halt. The Tories responded with a hail of gunfire, wheeled their horses, and rode off, with their pursuers firing after them. One Confederate loyalist, Lewis Pitchford, died in the exchange. A few weeks later, pro-Confederate vigilantes apprehended Jake Wofford, believed to have fired the shot that killed Pitchford. The mob stood Wofford on a plank with a rope around his neck hoping to force a confession, but the condemned man refused to say a word. Someone in the crowd finally jerked the plank away from Wofford's feet and sent him, with whatever secrets kept, to his death.[33]

Governor Brown ordered a force of state troops into northeast Georgia in early 1864, but the effort did little good. One Gilmer County Confederate wrote that "the Tories with their squirrel rifles, pick off our men from behind rocks and trees and all manner of hiding places. In this way they have killed six or eight of our soldiers." J. J. Findley of Dahlonega reported that "the District is overrun with Deserters, Tories,

---

[31]Davis, "White and Black in Blue," 357; John C. Inscoe, "Moving Through Deserter County: Fugitive Accounts of the Inner Civil War in Southern Appalachia," in Noe and Wilson, *Civil War in Appalachia*, 162.

[32]*Milledgeville Confederate Union*, 24 November 1863.

[33]*Savannah Morning News*, 16 November 1863; *Athens Southern Watchman*, 25 November 1863.

In 1864, Jefferson Davis publicly admitted that two-thirds of the army had deserted. When they reached home, many deserters joined layout gangs. They ambushed conscript and impressment companies, attacked army supply depots, and made war on Confederate authority wherever they found it. So violent did this inner civil war become that a Milledgeville newspaper wrote in 1863, "We are fighting each other harder than we have ever fought the enemy." Image from R. M. Devens, *Pictorial Book of Anecdotes and Incidents of the War of the Rebellion* (1866).

and Rogues...and that the condition of things is worse in that region than ever."[34]

Conditions were just as chaotic in northwestern Georgia, and had been for some time. As early as October 1862, deserters led by a man named Crawford terrorized the citizens of Marietta and Cobb County. Early the next spring in Walker County, Tories threatened to destroy the crops of any man who sided with the Confederacy. In March 1863, a group of Confederate loyalists wrote to Governor Brown begging him for assistance. One pro-Confederate had already been shot at, and another's house robbed. Violence also broke out in neighboring Dade County.[35]

Brown sent state troops to quell the Tory uprising, and asked for Confederate troops to help. In a letter to General Joseph E. Johnston, who commanded the Confederacy's western armies, Georgia's adjutant general Henry C. Wayne stressed the urgency of the problem but suggested a delicate handling. A heavy-handed invasion by Confederate soldiers might turn inactive layouts into active guerillas. "As these misguided people are our own citizens, His Excellency [Governor Brown] desires that...you will deal with them as gently as the heinousness of their offense will permit. It is thought that some of the insurgents are deserters from your armies." Gentle response or not, military efforts did little but make matters worse for loyal Confederates. By spring 1864, most had been driven out of LaFayette in Walker County.[36]

Confederates and layouts battled each other in southeastern Georgia as well. Colonel Duncan L. Clinch and his 4th Georgia Cavalry patrolled the Georgia coast mainly to ward off Union raids, but Clinch often sent detachments westward into the swamps, wiregrass, and piney woods in search of deserters. The first such expedition set out on May 19, 1863. Clinch ordered most of Company A to root out deserters in Irwin

---

[34]Henry C. Wayne to G. W. Lee, 23 January 1864, Adjutant General's Letter Books.

[35]*Atlanta Confederacy* in *Augusta Chronicle and Sentinel*, 28 October 1862; *OR*, series 1, vol. 23, part 2, 738.

[36]*OR*, series 1, vol. 23, part 2, 737–38; *Augusta Constitutionalist*, 7 May 1864.

County. The troopers spent a month patrolling Irwin and surrounding counties but their only success came on May 22, the day they arrived, when they apprehended twenty-two men and sent them to Savannah. Apparently losing the benefit of surprise, they made no other arrests. In July, Clinch sent another detachment into Charlton and Camden counties to "arrest and bring to these Hd Qrs all deserters at all hazzard." It had permission to go into Florida, if necessary, in pursuit of deserters. A month later it returned with only six deserters.

Ironically, Clinch's effort may have produced more desertion that it prevented. Many of his own troops deserted and joined those already hiding in the Okefenokee Swamp. Blackjack Island, one of the largest and most isolated in the swamp, held most of the resident deserters. Secure in fortified camps, they lived on deer, fish, and alligators, as well as cattle stolen from farms on the edges of the swamp.

Those troops who did not desert often expended little effort to catch those who did. In fact, they seem to have done the Confederate war effort more harm than good. Reports reached the War Department that cavalrymen stationed below the Altamaha River, apparently members of the 4th Georgia, were refusing to fight and spreading disaffection along the Georgia coast. Authorities would need to try something else if they wished to root out deserters from that region.

In November 1863, Major George Washington Lee, who a month earlier headed the Dahlonega expedition, took a battalion of state troops into south Georgia to search for deserters. His journey took him through Houston, Wilcox, Ware, and Coffee counties before landing him in Clinch County. There he met Captain Thomas Wylly, commander of Company H, 4th Georgia Cavalry, who had led his company to the area a few weeks before. Despite evidence to the contrary, both men considered reports of deserters hiding in and around the swamps to be exaggerated. They may have purposely underestimated deserter numbers to account for the few arrests they made. During the four months Lee's men were in south Georgia, they captured little more than twenty deserters and killed three more in a "sharp skirmish."[37]

[37]Carlson, "Loanly Runagee," 603–605.

So Much Rascality in this Confederacy

Deserters and conscripts with a bit of cash who wanted to remain at home but also wished to avoid skirmishing with armed troopers could still hire a substitute. For Confederate officials, however, the substitute system was much more trouble than it was worth. Confusion, corruption, and resentment plagued it from the start. Men frequently sold themselves as substitutes, deserted, then sold themselves again. Some operated individually, others were handled by brokers who ran what one Georgia paper called "a traffic in white human flesh—a blood-money speculation." Even more damaging to the Confederate cause was the ability of affluent men to hire substitutes in the first place. In May 1863, the *Milledgeville Confederate Union* pointed out what had been obvious to plain folk for some time: "The rich have it in their power to hire a substitute, whilst the poor man has not the power to avail himself of that privilege, for want of means.... Verily Solomon was right when he said: 'The poor is hated even of his own neighbor; but the rich hath many friends.'"[38]

Men with little or no money who wanted to keep out of the army had few legal options. Some sought light military details, such as those of enrollment officers, police patrollers, commissary agents, or impressment officers. Others claimed exemption as physicians although they had little if any medical knowledge. Still others claimed a teacher's exemption, although many who did so were barely literate. Because preachers were exempt as well, men of little acquaintance with Scripture were suddenly called to the ministry, sometimes with the help of their home church. In October 1863, Joel Swain, a member of Berrien County's Empire Primitive Baptist Church, deserted. Shortly after, the church licensed him to preach.[39]

---

[38]*Augusta Chronicle and Sentinel*, 21 August and 30 September 1862; *Savannah Morning News*, 10 November 1863; *Augusta Chronicle and Sentinel*, 20 August 1862; *Milledgeville Confederate Union*, 5 May 1863.

[39]Albert Burton Moore, *Conscription and Conflict in the Confederacy* (1924; repr., Columbia: University of South Carolina Press, 1996) 53; John G. Crowley, *Primitive Baptists of the Wiregrass South: 1815 to the Present* (Gainesville: University Press of Florida, 1998) 97.

Civil and judicial posts at all levels also offered sanctuary, but most of these positions went to the well-to-do. Political favors and newly created offices kept many well-connected men out of the army, so many that the *Southern Recorder*'s editor wrote, "It is discouraging to witness with what eagerness these offices are sought in every county by able bodied young men without families, hoping thereby to procure an exemption from the military duties demanded of them by our bleeding country."[40]

The ease with which wealthy men were "skulking" was a leading cause of discontent. "The bomb proof places they hold were, in most cases, bought with money—yes! Bought with money!" wrote the editor of Augusta's *Chronicle and Sentinel*. He reflected the outrage of thousands when he lashed out against those who bought their way out of combat. "They do not intend to pass sleepless nights and encounter dangers for the cause—not they!...is it any wonder that the masses are fast losing confidence in their Confederate leaders?"[41]

Plain folk hardly needed newspapers to point out the obvious. They saw it often enough for themselves. The citizens of Grooverville in Brooks County knew that W. R. Joiner had gained an exemption based solely on a petition signed by "some few special friends and some Ladies and a great many little children who cannot sign their own name." But officials rarely questioned a petition backed by local gentry. In fact, Brooks County's inferior court, without authority to do so, commonly granted exemptions to wealthy men. Clinch County's H. B. Hill was exempt as a doctor even though he had given up his practice, refused to see patients, and spent most of his time speculating. "We think it hard to give up our fathers and young brothers," citizens of Stockton wrote concerning Hill, "and have such an able bodied healthy man as he is allowed to remain at home who does nothing but is an injury to the county buying up all the provisions for speculation which poor women and children are needing."[42]

---

[40]*Milledgeville Southern Recorder*, 5 January 1864.

[41]*Augusta Chronicle and Sentinel*, 31 December 1864.

[42]Robert David Carlson, "Wiregrass Runners: Conscription, Desertion, and the Origins of Discontent in Civil War South Georgia" (master's thesis,

Officer's commissions with the state militia continued to provide a safe haven for those with money and connections to secure them. A Columbia County woman wrote complaining of "protection given to shirkers," as she called such men. She told of the wealthy and able-bodied being granted state commissions for the sole purpose of shielding them from the draft. Poor men, who had no money to buy state commissions, were the ones forced to leave wives and children and fight for rich men's liberty. That remained true even after Congress, responding to public rage against substitution, repealed the substitute law in December 1863. No longer able to hide behind his paid substitute, Jefferson Thomas, a prominent slaveholder in Richmond County, secured a commission in the state militia and remained at home.[43]

Outright bribery also provided a way out of front line service for reluctant conscripts. With enough ready cash, they could usually persuade enrollment officers to pass them by. One southwest Georgia editor wrote, "It is strange to us that the Government allows its officers to conscript poor men who have the appearance of *dead men*, while they turn loose rich ones who are *young, hale and hearty*."[44]

Very often, cash could purchase a post as conscript officer. Few such men had any interest in actually hunting down conscripts. Though most tried to maintain at least a show of adherence to duty, with some it was easy to see through their facade. One man wrote to Governor Brown from Pine Mount, "if they need men in the army, why don't they take these loafing enrolling officers who is doing the country more harm than that many Yankees could do."[45]

General knowledge of well-financed, and legal, draft dodging among the wealthy made poorer men even less willing to risk their lives

---

Valdosta State University, 1999) 16.

[43]Anonymous to H. C. Wayne, September 1862, Adjutant and Inspector General's Incoming Correspondence; Laura F. Edwards, *Scarlett Doesn't Live Here Anymore: Southern Women in the Civil War Era* (Urbana: University of Illinois Press, 2000) 89.

[44]*Early County News*, 30 March 1864.

[45]Knight to Brown, 22 February 1864, Governor's Incoming Correspondence.

for the Confederacy. With desertion and draft evasion rapidly depleting Confederate forces, Richmond decided to cast a wider conscription net. In February 1864, with its Third Conscription Act, Congress made all white males between the ages of seventeen and fifty subject to the draft. To discourage desertion, Congress also offered $100 in government bonds at 6 percent interest to any enlisted man who remained at his post. Neither effort worked to build up the ranks.

Thousands of letters poured into state and Confederate offices citing any number of reasons why men should be excused from the draft or discharged from the army. Isaac Bush of Colquitt asked for exemption on account of "my ankles swelling." A Stewart County woman, who had lost her husband, two brothers-in-law, and a brother to the war, now had only one brother left, and he was in the army sick with typhoid fever, measles, and a "hacking cough." She begged for his discharge so he could recover and care for his three children. "Their Mother is dead," she wrote, "and his Mother is a widow and not able to do anything for them."[46]

Pauline Wheeler of Columbia County considered Brown a "friend of the poor" and asked for her son's release. She had already lost her husband and two other sons to the war, and now badly needed help on her small farm. She described her work of hauling corn and wood, cutting crops, going to the mill, and tending stock. "Not having my son with me to do these things, I live in a state of some perplexity and vexation which is enough to drive me into insanity."[47]

The long hours of worry and work drove some women to their graves. Soldiers' wives in Baker County asked the governor to allow one of their men to remain at home to, among other things, build coffins. A

---

[46]Bush to Joseph E. Brown, 16 October 1863, Governor's Incoming Correspondence; Mrs. S. E. Cook to Brown, 16 August 1864, Governor's Incoming Correspondence.

[47]Wheeler to Brown, 31 October 1864, Governor's Incoming Correspondence.

sympathetic clerk in Brown's office summarized the petition on its outside fold, underlining for emphasis the words "build coffins."[48]

Adding to women's hardships were impressment companies that continued to roam the countryside. As food seizures became more frequent, so did complaints. The army's October 1863 attempt to impress every hog in southwest Georgia's Mitchell County met with considerable displeasure. A local grand jury called the effort "unwise, ungenerous, and unjust. Its execution would disorganize and demoralize the people." Even worse, it would "result in the starvation of the indigent." Impressment threatened indigents in north Georgia too. In spring 1864, under the heading "Starvation in the Mountains," an Athens paper reported that many people were living on roots and weeds. "Their means for making a crop this year are very lean—their oxen being impressed."[49]

One impressment officer threatened to beat a seventy-year-old Bibb County man if he did not hand over his horse. The man had already sent five sons into Confederate service, two of whom were dead. "We advise the people to resist them," wrote the *Atlanta Southern Confederacy*. The *Early County News* advised resistance as well. Otherwise "our military officers will soon think they own the whole country."[50]

Judge James Bush headed a meeting of Early County citizens who warned that corrupt and violent impressment officials were so numerous that they would "ultimately alienate the affections of the people from the government." They were right. In a letter to her brother, Nancy Mann of Harris County encouraged him to desert. She did not want to lose a member of her family to a cause she felt was not worth defending. "There is so much rascality carried on in this confedracy," she complained, "untill

---

[48]Ladies of Baker County to Brown, 26 October 1864, Talemon Cuyler Collection, Felix Hargrett Rare Book and Manuscript Library, University of Georgia, Athens.

[49]*Macon Telegraph*, 10 November 1863; *Athens Southern Watchman*, 18 May 1864.

[50]*Augusta Chronicle and Sentinel*, 31 May 1864; *Atlanta Southern Confederacy*, 27 February 1863; *Early County News*, 6 April 1864.

I think some times I do not no what will be come of the people and nor the confedracy and I do not care much."[51]

Though few people held either impressment or taxation in high regard, plain folk knew that the rich did not contribute in proportion to their wealth. Soon after Congress levied an income tax in April 1863, so many wealthy men refused to file tax returns that one Milledgeville citizen called on the state's superior court judges "to give the subject in special charge to their Grand Juries.... Our Government is entitled to support from the men who have been skulking from the field, while our brave boys have been pouring out their blood like water to protect their ill-gotten property."[52]

In response, the state levied a nominal penalty that was rarely enforced. Its superficiality had a devastating effect on morale. One man wrote an angry letter to Governor Brown in early 1864 warning him of widespread dissent among southwest Georgians. Their view of the tax system as inequitable had much to do with that dissent. "Poor people has to pay all the tax and do all the fighting, while the gentlemen and their sons are loafing."[53]

Impressment's lack of equity was just as obvious. Impressing agents typically sought out the most vulnerable targets first—the farmsteads of plain folk. Only when these farms were stripped bare did they turn to plantations. Even then, planters were reluctant to part with their surplus. Some used political connections to avoid impressment. Others simply had themselves appointed impressment agents—and profited by it. Mary Lane of Wilkes County complained to Governor Brown that William Sneed, a local slaveholder and impressment agent, was feeding confiscated produce to his slaves.[54]

---

[51] *Early County News*, 20 April 1864; Nancy Mann to Thomas Mann, 2 January 1864, Mann Civil War Papers, Georgia Department of Archives and History. James Bush, a prewar inferior court judge, was one of the first white settlers in Early County and is the author's great-great-great-grandfather.

[52] *Milledgeville Confederate Union*, 30 June 1863.

[53] Samuel Knight to Brown, 22 February 1864, Governor's Incoming Correspondence.

[54] Lane to Brown, 12 November 1864, Cuyler Collection.

Although the practice was not exclusive to planters, many hid supplies to avoid having them impressed. A Georgia soldier recalled how farmers "would hide their wagons under straw piles, and carry off their horses where you cannot come at them.... Some of these men rich—worth fifty thousand dollars." One southwest Georgia planter stashed at least a thousand bushels of corn in a large crib hidden deep in the woods. "What kind of a man can he be?" asked a local editor. "Is he a friend of the country? No; for no man who is will, at such a time as this, hide his corn from suffering Soldiers and their families." The editor insisted that he ought to be lynched. "He is a meaner man, by far, than any Yankee that ever invaded our country."[55]

As reluctant as planters were to give up produce and livestock, they were even less willing to part with their slaves. In 1862, after Fort Pulaski fell to the Federals, Georgia began impressing slave labor for work on Savannah's fortifications. Even though the state promised compensation for slaves killed or injured in its service, slaveholders still complained. Lee County planters led by C. M. Irvin drew up a resolution announcing their determination to resist slave impressment. Others acquiesced but demanded compensation. William Castleberry of Clay County wrote to Governor Brown protesting that he received no pay for his slaves' services. In a public letter addressed "To the Planters of Georgia," Brown expressed disappointment that so few had responded to his call for slave labor. He reminded planters of their stake in the Confederacy and of their earlier promises to support it. He wrote, "I will not believe that there was a want of sincerity in your professions of liberality and patriotism."[56]

That slaveholders were promised pay for lost labor only reinforced the widespread "rich man's war" attitude, especially among soldiers and

---

[55]Edmund Cody Burnett, ed., "Letters of Barnett Hardeman Cody and Others, 1861–1864," *Georgia Historical Quarterly* 23 (1939): 290; *Early County News*, 10 August 1864.

[56]*Augusta Chronicle and Sentinel*, 7 August 1862; *Americus Sumter Republican*, 8 August 1862; Castleberry to Brown, 1 August 1862, Governor's Incoming Correspondence; *Augusta Chronicle and Sentinel*, 4 November 1862.

their families. E. H. Grouby of the *Early County News* gave voice to many Georgians when he asked, "If a man of means is to be paid for a negro that dies while doing Government work, why should not a poor man or woman be also paid for the loss of a son while fighting for the country?" If anyone were to be paid, he insisted, it should be soldiers' families "instead of the rich man or woman who has lost a confounded negro, for which the poor people are now fighting. But," he lamented, "giving poor people their rights in this country has long since 'played out,' and so, we suppose, the poor will have to 'grin and endure' whatever the wealthy are a mind to require. So wags the world!"[57]

The wealthy, wrote a group of Spalding County women, "don't care what becomes of the poor class of people" as long as "they can save there niggroes." When Robert Toombs used political connections to have his slaves excused from impressment, one newspaper lashed out. "We believe Toombs, because he is rich, does pretty much what he wants...if he were a poor man he would be hanged." The editor concluded that "a *poor* man in this world has no more showing than a blind dog in a meat house with a dozen starving Yankees after him."[58]

Bread or Blood

Much of the suffering among plain folk was avoidable, arising from little more than corruption, incompetence, or neglect in the relief system. Frances Dorris, a soldier's wife, complained to Governor Brown that the Milton County inferior court refused to let women draw rations if they had "any thing attall." But her few provisions had been impressed, and there was nothing left for her starving children. Wiley Knight of Blackshear wrote that the inferior court of Pierce County "does not make an equal distribution of the money given by the State for the benefit of indigent families." Knight asked the governor to help him obtain a list of people who were supposed to receive help and the amount of funds given

[57]*Early County News*, 15 June 1864.

[58]Edwards, *Scarlett Doesn't Live Here Anymore*, 89; *Early County News*, 16 March 1864.

to the inferior court for distribution. "I believe," he wrote, "there is something [w]rong, and I can detect it if you will assist me."[59]

George Cleveland, justice of the peace for Miller County, also wrote Governor Brown that "there must be something wrong somewheare." Local soldiers' families had not drawn relief funds for several months because, according to a county agent, there was "no money on hand." Cleveland worried about the possibility of someone "swindling" the money, writing, "Please answer this as soon as it comes to hand and let Justice be done to the Brave soldiers suffering wives and children."[60]

Sarah Hudlow of Dawson County, an enfeebled seventy-three-year-old widow with children and grandchildren in the war, wrote that local officials of "the meanest carrecter" were misappropriating state corn. She begged the governor "to inquire into this bisnes for it is not manege rite for some draws corn that orte [ought] not." Sarah had applied for the badly needed corn herself, but had been turned down. She continued, "If I don't git help from the government I shal have to suffer if not pearish." Enraged citizens from Fannin County called on the governor to remove their inferior court justices "for want of energy, incapacity, [and] misapplication of the public fund corn."[61]

In April 1864, J. D. Hammack, clerk of Taliaferro County's inferior court, told Governor Brown of promises made and not kept. Many of the county's men had entered service early in the war, and now their families were destitute. They had joined believing "liberal promises from men of wealth that their families should be amply provided for." But those promises had "not been fully complied with." Hammack noted that the inferior court had tried to provide relief, but food was so scarce that there were few provisions available. Bacon was especially hard to come by.

---

[59]Dorris to Brown, 19 April 1864, Cuyler Collection; Knight to Brown, 16 July 1864, Governor's Incoming Correspondence. Milton later merged with Fulton County.

[60]Cleveland to Brown, 3 November 1863, Governor's Incoming Correspondence.

[61]Hudlow to Brown, 22 May 1864, Cuyler Collection; J. W. Henson, Maxwell Chastain, Jasper Ashworth, L. B. Crawford, and S. W. Bates to Brown, 1 July 1864, Cuyler Collection.

"The farmers in the County have little...and when you find one who could spare it, he dislikes to sell it to those families, because others can afford to pay higher prices."[62] By "others," he meant planters and speculators. In a bidding war for food, poor soldiers' families were inevitably the losers.

J. Paine of Quitman wrote the governor about starving women in Colquitt, Berrien, Clinch, Echols, Pierce, Ware, and Appling counties. Paine noted that the inferior courts were doing nothing to relieve suffering families. Area women told Paine that they had received no assistance since the war began and accused court officials of using government funds "for their own private purposes." Paine stressed that he was no planter and that his only interest in the matter was to help those in need.[63]

By the war's third winter, few in Georgia believed that planters had much interest in poor relief of any kind. Most tended to blame planters for destitution. A petition for help sent to Richmond from soldiers' wives in Miller County left little doubt who they blamed.

> Our crops is limited and so short...cannot reach the first day of march next.... But little [food?] of any sort to Rescue us and our children from a unanamus starveation.... We can seldom find [bacon] for non has got But those that are exzempt from service...and they have no humane feeling.... I tell you that with out som grate and speadly alterating in the conduckting of afares in this our little nation god will frown on it and that speadly.[64]

Women in Spalding County pointed the finger of blame even more directly. "The rich is all at home makeing great fortunes, and care nothing for nobody but themselves," complained these women. "They can speculate of soldiers wives [and] make fortunes [from] them.... Just look

[62]Hammack to Brown, 23 April 1864, Cuyler Collection.

[63]Paine to Brown, 28 March 1864, Cuyler Collection.

[64]Petition from Women of Miller County, Georgia, to Secretary of War James Seddon and President Jefferson Davis, 8 September 1863, Letters Received, Confederate Secretary of War, RG 109, Microcopy M 437, Roll 80, 776–80, National Archives, Washington, DC.

at ther women and children that are begging bread...they would see them pearish before they would give them one bushel of corn."[65]

To keep their heads above the flood tide of corruption and speculation, many soldiers' families went deep into debt for what food was available or traded what little they had for it. In cases of debt, interest rates were usually so high and money so scarce that loans could not be repaid. Then creditors could take whatever collateral could be had, very often in land. Frequently, land was the only commodity of any value that soldiers' families had with which to barter. The result was that many thousands of Confederate soldiers returned home to find their families destitute and their small landholdings much reduced or entirely gone.

Just as they had been doing since the war's second year, what women could not buy, beg, or trade for, they would steal if pushed to it. In late fall 1863, starving women rampaged through Thomasville for the "purpose of supplying themselves with goods." Threats of further rioting caused such fear among city officials that they called for help from as far away as Valdosta, forty miles to the east. Thannie Wisenbaker, a Valdosta resident, later remembered when the town's home guard "was ordered to Thomasville where some great excitement was reported.... When they arrived in Thomasville, they learned, to their utter chagrin, that some soldiers' wives had threatened to break into the government commissary to obtain food for their hungry children."[66]

At its December session, Thomas County's Superior Court called the riot a "disgraceful act" and warned that "misguided females" should refrain from "unlawful demonstrations in the future." Such warnings often went unheeded. Several months later, six armed Thomas County women stopped a wagon and stole its cargo of corn. Still, ineffective as they were, warnings were usually the extent official reaction when women resorted to theft. Criminal charges rarely followed. Most local officials

---

[65]Edwards, *Scarlett Doesn't Live Here Anymore*, 95.

[66]Thomas County Superior Court, December 1863, Minute Book 1858–1865; Thannie Wisenbaker Reminiscences, 19–20, South Georgia Regional Library, Valdosta.

knew that women were driven by circumstance and had much community sympathy.[67]

Another wave of rioting struck Georgia in spring 1864. In April, newspapers reported a "daring robbery" in Savannah. Armed women numbering between fifty and one hundred marched through the city calling for "bread or blood." They targeted the stores of A. F. Mira on Whitaker Street, John Gilliland on Congress Street, W. and R. McIntire on Saint Julian Street, and a Mr. Stroup's store on Bryan Street, helping themselves to whatever they needed. Mira tried to force payment but was pushed into a corner while his store was robbed. One of the McIntires offered the rioters rice and sugar free of charge, hoping to avoid a general ransacking. The gesture worked. They moved on to Gilliland's store, where they stole all his bacon. Gilliland tried grab back some of his pork, but most of women escaped with their plunder.

Although arrests were unusual in such cases, Sheriff Cole of Chatham County jailed three of the rioters. Mary Welsh was charged with theft. Anne McGlin and Julia McLane were charged with disorderly conduct. In the end, none were prosecuted. There was too much popular sympathy for them, especially since they were soldiers' wives. Store owners Gilliland and Mira later applied for reimbursement from Savannah's City Council. Gilliland asked for $250. Mira wanted $210. The council tabled their requests.[68]

---

[67]Thomas County Superior Court, December 1863, Minute Book 1858–1865; E. Merton Coulter, *Confederate States of America, 1861–1865* (Baton Rouge: Louisiana State University Press, 1950) 423. There was also a tradition in English common law dating back to the seventeenth century that women who engaged in rioting would not be prosecuted so long as their actions were spontaneous and driven by dire necessity. Though there is no evidence of a direct link, that may have helped local justices rationalize the lack of prosecutions. See Olwen Hufton, *The Prospect Before Her: A History of Women in Western Europe, Volume 1, 1500–1800* (New York: Alfred A. Knopf, 1996) 468–69.

[68]*Columbus Sun*, 22 April 1864; *Washington (DC) Daily National Intelligencer*, 10 May 1864, *Augusta Constitutionalist*, 23 and 24 April 1864; Savannah City Council Minutes, April 1864, Georgia Department of Archives and History.

On April 19, E. Yulee of Stockton reported that "thirteen women made their appearance here armed with pistols and knives and demanded admittance to the depot containing the provisions collected as tax in kind." Three guards tried without success to "pacify" the women. They shoved the men aside, broke open the door, and took more than one hundred pounds of bacon. Yulee believed that these women would be back for more supplies now that they knew they could "seize them with impunity." He suggested that the civil courts might offer a remedy, but "unfortunately these are now silent in the middle of our troubles."[69]

Just west of Stockton, Lowndes County saw more female rioting that month. A group of Valdosta women tried to buy cotton yarn, but the proprietor refused to take Confederate money. He would, however, trade for bacon. Having no bacon to exchange, the women "forcibly took all the yarns in the store." Around the same time, a dozen or more Valdosta women broke into a government warehouse and stole a wagonload of bacon. Shortly after, in the small Lowndes settlement of Naylor, women raided stores for both yarn and bacon.[70]

In May, Campbell County Justice of the Peace B. D. Smith found himself in an uncomfortable situation over the issue of women taking "impressment" into their own hands. In a letter to Governor Brown, Smith outlined circumstances that led two men to accuse him of "up holding the women presying provisions." The men in question were trying to avoid conscription by having Smith call bailiff elections and running for the positions themselves. Once elected, they would be draft exempt. To force the issue, they had tried to frighten a sixty-one-year-old bailiff into quitting his post, but neither Smith nor the bailiff would be intimidated. The would-be draft dodgers then accused Smith of supporting local women who stole provisions from a speculator's storehouse.

---

[69]E. Yulee to Joseph E. Brown, 19 April 1864, Governor's Incoming Correspondence. Most of the governor's incoming correspondence was read by clerks who wrote a short description on the outside of envelopes or letters for faster processing. Yulee's letter was marked "women outrages."

[70]*Savannah News* in *Augusta Chronicle and Sentinel*, 24 April 1864; *Augusta Constitutionalist*, 23 April 1864; Crowley, *Primitive Baptists of the Wiregrass South*, 94.

He denied the accusation, but then wrote, "I did not blame the women." Their victim was, he said, "staying at home" only to profit from a war in which he refused to fight. Though the man was well aware of how badly soldiers' families needed supplies and had "a right smart to [spare], he would not let them have it neither for money nor work but was speculating on it." Careful not to alarm the governor, Smith noted that the women's actions were peaceful. He refused to call the incident a riot, insisting that nothing of that sort, with all its violent connotations, had ever occurred in Campbell County.[71]

Destruction was usually not women's intent when taking provisions, but there was at least one raid that saw severe property damage. In June 1864, a number of armed Pierce County women broke into a storehouse, "carried off several wagon-loads of bacon, and burned some houses." These women boasted that they had plenty of men, including deserters hiding in the Okefenokee Swamp, who would back them up should they meet resistance. According to one source, "the people of property were much alarmed," so much so that one "prominent citizen" hurriedly boarded a train from Blackshear to Savannah and reported the attack to military authorities.[72]

The Negroes Do as They Please

Just as white women continued pressing for provisions, black folk continued pressing for freedom. In summer 1863, one news editor complained of blacks becoming "saucy and abusive," insisting that a police force was needed "as a check to their continued insolence." The Georgia General Assembly had already acted "to punish slaves and free persons of color for abusive and insulting language." Along with freedom of speech, blacks were taking freedom of assembly as well. In Blakely, the *Early County News* reported that blacks were "almost nightly running around where they have no business." A Columbus resident feared that blacks

---

[71]B. D. Smith to Brown, 16 May 1864, Governor's Incoming Correspondence. Campbell County, along with its seat of Campbellton, merged with Fulton County in 1932.

[72]*OR*, series 1, vol. 35, part 2, 544.

were forgetting their second-class status. "It is not uncommon," he wrote, "to see two or three in one whiskey shop."[73]

Though cause for concern among slaveholders, blacks taking small liberties were among the least of their worries. In October 1863, perhaps a hundred or more slaves in Hancock County laid plans for a mass revolt and escape to federal lines. When word leaked out prematurely, thirty-four slaves were arrested and tried for their part in the conspiracy—some in court, others by a vigilance committee. Four of the ringleaders were sentenced to hang. Other organizers received hundreds of lashes. One was a man named Cary, a slave belonging to Linton Stephens, brother of Alexander Stephens. The vice president himself witnessed and described the beatings. "They stretch them upon a log[,] make them fast—take off their britches—turn their shirts over their heads and strap them with a piece of buggy [leather]." Each whipping went on so long and became so painful than some victims involuntarily emptied their bowels. Cary and the others had been offered fewer lashes in exchange for testimony against fellow slaves. All refused.[74]

It is impossible to know how many such plots were hatched among enslaved Georgians. Slaveholders generally tried to keep such affairs out of the public eye, so eager were they to preserve the lie of generally contented slaves. Hancock County's vigilance committee attempted to suppress news of their abortive uprising, but a conspiracy that involved so many slaves was hard to hide. Milledgeville papers first printed the story, which was soon picked up by other outlets. The editor of the Augusta's *Constitutionalist* stressed that he would have preferred not to mention the incident, but did so anyway since word was already so widespread.[75]

Despite public insistence that slaves were content, slaveholders knew very well that resistance was the norm. That was certainly clear to Jane

---

[73] *Selma (AL) Morning Reporter*, 29 August 1863; *Milledgeville Southern Recorder*, 25 November 1862; *Early County News*, 16 March 1864; B. W. Clark to Joseph E. Brown, 30 January 1864, Governor's Incoming Correspondence.

[74] Bryan, *Confederate Georgia*, 127; Harris, *Plain Folk and Gentry*, 167–68.

[75] *Milledgeville Southern Recorder*, 6 October 1863; Harris, *Plain Folk and Gentry*, 169.

Eubanks of Columbia County, who wrote to Governor Brown about the need for more white men to control local slaves. There were four hundred slaves in her vicinity and few patrols to keep them subdued. John R. Edwards of Harris County wrote that in and around Waverly Hall, there were only four men available to ride patrol over seven hundred slaves. Slaveholding women in Schley County petitioned the governor to hire a local man who kept a pack of "Negro dogs" to hunt escaped slaves. Julia Brooks gathered signatures for a petition to have her husband, B. F. Brooks, sent home from the army to organize slave patrols.[76]

In December 1863, a slaveholding woman from Burke County wrote to Brown about the lack of white men in her area, most of them forced away by the draft. She urged Brown to create a police force for the protection of Georgia's "planting interest," insisting that the governor must "see to it, that [the planter] class of citizens are protected and not left to meet a fate worse than death." The General Assembly responded to such pleas by reinforcing laws forbidding slaves to travel without a pass and canceled exemptions from patrol duty.[77]

Nevertheless, patrols continued losing their power of intimidation. Some slaves boldly fought back. They often tied ropes or vines neck-high across a dark stretch of road just before patrols passed by. In Decatur County, roving blacks stood down patrollers simply by warning them that they had better move on if they knew what was best for them. When patrollers broke in on a prayer meeting near Columbus, one slave stuck a shovel in the fireplace and threw hot coals all over them. Instantly the room "filled with smoke and the smell of burning clothes and white flesh." In the confusion, every slave got away.[78]

---

[76]Eubanks to Brown, 18 July 1864, Governor's Incoming Correspondence; Edwards to Brown, 8 January 1864, Governor's Incoming Correspondence; Petition from Ladies of the County of Schley to Brown, August 1864, Governor's Incoming Correspondence; Brooks to Brown, 22 June 1864, Governor's Incoming Correspondence.

[77]Mrs. John Green to Brown, 11 December 1863, Governor's Incoming Correspondence; Bryan, *Confederate Georgia*, 126.

[78]Susan E. O'Donovan, *Becoming Free in the Cotton South* (Cambridge, MA: Harvard University Press, 2007) 105; W. B. Allen in George P. Rawick et

Try as they might, slaveholders had an increasingly difficult time controlling slaves. It was with good reason that William Mansfield of Stewart County wrote in early 1864 that local planters were terrified of their slaves. A short time later in neighboring Randolph County, a female planter moved her family to Cuthbert, saying that it was not safe to remain on her plantation without protection.[79]

That August, Julie Pope Stanley of Clarke County wrote to her husband in the army, "there are so few men in the neighborhood and they do not visit the plantation at all, the Negroes do as they please." They had been doing the same all over Georgia, subtly and overtly, for some time. In the process, they were ending slavery on their own. After the Hancock County slave conspiracy of October 1863, Linton Stephens wrote to his brother Alexander that "the institution of slavery is already so undermined and demoralized as never to be of much use to us, even if we had peace and independence to day." With or without Confederate victory, blacks were taking steps to ensure that they would never be fully enslaved again.[80]

Even so, the Confederacy remained committed to slavery in concept, and blacks generally did all they could to undermine the hated regime. Their efforts often included assisting any whites they considered allies in the cause. Confederate deserters traveling home knew that slave cabins were their safest bet for food, shelter, and support. One deserter killed Georgia planter William McDonald when the slaveholder discovered him hiding in his slave quarters. McDonald's slaves did not intervene. Nancy Johnson, enslaved on a Liberty County plantation, told how "some of the rebel soldiers deserted and came to our house and we fed them. They were opposed to the war and didn't own slaves and said they would die rather than fight. Those who were poor white people, who

---

al., comp., *The American Slave: A Composite Autobiography* (Westport, CT: Greenwood Press, 1972 and 1977) supplement, series 1, vol. 3, part 1, 7–8.

[79]Mansfield to Brown, 26 May 1864, Governor's Incoming Correspondence; O'Donovan, *Becoming Free in the Cotton South*, 97.

[80]Mark A. Weitz, *A Higher Duty: Desertion among Georgia Troops during the Civil War* (Lincoln: University of Nebraska Press, 2000) 161–62; Harris, *Plain Folk and Gentry*, 167.

Enslaved people who did not escape found many ways to work against the Confederacy. After the war, Nancy Johnson told how she and her husband helped escaping Union prisoners and Confederate deserters. "There was a Yankee prisoner that got away and came to our house . . . . My husband slipped him over to a man named Joel Hodges and he conveyed him off so that he got home. . . . Some of the rebel soldiers deserted and came to our house and we fed them." Image from Junius Henri Browne, *Four Years in Secessia* (1865).

didn't own slaves were some of them Union people. I befriended them because they were on our side."[81]

Defining deserters and Unionists as "on our side" became easier for Southern blacks as word of the Emancipation Proclamation spread. Increasingly blacks came to identify freedom with the Union cause, with white Southern Unionists, and with Union soldiers. Blacks did not always know what to make of their new allies' motives, nor did they always trust them entirely. But with freedom and the Union joined together, blacks were more eager than ever to join whites in any effort that might serve the interests of both. As an escaping Union prisoner of war recalled, "They were always ready to help anybody opposed to the Rebels. Union refugees, Confederate deserters, escaped prisoners—all received from them the same prompt and invariable kindness."[82]

Black women in Savannah took great risks in smuggling food to Union prisoners. Susie King Taylor, a Savannah native, wrote of the city's prison stockade as "an awful place. The Union soldiers were in it, worse than pigs, without any shelter from sun or storm, and the colored women would take food there at night and pass it to them through the holes in the fence. The soldiers were starving, and these women did all they could towards relieving those men, although they knew the penalty should they be caught giving them aid."[83]

Blacks sometimes assisted white anti-Confederates escape imprisonment. In December 1863, Robert Webster, a black Atlanta barber, helped an aging Tennessee Unionist named William Clift break out of the city's military prison. Clift had served as a courier for the Federals in his home state until being arrested by his own son, a Confederate cavalry officer. Webster smuggled a rope to the old man, who soon after made

---

[81] *Augusta Constitutionalist*, 5 May 1864; Ira Berlin et al., eds., *Freedom: A Documentary History of Emancipation, 1861–1867*, series 1, vol. 1, *The Destruction of Slavery* (New York: Cambridge University Press, 1985) 151 (hereafter cited as *Destruction of Slavery*).

[82] Albert D. Richardson, *The Secret Service, the Field, the Dungeon, and the Escape* (Hartford, CT: American Publishing, 1866) 445.

[83] Susie King Taylor, *Reminiscences of My Life in Camp* (1902; repr. with introduction by Catherine Clinton, Athens: University of Georgia Press, 2006) 68.

his escape. Along their routes to Union lines, people like Clift could expect safe haven and escorts among black folk. Nancy Johnson told of a Yankee fugitive who showed up at her doorstep one evening. After keeping him hidden through the next day, Nancy's husband "slipped him over to a man named Joel Hodges and he conveyed him off so that he got home."[84]

In late spring 1864, John Kellogg was among a group of Union prisoners escaping through the Georgia mountains with the aid of local blacks. They impressed Kellogg with their "telegraph line," a verbal information network also known as the "grapevine telegraph." They told Kellogg and his comrades of Union troop movements between Chattanooga and Atlanta, some at a distance of 150 miles. Such intelligence was essential to planning the safest route to federal lines. Kellogg found his black allies "better informed of passing events" than most Southern whites.[85]

Whatever assistance blacks rendered to whites was usually of a covert nature. If it came to light, dire consequences could result. Such was the case in August 1864 when three slaves—Nelson, George, and Sam—along with a white man named John Vickery, tried to organize a slave rebellion in south Georgia's Brooks County. Vickery was a man of modest means for whom no evidence can be found of prior trouble with the law. In fact, Vickery was listed on Brooks County jury rolls in 1863. He next appears in the public record a year later at the end of a hangman's rope. Vickery's motives remain unclear and details of events leading to his execution vary, but all sources agree that Vickery, with the assistance of Nelson, George, and Sam, planned a violent uprising aimed at some of the county's wealthiest slaveholders.

After arming themselves and killing local planters, the small slave army would set the county seat of Quitman afire. From there they would head south toward Madison, Florida, and burn it as well. Hoping to be reinforced by deserters and Union troops on the Gulf Coast, the men

[84]Dyer, *Secret Yankees*, 88–89; Berlin et al., *Destruction of Slavery*, 151.

[85]John Azor Kellogg, *Capture and Escape: A Narrative of Army and Prison Life* (n.p.: Wisconsin Historical Commission, 1908) 146–47, 149.

would return to Quitman, set free the rest of Brooks County's slaves, and secure a Union foothold in southern Georgia.

As early as January 1863, Confederate officials were warned that Dead Man's Bay on the Gulf Coast could be a prime landing site for Union forces. It was in Taylor County, already a deserter stronghold. The ground was firm, no natural obstructions blocked the roads between the bay and the interior, and there was a direct route from there to Madison. Just such a landing occurred one week prior to the planned Brooks County uprising. Eight hundred Union troops disembarked at the mouth of the Aucilla River, with another five hundred at Dead Man's Bay. It is unclear whether Vickery, or anyone else, was in contact with the landing force or whether its timing prompted Vickery and his comrades to action. In any case, there would be no rendezvous at Madison.

On the eve of the planned uprising, local authorities learned of its details from a slave arrested for theft. After torturing information from other slaves, Brooks County's police patrol arrested Vickery and his three leading slave coconspirators.

The Brooks County home guard, composed of some of the same slaveholders allegedly targeted, determined to use the conspirators as warning examples against further rebellion. Although not authorized to do so, a home guard court quickly convened. After a mock trial, the vigilantes rendered their verdicts: John Vickery—guilty of arson, inciting slaves to insurrection, and aiding slaves to flee to the Yankees; Sam—guilty of insurrection and inducing slaves to insurrection; Nelson—guilty of insurrection; George—guilty of insurrection. All were condemned to death by hanging. At six o'clock that evening the sentence was carried out on Quitman's courthouse square.[86]

---

[86]Sarah Jones to Joseph E. Brown, 22 August 1864, Governor's Incoming Correspondence; *Augusta Chronicle and Sentinel*, 26 August 1864; *Columbus Sun*, 27 August 1864; *Augusta Constitutionalist*, 26 August 1864; *Macon Telegraph*, 26 August 1864; *OR*, series 1, vol. 14, 752; *Augusta Constitutionalist*, 24 and 31 August 1864. See also Christopher C. Meyers, "'The Wretch Vickery' and the Brooks County Civil War Slave Conspiracy," *Journal of Southwest Georgia History* 12 (1997): 27–38. In 2010, the Georgia Historical Society and the city of Quitman erected a marker in front of city hall commemorating the conspiracy.

Such efforts to maintain the slave regime through terror were ultimately doomed. Even as Union troops were landing on the Gulf Coast, a far greater threat was reaching its culmination far to the north. Federals were bearing down on Atlanta, the South's busiest transportation hub. Within days, the city would be in Union hands.

Georgia Will Soon Go Under

In early May 1864, from his base in Chattanooga, General William Tecumseh Sherman led a Union force of more than a hundred thousand men into northern Georgia. They headed for Dalton where a Confederate army of less than half their number under General Joseph E. Johnston was waiting for them. Johnston had expected to have more men, anticipating that the threat of Yankees on their doorstep might spur more Georgia men to volunteer. Some did, but most did not. Even among those who led drum-beats for the Confederate cause, patriotism was often more apparent than real. Johnston wrote to Jefferson Davis that "many persons in Georgia…are recruiting for cavalry, ostensibly under authority of the War department." But they "never complete their companies—have no other object than to keep themselves and a few friends out of service." In his own command, Johnston added, "desertion is becoming more frequent."[87]

As federal forces approached Dalton, Johnston hoped to lure Sherman into hurling his men against fortified entrenchments on high ground straddling the rail line leading into town. Sherman refused to take the bait. Instead, he swung his army south through Snake Creek Gap trying to cut Johnston's supply line from Atlanta at Resaca. Johnston quickly countered the move, rushing his men south by rail to defend Resaca before Sherman could bring up his full force. There Johnston met reinforcements from Alabama, bringing his troop strength to nearly sixty thousand. For three days, in a series of attacks from May 13–15, Sherman tried without success to break through Johnston's defenses and capture the railroad. When that effort failed, Sherman again shifted his men

---

[87]Bryan, *Confederate Georgia*, 148.

south around Johnston's left flank, threatening the vital rail line. Again, Johnston was forced to fall back.[88]

The Confederates took up a strong position astride the rails at Cassville, once more hoping that Sherman would attack. After surveying Johnston's line, Sherman opted for another flanking maneuver, this time sending his armies south across the Etowah River and turning southeast to threaten Marietta. Johnston moved swiftly to intercept Sherman near Dallas. What followed on May 25–28 was a series of battles at New Hope Church, Pumpkin Vine Creek, and Pickett's Mill during which Johnston's men beat back Sherman's advance. Sherman then tried going around Johnston, shifting his men left in a move toward the rail line into Marietta. Johnston hurried to keep himself between Sherman and Marietta, establishing a strong defensive position north and west of the town with Kennesaw Mountain at his center.

Believing that the Confederates had been worn down by the weeks of campaigning, Sherman delivered a blow that he hoped would break Johnston's line and destroy his army. On June 27, Sherman threw his men into headlong assaults against Confederate earthworks on Kennesaw Mountain. The entrenched defenders threw back their adversaries, inflicting nearly three thousand casualties while suffering perhaps five hundred themselves.[89] Unable to break through at Kennesaw, Sherman once again flanked Johnston. He sent his army east, crossed the Chattahoochee River at Roswell, and headed for Atlanta. Johnston fell back within the city's ring of fortified, entrenched defenses and prepared to repel Sherman's expected assault.

As Sherman's columns bore down on Atlanta, Governor Brown asked President Davis to send more men. Davis refused, writing that he had already sent as many as he could spare. Throughout May and into June, Brown had tried to raise troops himself, ordering non-essential state and local officials into militia units for service in Atlanta. He finally

---

[88]See Philip L. Secrist, *The Battle of Resaca* (Macon, GA: Mercer University Press, 2010).

[89]See Earl J. Hess, *Kennesaw Mountain: Sherman, Johnston, and the Atlanta Campaign* (Chapel Hill: University of North Carolina Press, 2013).

issued a general call, published in newspapers across the state, ordering every white male from ages sixteen to fifty-five to assemble in Atlanta. He cancelled all exemptions as well as any previous orders detailing Georgia militiamen to other parts of the state. Home guards, state and local officials, even exempted planters were all ordered into militia units.

A few thousand answered the call, but many thousands more did not. Some continued to claim Confederate exemption, saying they had been "mustered into Confederate Service for local defense." Brown urged Richmond to cancel such exemptions immediately. "The thousands who have such details," he insisted, "cannot be permitted to hide behind them when the State is being overrun." Others claimed exemption as county officeholders. D. A. Johnson, a bailiff in Berrien County, was one of many who refused to go. A neighbor, who anonymously signed his letter "Over Fifty," wrote to Governor Brown that Johnson was "a Tory, and ought to be in front of some good man." Hall County Justice of the Peace William O'Kelley had two brothers who were already deserters from the Georgia militia. Hardly a Brown supporter to begin with, O'Kelley declined to take up arms. An acquaintance told Brown of O'Kelley, "I have heard him say myself that he had rather shoot you than a deer."[90]

As Brown's call circulated across Georgia, one man, apparently a farmer, published a Shakespearian-like expression of his attitude in the *Milledgeville Confederate Union*.[91] It gave voice to many who faced the same dilemma.

> To go or not to go, that is the question:
> Whether it pays best to suffer pestering
> By idle girls and garrulous old women,

---

[90]Brown to Jefferson Davis, 19 July 1864, Governor's Letter Book; J. A. Seddon to Brown, 21 July 1864, Governor's Letter Book; Brown to J. A. Seddon, 22 July 1864, Governor's Letter Book; Anonymous to Brown, 6 June 1864, Governor's Incoming Correspondence; Moses W. Finger to Brown, 14 May 1864, Governor's Incoming Correspondence; Henry Collom to Brown, 27 May 1864, Governor's Incoming Correspondence.

[91]*Milledgeville Confederate Union*, 28 June 1864.

Or to take up arms against a host of Yankees,
And by opposing get killed—To die, to sleep,
(Git eout) and in this sleep to say we "sink
To rest by all our Country's wishes blest"
And live forever—(that's a consummation
Just what I'm after). To march, to fight—
To fight! perchance to die, aye there's the rub!
For while I'm sleep, who'll take care Mary
and the babes—when Billy's in the low ground,
Who'll feed 'em, hey! There's the respect
I have for *them* that makes life sweet;
For who would bear the bag to mill,
Plough Dobbin,[92] cut the wheat, dig taters,
Kill hogs, and do all sorts of drudgery
If I am fool enough to get a Yankee
Bullet on my brain! Who'll cry for me!
Would patriotism pay my debts, when dead?
But oh! The dread of something after death—
That undiscovered fellow who'll court Mary,
And do my huggin—that's agony,
And makes me want to stay home,
Specially as I aint mad with nobody.
Shells and bullets make cowards of us all,
And blam'd my skin if snortin steeds,
And pomp and circumstance of War
Are to be compared with feather beds,
And Mary by my side.

If many Georgians were unwilling to help Brown, some were willing to help Sherman. When Brown issued his call, several Dawsonville citizens told the governor that their county surveyor, Elias Darnel, "instead of obeying your proclamation went about organizing a federal home guard to assist the enemy." Mary Gordon of Walker County and Carrie

[92]A colloquialism referring to a plodding work horse.

King, a Columbus native, assisted the enemy too. Both served as spies for the Union army. James George Brown of Murray County led a network of Unionist spies who operated throughout northeast Georgia. James C. McBurney of Macon, who had previously guided a federal raid through Alabama and Georgia, provided Sherman with information on Georgia's resources and railroads. In Gordon County, a group of local Unionists captured nine Confederate soldiers and turned them over to the Federals. One hundred twenty-five Pickens County men formed a Union home guard to protect themselves from Confederate militia, to raid pro-Confederate plantations, and to assist the advancing Federals. One Union officer was sure that hundreds more men in neighboring counties could be called to arms.[93]

The Federals did just that in summer 1864. Hoping to form not simply a home guard but a regular fighting force, they recruited about 300 northeast Georgia men. Some were sent directly to the 5th Tennessee Mounted Infantry. Others formed an independent company operating in Fannin County attached to the 5th Tennessee. The rest enrolled as the 1st Georgia State Troops Volunteer Battalion. Though well-armed, the 1st Georgia was ill trained and never of much use to the Federals in regular combat. But driven by a desire to protect their families from, and to take revenge against, Confederate home guards and state militia, the men of the 1st Georgia fought a guerrilla war that kept Confederate loyalists busy who might otherwise have been put into battle against the Federals.[94]

---

[93]John D. Palmour and others to Brown, 20 March 1865, Governor's Incoming Correspondence; John Hammond Moore, "Sherman's 'Fifth Column': A Guide to Unionist Activity in Georgia," *Georgia Historical Quarterly* 68 (1984): 386; Dyer, *Secret Yankees*, 149, 151; Davis, "White and Black in Blue," 357; Bryan, *Confederate Georgia*, 150; *OR*, series 1, vol. 38, part 2, 866; *OR*, series 1, vol. 52, part 1, 107; *OR*, series 1, vol. 38, part 5, 299.

[94]Davis, "Forgotten Union Guerrilla Fighters," 30–33; Jonathan Dean Sarris, "Anatomy of an Atrocity: The Madden Branch Massacre and Guerrilla Warfare in North Georgia, 1861–1865," *Georgia Historical Quarterly* 77 (1993): 704–705. For more on the 1st Georgia State Troops Volunteer Battalion see Davis, "White and Black in Blue," 360–66.

In Atlanta, by early July, morale among Confederate soldiers was at a low ebb. General Johnston still held the city and maintained a functioning army, but he had lost eighty miles of ground and roughly ten thousand men over the previous two months. Even safely behind Atlanta's defenses, he was losing more men to desertion every day. One Georgia soldier wrote to his wife,

> The men is all out of heart and say that Georgia will soon have to go under and they are going to the Yankees by the tens and twentys and hundreds most every night. Johnston's army is very much demoralized[,] as much so as a army ever gets…I see that the Officers is down in the mouth and their faces looks very long and some of them say that they are fearful that all their men will go to the Yankees.[95]

On July 17, trying to breathe new life into the army, President Davis removed Johnston and replaced him with one of Johnston's corps commanders, General John Bell Hood. Three days later, on July 20, the aggressive Hood launched a northward attack on Sherman's right wing at Peachtree Creek. Failing to budge the Union line, Hood moved his men back south through Atlanta, then turned east and hit Sherman's left flank on July 22, again with little result. He then struck west on July 28, trying to turn the Federals back near Ezra Church. None of Hood's efforts did much to weaken Sherman's forces. The Confederates, in fact, suffered more damage than they inflicted. By August, Hood's army numbered barely thirty-five thousand men.

As Sherman tightened his noose around Atlanta, Hood made one last desperate assault on August 31, this time trying to keep the rail line to Macon open at Jonesboro. Again, his men failed to stop the encircling Federals. Hood knew that he if he stayed put, he and his army would be surrounded, cut off from their lines of supply, and forced to surrender. It was time to abandon Atlanta.

---

[95]Celathiel Helms to his wife, Mary Helms, 6 July 1864, Confederate Letters Collection, United Daughters of the Confederacy, Georgia Department of Archives and History.

Chapter 5

1864–1865: End of the Revolution

Explosions rocked Atlanta on the first day of September as General Hood prepared to evacuate the city. Departing Confederates destroyed anything that might be of use to Sherman's army—locomotives, rail tracks, war materiel and accouterments—all were sabotaged or set alight. As darkness descended on the city, one Atlanta woman called the blaze "a most beautiful spectacle.... The Heavens were a perfect glow."[1] Around midnight, dozens of rail cars filled with ammunition blew up on the tracks. The blasts, which went on for half an hour, shattered windows throughout town. Sherman himself heard the noise fifteen miles away at his Jonesboro headquarters.

God Have Mercy on the Land

Before leaving Atlanta, Hood opened government food stores to the public, but it was hardly enough to satisfy Atlanta's population of hungry civilians. The next day, as federal troops began entering Atlanta, hundreds of destitute women, most of them barefoot and clothed in little more than rags, swarmed through the streets breaking into stores and taking what food they could find. Soldiers joined in the looting. So did former slaves who knew that, with Sherman's arrival, they were legally free. "Our negro property has all vanished into air," wrote Atlanta merchant Sam Richards. He briefly caught sight of his brother's ex-slave Sally strolling through the streets "as independent as can be."[2]

Over the next few days, an unexpected calm settled over Atlanta. It seemed that life for city residents might go on as well as before, perhaps

---

[1]Wendy Hamand Venet, *A Changing Wind: Commerce and Conflict in Civil War Atlanta* (New Haven, CT: Yale University Press, 2014) 172.

[2]Ibid., 173.

better than it had for some time. Sam Richards conceded that the Yankees "generally behaved pretty well." One young woman went so far as to say, "I think I shall like the Yankees very well." On Sunday morning, September 4, Union soldiers attended church services across the city. That afternoon, many knocked on doors asking for home-cooked meals and offering pay to those who could feed them. Some soldiers took pity on those who could not. General John W. Geary wrote to his wife of a woman weakened by hunger with a "starving child, so poor as scarcely to live." Unable to stand by and watch women and children perish, Union soldiers began giving their own rations to the needy. One estimate put the ration distribution at between two and three thousand a day.[3]

Within days, attitudes began to change, at least toward Sherman if not toward his soldiers. In mid-September, Sherman ordered all civilians not essential to army operations to leave the city. He gave no clear reason, saying only that "Atlanta is no place for families or non-combatants." Most likely, Sherman simply wanted no part of becoming caretaker to Atlanta's many destitute people. Mayor John M. Calhoun begged Sherman to reconsider. The expulsion would, he said, place an "extraordinary hardship" on poor women and children. Sherman's own quartermaster, Colonel William Le Duc, warned his commander that "this order won't read well in history."[4] Still Sherman would not relent.

Long columns of refugees were soon filing out of town. Sherman allowed them to take their belongings and go where they pleased, but most had nothing to carry and nowhere to go. Untold numbers died of illness brought on by exposure and hunger. Many of the survivors landed in Macon, where residents tried to raise funds for their care, but the response was too meager and the need too great. Hundreds remained homeless and hungry.[5]

---

[3]Ibid., 174.

[4]T. Conn Bryan, *Confederate Georgia* (Athens: University of Georgia Press, 1953) 163; *Athens Southern Banner*, 28 September 1864; Venet, *A Changing Wind*, 174.

[5]Venet, *A Changing Wind*, 177.

As Atlanta's people were leaving their homes, Sherman wrote Governor Brown offering to meet with him about making peace and returning Georgia to the Union. Brown refused, saying that the legislature had conferred no authority upon him to surrender his state. Although Brown declined Sherman's peace proposal, news of the offer so alarmed Jefferson Davis that he hurried to Georgia to shore up resolve. He visited Hood's army south of Atlanta to inspire the troops. He gave public addresses as well, blaming Confederate reverses on "croakers" who refused to join the army and deserters who refused to return. "Two-thirds of our men are absent," he lamented, "most of them without leave.... If one-half the men now absent without leave will return to duty, we can defeat the enemy."[6]

Brown too was begging Georgia men to rally, but his pleading was in vain. Even those already gathered were giving up and going home. From Spalding County's Camp Stephens, one of the state militia's main assembly points, William Dickey wrote that there was "great dissatisfaction" in the ranks, especially among those who thought they were exempt. Some believed Brown had no legal right to hold them. By the time of Dickey's letter in late October, two hundred had deserted Camp Stephens alone.[7]

Dickey was among the few firm Confederate loyalists still left, and was disgusted at the lack of Rebel patriotism he witnessed among his fellow Georgians. Hardly anyone was willing to fight for the Confederacy. "I wish," wrote Dickey, "they would get every man that is able to carry a gun out at once irrespective of exemptions, details, or anything else." If only they would come, Dickey thought, Atlanta might be saved.[8]

---

[6]Bryan, *Confederate Georgia*, 164; *Athens Southern Banner*, 12 October 1864; *Macon Telegraph*, 24 September 1864.

[7]Dickey to his wife, Anna, 26 October 1864, Civil War Miscellany, Georgia Department of Archives and History, Morrow. Named for Alexander H. Stephens, Camp Stephens was located just north of Griffin on McIntosh Road. See Kenneth K. Krakow, *Georgia Place-Names* (Macon, GA: Winship Press, 1975) 34.

[8]Dickey to his wife, Anna, 26 October 1864, Civil War Miscellany.

Far from aiding the Confederacy, many were aiding those opposed to it. Friends and family regularly befriended draft dodgers and deserters, ever more so as the war neared its end. Some Georgians would assist anyone trying to avoid Confederate entanglements, Yankees included. In late 1864, two escapees from Andersonville prison showed up at J. B. Norman's farm in Colquitt County. Norman fed the men and allowed them to stay the night. Next day, he gave them steak before they continued their journey south toward federal outposts in Florida.[9]

Traveling that far was risky business for Union prisoners, but hardly more so than remaining where they were. Andersonville was by far the country's most deadly stockade, North or South. Death rates in Civil War prison camps averaged about 14 percent. At Andersonville, the rate was close to a third. Only Elmira prison in New York state, with a death rate of nearly one-fourth, came close. Of the forty-one thousand men imprisoned at Andersonville, roughly thirteen thousand died there. Over crowded, ill-clothed, ill-fed, and housed hardly at all, the prisoners died of malnutrition, disease, exposure, and neglect at a rate of more than thirty a day. Many of the survivors, often barely alive, never fully recovered, suffering physical and mental anguish for the rest of their lives. One Georgia woman who visited Andersonville wrote of the suffering prisoners, "My heart aches for these poor wretches, Yankees though they are, and I am afraid God will suffer some terrible retribution to fall upon us for letting such things happen. If the Yankees should ever come to South-West Georgia, and go to Anderson and see the graves there, God have mercy on the land!"[10]

---

[9]W. A. Covington, *History of Colquitt County* (Atlanta: Foote and Davies, 1937) 37.

[10]Lonnie R. Speer, *Portals to Hell: Military Prisons of the Civil War* (Mechanicsburg, PA: Stackpole Books, 1997) 16; Gerald F. Linderman, *Embattled Courage: The Experience of Combat in the American Civil War* (New York: Free Press, 1987) 236; William Marvel, *Andersonville: The Last Depot* (Chapel Hill: University of North Carolina Press, 1994) ix, 238–39; Michael Horigan, *Elmira: Death Camp of the North* (Mechanicsburg, PA: Stackpole Books, 2002) 193; Eliza Frances Andrews, *The War-Time Journal of a Georgia Girl* (New York: D. Appleton, 1908) 78–79.

Burying the dead at Andersonville. On average, more than thirty men died there every day. One young Georgia woman who visited the stockade wrote of its suffering prisoners, "My heart aches for these poor wretches, Yankees though they are, and I am afraid God will suffer some terrible retribution to fall upon us for letting such things happen. If the Yankees should ever come to South-West Georgia, and go to Anderson and see the graves there, God have mercy on the land!" Image courtesy of the National Archives.

The Yankees did eventually reach Andersonville and saw its many graves. They also heard gruesome tales from the prisoners who lived to tell them. And they had no mercy on the prison's commandant, Captain Henry Wirz. Convicted of war crimes by a U.S. military commission, he was hanged at Washington's Old Capitol Prison in November 1865.

Like J. B. Norman, Willis Bone of Irwin County was also willing to help escaped Union prisoners. He had operated a refuge for deserters and draft dodgers on his lands for some time. He even harbored runaway slaves. Originally from South Carolina, Bone immigrated to Georgia in the 1850s and settled at Bone Pond (now Crystal Lake) in Irwin County's Third District. A staunch Unionist, Bone was exempt from Confederate service because he owned a small grist mill, which rendered what was by law an essential service. Shielded himself, Bone turned his attention to protecting other Georgians from Confederate authority.

Bone was little different from most people of his community. Irwin was south Georgia's third least populated county and one of the poorest. The district in which Bone lived had just fourteen families, all of whom raised cattle, sheep, and hogs, and grew subsistence crops of corn, peas, and oats. There were only nine slaves spread among four white families in the district, none of whom belonged to Bone. What land he held was mostly undeveloped. He grew corn, sweet potatoes, and a little cotton. He owned one horse, one mule, one ox, eight head of cattle, eighteen hogs, and nineteen sheep. Most of his small earnings came from the mill. Hardly any better or worse off than his neighbors, he was no leading light of the county. Neither was he a social outcast, despite his political views. Bone was regularly seated as a petit juror beside his neighbors.[11]

Either Bone was very good at hiding his Unionism or most of his contemporaries were largely tolerant of it. By late 1864, most simply longed for end to the war. That wish for peace among Georgians would become even more earnest after Sherman's March to the Sea.

[11]Robert David Carlson, "Wiregrass Runners: Conscription, Desertion, and the Origins of Discontent in Civil War South Georgia" (master's thesis, Valdosta State University, 1999) 93–95.

Forage Liberally on the Country

When Hood's forces abandoned Atlanta in early September 1864, they retreated to Palmetto, southwest of the city, where Hood laid plans for his next move. Knowing he could not drive Sherman out of Atlanta, Hood hoped to draw him out by threatening his supply line from Chattanooga. Crossing the Chattahoochee and heading north, Hood's army reached the railroad near Allatoona on October 1. There it brushed aside a small federal detail, cut the telegraph line, and spent four days tearing up track. Hood then headed west to avoid a larger federal garrison at Rome, crossed the Coosa River, and turned northeast to hit the rail line again at Resaca. Hood continued north and on October 13 captured Dalton.

As Hood had expected, Sherman pursued him with a force of sixty thousand men, nearly twice that of the Confederates. Sherman planned to catch up to the Rebels and crush them, but Hood had no intention of allowing that to happen. He quickly headed his army southwest, fighting a small skirmish at Snake Creek Gap on October 15, then hurried on to Gaylesville, Alabama. Sherman obligingly followed. When Hood still refused to give battle, moving his army further west to Gadsden, Sherman realized that he was being led on something of a wild goose chase. Leaving a portion of his army to counter any further moves Hood might make, Sherman took most of his men back to Atlanta.[12]

There Sherman prepared for a deeper strike into the Confederacy. Rather than hold Atlanta, he would destroy the city's war-making capacity, abandon his communication and supply lines to Chattanooga, and move with his full force as quickly as he could across Georgia to capture Savannah.

On November 15, Atlanta's destruction commenced. Union soldiers tore down the rail depot and set fire to machine shops, rolling mills, iron works, factories, and warehouses. Sherman gave orders that facilities of no military value be spared, but once the burning began, it quickly spread

---

[12]Hood turned north into Tennessee, where his remaining men were destroyed as a fighting force at the battles of Franklin (30 November) and Nashville (15 December).

out of control. Small businesses, private residences, offices, theaters, markets, grog shops, and shanties were caught in the conflagration. "The heaven is one expanse of lurid fire," wrote one Union soldier that night. "The air is filled with flying, burning cinders; buildings covering two hundred acres are in ruins or in flames." Sheets of fire shooting skyward could be seen from fifty miles away. By morning, a few hundred homes, several churches, and city hall were nearly all that remained.[13]

Heading out of Atlanta, Sherman divided his army of more than sixty thousand into two broad columns. Failing to concentrate one's forces in enemy country ran counter to military doctrine, but, moving too rapidly to maintain supply lines, Sherman spread his men out so they could "forage liberally on the country." Besides, Sherman knew he had little to fear. There was hardly any will among Georgians to oppose him and no force that could effectively do so. Macon's *Telegraph* vainly called for Georgia's people to "come down upon Sherman like wolves on a sheepfold.... Fight him in the front, fight him in the flank, fight him in the rear."[14] A few tried, but to no avail. When elements of the Georgia militia made a stand at Bear Creek Station near Griffin, the Federals cut them cut to pieces. One militiaman recalled that "we were so completely run over that we were scattered in every direction, those of us who were not killed or captured."[15]

The militia suffered an even greater tragedy at the Battle of Griswoldville. On November 22, a small force moving east out of Macon heading for Augusta ran into Sherman's right flank. The militia's commander, General Pleasant J. Philips, had orders to avoid contact with Sherman's army, but the impulsive Georgian—a pre-war planter and banker who had tried and failed to make a name for himself in the Confederate army—ignored his instructions and ordered an attack. Three times the militia advanced, and three times they were beaten back. By the

---

[13]Bryan, *Confederate Georgia*, 165; Venet, *A Changing Wind*, 179. See also Stephen Davis, *What the Yankees Did to Us: Sherman's Bombardment and Wrecking of Atlanta* (Macon, GA: Mercer University Press, 2012).

[14]Iobst, *Civil War Macon*, 343.

[15]Bryan, *Confederate Georgia*, 167.

On November 15, 1864, Atlanta's destruction commenced. Sherman ordered that facilities of no military value be spared, but once the fires began, they quickly spread out of control. "The heaven is one expanse of lurid fire," wrote one Union soldier that night. "The air is filled with flying, burning cinders; buildings covering two hundred acres are in ruins or in flames." Sheets of fire shooting skyward could be seen from fifty miles away. In this scene, Sherman's men march out of Atlanta as the city burns behind them. Image from *Harper's Weekly* (1865).

time Philips called off the hopeless effort, more than five hundred of his soldiers—nearly a quarter of his force—lay dead or wounded.[16]

Hardly seasoned veterans, the militiamen at Griswoldville were, as one astonished Union officer described them, mostly "old grey-haired and weakly-looking men and little boys, not over 15 years old." Walking among the casualties, Union soldiers heard a groan from under a pile of corpses. "We moved a few bodies," recalled Theodore Upson, "and there was a boy with a broken arm and leg—just a boy 14 years old." That was not the worst of it. "Beside him, cold in death, lay his father, two brothers, and an uncle. It was a harvest of death. We brought the poor fellow up to the fire. Our surgeons made him as comfortable as they could."[17]

Aside from the dead at Griswoldville, Upson and his fellow soldiers killed few Georgians during their March to the Sea, mainly because so few opposed them. What damage they did was limited mainly to industry, rail lines, and food stocks. At Madison, they burned the commissary and depot. Eatonton lost its cotton mill. When Sherman's men reached Milledgeville, they destroyed arsenals, factories, and depots. Adding insult to injury, they held a mock legislative secession at the state capitol and voted Georgia back into the Union.

Not infrequently, the estates of wealthy planters were prime targets. Sherman's men had orders not to harm personal property, especially that of the poor, who were, as they observed, "usually neutral or friendly." But when it came to plantations, few soldiers held themselves in check. "The Yankees took all my hams, and chickens, and turkeys, and all my lard, and sugar," wrote one planter from Eatonton. The soldiers did not limit themselves to his foodstuffs. "They broke open my closets, took my tin ware, some of my china, and nearly all of my blankets." Another planter reported that "all our provisions, crockery, silver, bed clothing, our own clothing…were taken or destroyed." Some federal commanders tried to

[16]William R. Scaife and William Harris Bragg, *Joe Brown's Pets: The Georgia Militia, 1861–1865* (Macon, GA: Mercer University Press, 2004) 73–88.

[17]Scaife and Bragg, *Joe Brown's Pets*, 79; Theodore F. Upson, *With Sherman to the Sea* (Bloomington: Indiana University Press, 1958) 38.

stop the stealing with inspections, but the men simply hid or buried their loot until the officers moved on.[18]

Ironically, among the most destructive of Sherman's men were themselves Southerners, some of them Georgia natives. Units such as the Union's 1st Alabama Cavalry Regiment, which included dozens of Georgians, were composed mainly of poor farmers who blamed planters for the war and relished any opportunity to sack their plantations. In late November, the 1st Alabama's commander received a letter from his superior informing him that "the outrages committed by your command during the march are becoming so common, and are of such an aggravated nature, that they call for some severe and instant mode of correction." Every officer in the regiment was threatened with arrest and dishonorable discharge if they did not put a stop to the plundering.[19] Such threats had little effect.

Not only did officers fail to halt the looting, they sometimes participated in it. One of the most destructive of the 1st Alabama's officers was David Snelling, a native of Baldwin County, Georgia, who had deeply personal reasons for his Union stand. David's father, William, a man of modest means, died of fever when David was five. His mother, Elizabeth Lester Snelling, whose family had never approved of her marriage, was given a small plot of land adjoining the plantations her brothers owned. When Elizabeth died a few years later, young David was taken in as a farm hand by his uncle, David Lester. While Lester sent his own sons away to school, he put David to work in the fields along with his slaves. Treated much as a slave himself, David came to detest slavery and to hold an abiding disdain for slaveholders.

In May 1862, under threat of conscription, David joined the Confederate army. That summer he deserted and signed up with the Feder-

---

[18]*War of the Rebellion: A Compilation of the Official Records of the Union and Confederate Armies* (Washington, DC: Government Printing Office, 1880–1901) series 1, vol. 39, part 3, 713 (hereafter cited as *OR*); Bryan, *Confederate Georgia*, 168, 169.

[19]Joseph T. Glatthaar, *The March to the Sea and Beyond: Sherman's Troops in the Savannah and Carolinas Campaigns* (New York: New York University Press, 1985) 147, 150; *OR*, series 1, vol. 44, 504–505.

als. Two years later, as a lieutenant commanding Sherman's personal cavalry escort during the March to the Sea, David went out of his way to lead a raid on his uncle's plantation a few miles from Milledgeville. His troops seized provisions and livestock, then burned the gin house to the ground.[20]

Members of the 1st Alabama were not the only Southerners to do such damage. Confederate cavalry under General Joseph Wheeler, instructed to harass Sherman's men, did more harm to Georgians than to the invaders. Alexander Walker, a Burke County planter, called Wheeler's men a "plundering band of horse stealing ruffians." Another contemporary wrote that "the whole of Georgia is full of bitter complaints of Wheeler's cavalry." State officials presented his superiors with evidence of at least forty acts of looting and destruction, ruined plantations included, but Wheeler retained his command.[21]

Planters often buried their silverware, tea sets, and other valuables, trying to hide their treasure from plundering soldiers, but their slaves frequently revealed those locations. "They very readily tell us where anything is concealed," a Union army chaplain remarked, "and seem well pleased when we find various articles." Wrote another of Sherman's men, the slaves "were proud to offer any service to the soldiers. They would risk their lives to aid them, and would give them the food from their mouths or the garments from their backs." When one elderly slave noticed worn out shoes on a foraging soldier, he removed his own and handed them over. The soldier at first refused to take them, but the old man bent down, put them on the young man's feet, and laced them up. "Massa soldier boy," he insisted, "you can't fight without no shoes. Them's *your* shoes, they ain't mine. Soldier, honey, don't you know that *I'se glad to go barefooted* to help you fight the battle of freedom?"[22]

---

[20]James C. Bonner, "David R. Snelling: A Story of Desertion and Defection in the Civil War," *Georgia Review* 10 (1955): 275–82.

[21]Bryan, *Confederate Georgia*, 171.

[22]Edmund L. Drago, *Black Politicians and Reconstruction in Georgia: A Splendid Failure* (Baton Rouge: Louisiana State University Press, 1982) 9; John Richards Boyle, *Soldiers True: The Story of the One Hundred and Eleventh Regiment Pennsylvania Veteran Volunteers* (New York: Eaton and Mains, 1903) 263.

David Snelling of Baldwin County joined the Confederate army under threat of conscription in May 1862. He deserted that summer and signed up with the Federals. Two years later, as a lieutenant in charge of Sherman's cavalry escort, Snelling went out of his way to lead a raid on his uncle's plantation. It was Southerners themselves who did much of the damage during Sherman's March, blaming planters for the war and relishing the opportunity to sack plantations. Image courtesy of the Russell Library, Georgia College and State University.

Slaves sometimes took pity on their owners as well. One planter wrote that nearly all that remained to his family after Sherman's men passed through "was what was returned to us by our own and other negroes." His wife and children had no food except a few potatoes and what "the negroes fed them from the leavings of the Yankees."[23] For slaves who remained with their owners, and most did, such expressions of sympathy also reflected a self-interested reality. Taught from birth to distrust all whites, blacks often preferred to deal with the devil they knew. Besides, as surely as the Federals came they would go, leaving blacks to fend for themselves in a world still dominated by slaveholders. As one elderly black man told Sherman, "you'll go away tomorrow, and another white man will come."[24]

For those determined to escape slavery, following Sherman's men seemed to be the safest option. They knew that they were taking a risk, but for tens of thousands, even an uncertain future outside of slavery was worth the gamble. "We went to sleep one night with a plantation full of negroes," wrote one slaveholder, "and woke to find not one on the place—every servant gone to Sherman." It seemed to surprise him that all his slaves left. "We had thought there was a strong bond of affection on their side as well as ours!" That slaveholders could view any degree of slavery as a show of affection hints at the depths of their self-delusion, and at how easily they could be, and had been, deluded by their slaves. As mass escapes finally lifted the delusion, slaveholders' anger toward their former chattel was palpable. "When Sherman came along," recalled one disgusted planter, "every last skunk of 'em run away."[25]

Sherman's men rarely welcomed the refugees who showed up at their camps and followed in their wake. They had little food or supplies to spare, and little inclination to share it with blacks when they did. Still blacks came. One of Sherman's columns reported seventeen thousand escapees trailing behind. Union commanders did their best to keep blacks

---

[23]Bryan, *Confederate Georgia*, 169.

[24]George Ward Nichols, *The Story of the Great March, From the Diary of a Staff Officer* (New York: Harper, 1865) 59.

[25]Drago, *Black Politicians and Reconstruction in Georgia*, 4.

at bay, often with disastrous results. Some blacks died of exposure, others of starvation. With Confederate cavalry hot on their heels, Sherman pulled up his pontoon bridges after crossing Ebenezer Creek just west of Savannah, leaving more than five hundred terrified refugees stranded on the opposite bank. Some were shot down by the pursuing Rebels. Others, with children clinging to their backs, jumped into the swollen creek and drowned. Survivors were rounded up and carried back to their owners. Reflecting on the callousness of his army's role in the affair, one appalled Union soldier asked, "Where can you find in all the annals of plantation cruelty anything more completely inhuman and fiendish than this?"[26]

Expressions of sympathy for blacks were infrequent among Union soldiers. Most had opposed making the war a crusade against slavery, and tens of thousands had resigned or deserted after Lincoln issued his Emancipation Proclamation. Compiled reports for all Union armies from February 1863, a month after the Proclamation went into effect, showed a third of the men absent without leave. Most who remained tended to support emancipation grudgingly, viewing it as a way to punish secessionists or as a means of avoiding another civil war. When Georgia slaves greeted his comrades as liberators, an exasperated Michigan soldier exclaimed: "Tain't right…to have them thinking we're here just to free slaves. We're fighting secession. This slavery business has just been hung onto us." One federal trooper told whites in Liberty County that if only he had enough powder, he would blow the brains out of every black he met.[27]

Regardless of why the Federals came, blacks saw in the coming what they wished to see. When Sherman's men marched through Savannah's streets on December 22, Reverend James Simms declared that they "had

[26]Paul D. Escott, "The Context of Freedom: Georgia's Slaves during the Civil War," *Georgia Historical Quarterly* 58 (1974): 85; Glatthaar, *March to the Sea and Beyond*, 64.

[27]Ella Lonn, *Desertion During the Civil War* (New York: Century Co., 1928) 145, 151; Drago, *Black Politicians and Reconstruction in Georgia*, 10–11.

come for our deliverance…and the cry went around the city from house to house among the race of our people, 'Glory be to God, we are free!"[28]

Upon Their Hands Is the Blood of Slain Thousands

A few days before Sherman reached Savannah, he sent a portion of his command to take Fort McAllister, just south of the city on the Ogeechee River. With his flank secure, Sherman drove on toward Savannah. Its ten thousand defenders under Georgia native General William J. Hardee, knowing that they were no match for the Federals, fled into South Carolina on December 20. Early the next morning, leading units of Sherman's columns filed into Savannah, escorted by the mayor and several city councilmen who had rushed out to surrender the city. When Sherman arrived a day later, he sent a telegram to President Lincoln reading, "I beg to present you as a Christmas-gift the city of Savannah, with one hundred and fifty heavy guns and plenty of ammunition, also about twenty-five thousand bales of cotton."[29]

As Sherman's men moved in, hungry people, white and black, raided stores all over town looking for food. One Union officer described "the poor classes" as "apparently well pleased with the change, for they had nothing to lose, and had suffered much during the war." Wealthier folk seemed less pleased. Most of them kept out of sight. City leaders, pleased or not, gave in to the reality of Union occupation and drew up resolutions asking Governor Brown to call a statewide peace convention and get Georgia out of the war.[30]

Similar petitions came from all over Georgia in the wake of Sherman's March. A Hart County meeting, with a "a large number" attending, asked Brown for a state convention and "a speedy peace." Citizens in

---

[28]James M. Simms, *The First Colored Baptist Church in North America* (Philadelphia: J. B. Lippincott, 1888) 137.

[29]William T. Sherman, *Memoirs of W. T. Sherman*, vol. 2 (New York: Charles L. Webster, 1891) 231.

[30]Jacqueline Jones, *Saving Savannah: The City and the Civil War* (New York: Alfred A. Knopf, 2008) 207; David Power Conyngham, *Sherman's March through the South, with Sketches and Incidents of the Campaign* (New York: Sheldon and Co., 1865) 293; Bryan, *Confederate Georgia*, 172.

Lumpkin County did the same. "All most to a man," wrote Dahlonega resident James Findley, they were eager for peace. When Jackson County men tried to hold an antiwar meeting, Confederate cavalry broke it up. Undeterred, they met again and drew up resolutions urging an end to the "bloody and destructive war." They sent a list of their demands to Governor Brown and to Athens's *Southern Watchman*. The *Watchman*'s sympathetic editor published their letter and called the cavalry's action "an assumption of power unparalleled in any professedly free Government."[31]

Asserting their "inalienable right of popular assemblage," Jasper County folk met at the courthouse and demanded an end to "the great sufferings of our people." Upson County citizens met at Thomaston and voted "to stop the war on any terms." According to one attendee, "some of the citizens go so far as to say that they will be glad to see Lincoln in possession of the state." One assembly in a rural district of Bibb County was especially aggressive in its demands. A crowd of about sixty voters, all but four of them antiwar men, met to vote for local judges. After the balloting, one of the newly elected officials threatened to drive every pro-Confederate office holder out of Macon and "pledged himself to raise 300 men in twenty-four hours for that purpose if required."[32]

In south Georgia, Echols County's citizens called for a state convention so that a "free discussion may be had relative to the situation of our bleeding country." Thomas County's peace meeting turned violent when the assembly was forced to beat back an assault by pro-Confederates. An antiwar gathering in Wilcox County urged Governor Brown "to settle this Bloody conflict at once by negotiations before the whole white male population is butchered up." So did citizens in Berrien and Pierce counties. Men from Tatnall and Liberty counties in-

[31]*Athens Southern Watchman*, 25 January 1865; Findley to Joseph E. Brown, 26 January 1865, Governor's Incoming Correspondence, Georgia Department of Archives and History; *Augusta Chronicle and Sentinel*, 29 January 1865; *Athens Southern Watchman* 18 January 1865.

[32]*Augusta Chronicle and Sentinel*, 26 February 1865; W. A. Thomas to Howell Cobb, 18 January 1865, Howell Cobb Papers, Felix Hargrett Rare Book and Manuscript Library, University of Georgia; J. T. Smith to Brown, 25 February 1865, Governor's Incoming Correspondence.

sisted that they would rejoin the Union whether Georgia did or not. Already under Union occupation, Savannah effectively severed its ties to the Confederacy.[33]

Willis Bone and other Unionists, along with "a large number of deserters," convened an antiwar meeting at Irwinville. They adopted several resolutions, one calling for the Confederacy's surrender. When a militia lieutenant tried to break up the meeting, Bone knocked the officer down with his musket and led three cheers for Abraham Lincoln. The assembly then drove the lieutenant, and every other pro-Confederate, out of town.[34]

Private letters begging him to get Georgia out of the war also flooded the governor's office. One was especially poignant. J. T. Smith of Bibb County had sacrificed as much as anyone for the Confederacy. One son had been killed in battle. Another was maimed for life. Three more remained in the army, and all his property was ruined. He encouraged Brown to "leave the sinking ship." The cause was lost, and there was no point in losing any more. "Stop it, my friend, stop it. All the enlightened world is against us, and God himself is against us!"[35]

There was at least one pro-Confederate rally in Georgia that winter. In February 1865, Augusta's *Chronicle and Sentinel* editor sarcastically wrote of "the 'great' war meeting—with a slim attendance, recently held in Coweta County." The paper noted that only five of those present had ever been in the army. The rest were exempts "occupying profitable bomb-proof positions—and of course wanted the war to go on." The editor hardly found that surprising. "They want our difficulties settled?

---

[33]*Milledgeville Confederate Union*, 28 February 1865; *OR*, series 1, vol. 47, part 2, 31; Citizens of Wilcox County to Brown, 14 January 1865, Joseph E. Brown Papers, Felix Hargrett Rare Book and Manuscript Library, University of Georgia; *Augusta Chronicle and Sentinel*, 2 February 1865; Berrien County Inferior Court, Minutes, 18 January 1865, Georgia Department of Archives and History; *OR*, series 1, vol. 47, part 3, 262; *OR*, series 1, vol. 44, 827–28; *Augusta Register* in *Sumter Republican*, 21 January 1865.

[34]*Albany Patriot*, 23 February 1865.

[35]Smith to Brown, 25 February 1865, Governor's Incoming Correspondence.

Not a bit of it! ...they would be obliged to come down to the level of common people.... This kind of patriotism is altogether too prevalent." One southwest Georgia man who signed himself "An Old Soldier" wrote that one way to get rich at the life insurance business would be to take "only those applicants who are shouting for their fellow citizens to go to the front." The *Columbus Sun* agreed. It seemed to the editor that those most likely to advocate "fighting it out" were among the least likely to do so. "We know men of this stamp in Columbus."[36]

Men of that stamp still held sway in the General Assembly. Although the vice president's brother Linton Stephens introduced resolutions as early as November 1864 calling for a state convention and peace negotiations, war supporters countered with resolutions of their own. All peace resolutions were consistently voted down. After President Davis informed Georgia that only his administration could negotiate peace in any case, Governor Brown, in February 1865, asked the Assembly to call for a convention of all Confederate states for the purpose of ousting Davis. Only two members of the lower house voted in favor of Brown's request. The senate also turned him down and passed a resolution supporting continued military action.[37]

Even so, as they began to recognize the inevitability of Confederate defeat, many prominent secessionists changed their minds. Among those at the Thomas County meeting urging a reconstruction of the old Union were Judge Peter E. Love and Congressman James L. Seward. Both had held strong secessionist views before the war. Fifteen years earlier, Love had disrupted a "Friends of the Union" meeting in Thomasville held to support the Compromise of 1850. Seward had been a driving force for secession in the Thomas County Democratic Party. But times had changed and attitudes with them, although some, like the *Countryman*, were not willing to let Love and Seward off the hook so easily.

> These men, and such as they, are the ones who have plunged this country into war. Upon their hands is the blood of slain thousands.

---

[36] *Augusta Chronicle and Sentinel*, 11 February 1865; *Early County News*, 14 December 1864; *Columbus Sun*, 5 February 1865.

[37] Bryan, *Confederate Georgia*, 97.

> Once, none were so blood-thirsty, and ferocious as they. To hear them talk, you would think they could swallow the universal yankee nation at one mouthful. It was this class who were ready to drink all the blood shed in this revolution. Seward was a noted fire-eater.... And yet, now, you find him leading a Union meeting in Thomasville.[38]

If some among Georgia's upper classes were willing to give up the Confederacy, they were not willing to give up cotton. They never had been. Although production was down from its 1862 wartime high, cotton still dominated much of Georgia's landscape. A visitor to Macon in early 1864 reported that "the cotton warehouses are loaded, I may say densely packed and overflowing." In September, at least 440 bales shipped out from Griffin. Other Black Belt towns reported similar shipments through that fall and into the winter. Sherman's men found 25,000 cotton bales stockpiled in Savannah after they captured the city in December. When Columbus fell to a federal raid the next April, there were 125,000 bales packed into the city's warehouses and lining its wharves.[39]

While planters devoted prime farmland to cotton, common folk continued to go hungry. In March 1865, a commissary agent wrote from Atlanta that "the suffering for [lack of] food is absolutely heart rending." Knowing that poor women might take what they wanted in any case, he regularly opened his doors to them. His office was "almost constantly thronged with women and children begging for bread.... During the late freezing weather, females walked as far as sixteen miles in the mud and ice, for the purpose of getting meal, which they would carry home upon

---

[38]Carlson, "Wiregrass Runners," 103–104; *Turnwold Countryman,* 14 February 1865.

[39]G. S. Plumley, "In Dixie," *Harper's New Monthly Magazine* 29 (July 1864): 233; Griffin Cotton Receipts, Box 20, Folder 23, Talemon Cuyler Collection, Felix Hargrett Rare Book and Manuscript Library, University of Georgia, Athens; Columbus Cotton Receipts, Box 20, Folder 23, Cuyler Collection; Cotton Receipts, Box 20, Folder 25, and Box 21, Folder 2, Cuyler Collection; Sherman, *Memoirs*, 231; David Williams, *Rich Man's War: Class, Caste, and Confederate Defeat in the Lower Chattahoochee Valley* (Athens: University of Georgia Press, 1998) 181.

their sho[u]lders." It was a pitiful sight, he wrote, to see them come in from the cold with their bonnets and shawls crusted with ice.[40]

Not all Georgians were struggling so in the war's closing months. Finer foods were still available for those who could afford them. Blockade runners had long since given up importing necessities, preferring to smuggle in items they knew would bring top dollar from the wealthy. In December 1864, T. J. MacGare, owner of Augusta's Morgan Restaurant, placed an ad in local papers aimed at "lovers of good living and drinking." The *Chronicle and Sentinel* editor, who had visited the establishment, praised its "delicacies and luxuries" as well as its "excellent assortment of the finest kind of liquors." As late as March 1865, only weeks before the war's end, one lady wrote of a meal at the Cook House, a posh Columbus inn, where the table was so heavy with food it "*actually groaned.*" There were sausages, roast pork, cold turkey, biscuits, hot rolls, cornbread, and cake. The next morning at breakfast there was real coffee, not the more common substitutes, with milk and sugar.[41]

That planters, speculators, industrialists, and high-ranking officials could indulge themselves with riches squeezed from a society in its death throes, most while proclaiming their commitment to the cause, seemed the height of hypocrisy. In February 1865, a Columbus paper soundly chastised such people for their continuing self-interested callousness.

> That is right. Pile up wealth—no matter whether bread be drawn from the mouth of the soldier's orphan or the one-armed, one limbed hero who hungry walks your streets—take every dollar you can, pay out as little as possible, deprive your noble warriors of every comfort and luxury, increase in every way the necessaries of life, make everybody but yourself and non-producers bear the taxes of the war; but be very careful to parade everything you give before the public—talk boldly on the street corners of your love of country, be a grand home general—and, when the war is over, point to your princely palace and its magnificent

---

[40]*Augusta Constitutionalist*, 10 March 1865.

[41]*Augusta Chronicle and Sentinel*, 3 December 1864; Kate Cumming, *The Journal of Kate Cumming—A Confederate Nurse 1862–1865*, ed. Richard Harwell (Savannah: Beehive Press, 1975) 244.

surroundings and exclaim with pompous swell, "These are the results of my patriotism."[42]

Such inequities were a sure formula for continued and, at times, violent discontent. As a symbol of planter prosperity in the face of widespread hardship, cotton was sometimes the target of that violence. In December 1864, a band of captured deserters broke out of their Albany barracks and set fire to several buildings containing at least five hundred bales of cotton. The next February, a fire of mysterious origin blazed through Valdosta. "A considerable amount of cotton" was destroyed, most of it belonging to local planter L. D. Rountree. Shortly after, an Early County resident clearly expressed plain folk's ongoing frustration when he wrote that planters would give nothing to poor soldiers or their families, even those sick and dying. The man sarcastically asked, "Ain't it a pity but what the Yankees would take every thing such men have, and leave them without a single mouthful of anything? We hope to live to see the day."[43]

Georgia women were not waiting for the Yankees. During winter 1864–1865, soldiers' wives and widows, mothers and daughters, in Early County and neighboring Miller County were stealing livestock on a regular basis. In February, fifty women raided the government depot in Colquitt, Miller County's seat. Armed with axes, they broke open the doors and took a hundred bushels of government corn. One report noted that the women were soldiers' wives and blamed judges of Miller County's inferior court for their destitute condition. In an open letter, a local resident accused the judges of being more focused on their own interests than the well-being of hungry women and children. Accusations of callousness did not stop with county officials. State officials, including Governor Brown, were also at fault. Augusta's *Chronicle and Sentinel* shared the writer's sentiments, especially regarding improper administration of poor relief: "The Government has lost the corn. Would it not

---

[42]*Columbus Sun* in *Augusta Chronicle and Sentinel*, 17 February 1865.

[43]*Augusta Chronicle and Sentinel*, 21 December 1864; *Columbus Sun*, 24 February 1865; *Early County News*, 5 April 1865.

have been much better to have given it freely to the sufferers? We think so."[44]

February also saw a band of Macon women rampaging from store to store on what one city editor called a "pillaging expedition." Soldiers were ordered to break up the mob, although, as with most such riots, there were no reported injuries. Not so a few weeks later in Augusta. A women's "bread riot" there turned violent, with tragic consequences. One source called it "quite a serious affair...several persons were shot dead."[45]

Among women's staunchest supporters were former soldiers back from the war, with or without leave. In March 1865, Hart County men arriving home from the Army of Tennessee were appalled at the destitution they found. Realizing that no help was coming from the county's inferior court justices, these men raided a local grist mill and distributed sacks of government flour to about fifty hungry women.[46]

Going Home as Fast as They Can Get There

With Confederate defeat increasingly assured and soldiers' families in dire need of help, requests for discharges and extended furloughs flooded Confederate and state offices. From Randolph County came a petition to have Private B. F. Brooks relieved of duty. His wife, Julia, headed a list of twenty-six names pleading on his behalf. In October 1864, Martha Tyler of Lowndes County wrote that she and her five children, all younger than nine years, were "destitute of food and clothing and without help we will suffer." Her husband had been in the army for most of that year and had never been paid. Long a man of poor health, Martha noted that she and her husband had "been married eleven years [and] he has been afflicted ever sinc[e]." Now she was asking for his discharge.[47]

---

[44]*Early County News*, 8 February 1865; *Macon Telegraph*, 24 February 1865; *Augusta Chronicle and Sentinel*, 8 March 1865.

[45]*Atlanta Southern Confederacy* in *Salem (MA) Register*, 16 February 1865; *Albany (NY) Evening Journal*, 22 May 1865. At the time, the *Atlanta Southern Confederacy* was being published in Macon.

[46]*Milledgeville Confederate Union*, 7 March 1865.

[47]Julia A. Brooks and others to Brown, 22 June 1864, Governor's Petitions, Georgia Department of Archives and History; Tyler to Brown, 11 October

Already at home on leave, Daniel Chessy of Decatur County asked for an indefinite furlough. West Sheffield of neighboring Miller County did the same.[48] Unlikely as approval was, most soldiers never bothered to ask. They simply abandoned their posts and never went back. Between October 1864 and early February 1865, at least seventy-two thousand men deserted from units east of the Mississippi River. That rapid manpower drain was reflected in General Lee's dispatches to Richmond from the Army of Northern Virginia, which contained dozens of Georgia regiments.

> November 18, 1864: Desertion is increasing…not withstanding all my efforts to stop it.
>
> January 27, 1865: I have the honor to call to your attention the alarming frequency of desertions.
>
> February 25, 1865: Hundreds of men are deserting nightly and I cannot keep the army together unless examples are made of such cases.
>
> March 27, 1865: The number of desertions from the 9th to the 18th…1,061…. I do not know what can be done to put a stop to it.[49]

One estimate put the number of Georgia troops deserting at 60 percent or more by early 1865. Some were sure that the number was much higher. A Bibb County man wrote to Governor Brown in February that nine-tenths of Georgia soldiers were "going home as fast as they can get there. The country is full of deserters and almost every man in the community will feed them and keep them from being arrested."[50]

1864, Governor's Incoming Correspondence.

[48]Daniel Chessy to Brown, 7 October 1864, Governor's Incoming Correspondence; West Sheffield to Brown, 30 September 1864, Governor's Incoming Correspondence.

[49]Kenneth Radley, *Rebel Watchdog: The Confederate States Army Provost Guard* (Baton Rouge: Louisiana State University Press, 1989) 154.

[50]James A. Riley, "Desertion and Disloyalty in Georgia during the Civil War" (master's thesis, University of Georgia, 1951) 106–107; J. T. Smith to Brown, 25 February 1865, Governor's Incoming Correspondence.

Georgia was full of draft-dodging conscripts as well, who received the same sort of help. For those who refused to help, it was no uncommon thing for them to be visited by layout gangs made up of draft dodgers or deserters or both. In late 1864, Mollie Dunlap of Meriwether County wrote to her brother that layout gangs were "traveling all through the whole country and they are stealing horses and doing everything else that is mean." Citizens in Worth County informed Governor Brown that layouts were "prowling over the country stealing and committing depredations of various kinds." From neighboring Colquitt County, Elizabeth Fields wrote Brown that such gangs were stealing "nearly all there is in the country. I am here in the midst of them, and, because I will not be a friend to them, they are mad and has threatened to burn my house."[51]

In December 1864, B. J. Fry reported to General Cobb from Augusta that "the whole country from here to the Ocmulgee [a stretch covering the east-central part the state] appears to be full of stragglers.... Complaints are made here almost daily from the surrounding counties of their depredations." In Walton County, bands of armed deserters and draft dodgers controlled the countryside. The same was true in Morgan County. In the west Georgia counties of Marion and Chattahoochee, layout gangs fought running battles with what Confederate authorities remained.[52]

Layouts regularly raided Blackshear in Pierce County, ransacking local stores. Just to the west in Ware County, a Confederate inspector reported that south of the Altamaha River there were more deserters than ever, all swearing to fight efforts to arrest them.[53] In Coffee County, Ben Pearson accused a layout gang headed by "Old Man" Bill Wall of stealing his produce and livestock. Trouble had been brewing between Pearson and Wall's men for some time. At one point, Pearson found a grave dug outside his front

---

[51]Dunlap to Billie Dunlap, 11 August 1864, *Confederate Reminiscences and Letters*, 7 vols. (Atlanta: United Daughters of the Confederacy, 1997), 6:179; Citizens of Worth County to Brown, 4 October 1864, Governor's Petitions; Fields to Brown, 8 November 1864, Cuyler Collection.

[52]B. J. Fry to Howell Cobb, 16 December 1864, Cobb Papers; T. T. Eason to Howell Cobb, 28 March 1865, Cobb Papers; Bryan, *Confederate Georgia*, 264, n. 84; *Milledgeville Confederate Union*, 20 December 1864.

[53]Bryan, *Confederate Georgia*, 153–54; *OR*, series 1, vol. 47, part 2, 1391.

door. He finally issued a public demand that Wall turn his men over to local authorities, offering a reward and amnesty to Wall himself. Wall could not resist poking fun, in poetic form, at Pearson's assumption that he might do such a thing.

> If it is my choice to stay at home,
> and the woods in beauty roam;
> Pluck the flowers in early spring,
> and hear the little songsters sing!
>
> Why, then, should I, for the sake of gain,
> leave my conscience with a stain.
> A traitor! who could hear the name
> with no respect for age or fame;
>
> Who, for the sake of a little gold,
> would have his friends in bondage sold?
> I would rather take the lash
> than betray them for Confederate trash.
>
> You say they kill your sheep and cows,
> You say they take your hoss and your plows,
> You say they took your potatoes away,
> You say they dug your grave one day.
> All this may be true;
> It makes me sorry for you.
>
> Yet, sir, if I, these men betray
> and they were all taken away,
> And they did not in the battlefield fall,
> They would the come back and kill
> "Old Man Bill Wall"[54]

---

[54]Warren P. Ward, *Ward's History of Coffee County* (1930; repr., Spartanburg, SC: Reprint Co., 1985) 141–42.

In summer 1864, Brown increased the number of slave patrols and expanded their authority to include going after layouts. Though partially intended to keep draft evaders in check, the new patrols often became a haven for them. Complaints of fraud in the selection of the patrol members were almost universal, and the state inspector general's office questioned the legality of appointments in many Georgia counties.[55]

Brown also ordered state cavalry and home guards to step up operations against layouts, but their efforts had little effect when they put forth any effort at all. Captain Caleb H. Camfield was stationed at Bainbridge with 150 cavalrymen to root out local conscripts and deserters. In early 1865, after fierce battles with area layouts, Camfield retreated and left the region with no effective state or Confederate authority.[56]

By winter 1864–1865, every effort to round up deserters and conscripts in Georgia had failed. District sub-enrolling officers and captains of police patrols were rapidly resigning their positions under threat of assassination. Such threats were taken most seriously. Reporting on conflict between layouts and Confederates that had been going on for some time "with fierce fatality," a Macon newspaper wrote that "not a few have been found in secluded by-ways, dangling their pitiful carcasses from swinging limbs."[57]

In southeast Georgia's first congressional district, the largest by area in the state, Lieutenant Alfred Prescott reported that "all law, both civil and Military seems to be overthrown." The region was, he said, "to a greater or lesser extent, disloyal.... No officer of the C. S. Army who is a stranger to the people can travel through these counties with safety." In an open letter, "the few loyal people" of the region begged their district's commanding general for help against Tories and deserters. Otherwise, they would have to "join in with them." Deserters had already stolen supplies from government storehouses at Blackshear and Homerville, and had run conscript officers out of Berrien and Irwin counties. The district

[55]David Carlson, "The 'Loanly Runagee': Draft Evaders in Confederate South Georgia," *Georgia Historical Quarterly* 84 (2000): 610–11.

[56]Carlson, "Wiregrass Runners," 95, 102.

[57]*Georgia Journal and Messenger*, 20 July 1864.

enrolling officer, Duncan Clinch, told General Cobb that "not only the deserters, but almost the entire population of Appling County, as well as Coffee, Pierce, Berrien, Clinch, Ware, Wayne and adjacent countys" were resisting Confederate authority. And, he wrote, they were determined to drive him off.[58]

In northern Georgia, Paulding County's conscript officer had to protect himself with posted guards. Further to the northeast, one Confederate loyalist wrote that Georgia's mountain region was in a "deplorable condition—desertions from the army, straggling to an incredible degree, and all kinds of irregularity." These irregularities were "not only tolerated, but I must say connived at by those whose duty it is to rectify these evils." Even officials who did not support layouts usually turned a blind eye to their activities. Some state militia units, like the command at Dahlonega headed by Colonel James J. Findley, hardly bothered with an occasional muster. When General A. W. Reynolds went to investigate, he found Findley's men "scattered over the country, as if quartered at home."[59]

In January 1865, Richmond sent a detachment to the area under General W. T. Wofford to arrest all stragglers and deserters. Findley warned that it would do little good. He knew his men could keep themselves well hidden in the hills. It would be impossible for Wofford's force to track them all down. Reynolds agreed that it was a wasted effort. Even if they could be captured and returned to the army, Reynolds knew they would simply go home again or desert to the Federals.[60]

---

[58]Prescott to P. Looney, 27 February 1865, Confederate Bible Records, United Daughters of the Confederacy, Georgia Department of Archives and History; *Albany Patriot*, 23 March 1865; B. F. White to Lamar Cobb, 6 January 1865, Cobb Papers; J. Williams to J. A. Davis, 26 February 1865, Cobb Papers; Clinch to Howell Cobb, 4 April 1865, Cobb Papers.

[59]Findley to Brown, 26 January 1865, Governor's Incoming Correspondence; A. W. Reynolds to Howell Cobb, 22 January 1865, Cobb Papers.

[60]Andrew J. Hansell to Howell Cobb, 10 January 1865, Cobb Papers; Joseph Henry Lumpkin to J. A. Campbell, 31 December 1864, Cobb Papers; *OR*, series 1, vol. 49, part 1, 963; *OR*, series 1, vol. 45, part 2, 805.

To make matters worse for Confederate officials, whole units sent to assist enrolling efforts would often neither perform that duty nor return to the army. Clinch's 4th Georgia Cavalry, assigned to help patrol southeastern Georgia, were out of control, vowing to ignore orders calling them back to their commands. They were certainly well equipped to resist Confederate authority. Clinch had recently supplied his men with new clothing, rifles, revolvers, sabers, ammunition, tents, spurs, saddles, and other gear.[61]

By late 1864, even long-time soldiers who had risked all and given much for the cause were turning their backs on the Confederacy. Captain Robert Hardee, Brooks County's enrollment officer and himself a wounded veteran, wrote to members of his old company encouraging them to desert. Almost the entire company did so. Hardee, who also commanded the local police patrol, refused to arrest members of the militia who would not report for duty. Some officials suggested abolishing the draft. Enforcement efforts had become useless anyway. In March 1865, the General Assembly passed a resolution calling on Congress to do just that.[62] It was a useless gesture. Time and tide were turning too quickly against the Confederacy.

So many soldiers were deserting their ranks that Confederate officials began to consider what until then had been, for most of them, unthinkable—arming the slaves. The idea was hardly a new one. As early as summer 1861, just after the Confederacy's victory at Manassas, General Richard Ewell warned Davis that there was but one way to secure ultimate Confederate success—"emancipating the slaves and arming them."[63] In late 1863, other high ranking Confederate officers began to advocate black enlistment. Some had faced black Union soldiers on the battlefield and knew that they could be effective soldiers. As prospects for

---

[61]Carlson, "Wiregrass Runners," 101.

[62]Ibid., 103; James J. Findley to Brown, 26 January 1865, Governor's Incoming Correspondence; *Augusta Constitutionalist*, 10 March 1865.

[63]Bruce Levine, *Confederate Emancipation: Southern Plans to Free and Arm Slaves During the Civil War* (New York: Oxford University Press, 2006) 17.

Confederate victory became ever more dim, support for arming slaves began to grow.

There were civilians as well who, for reasons of their own, supported slave enlistment. In 1862, a Putnam County woman, upset that wealthy slaveholders were "heaping up money on sufferings of the poor," insisted that "rich speculators and extortioners should be compelled to send a part of their negros to fight." As it stood, she wrote, slaves were being used only to "uphold their aristocratic owners who are nothing but Vampires."[64]

By late 1864, desperate for men, both Jefferson Davis and Robert E. Lee came to favor enrolling blacks. In January 1865, Lee wrote to a friend that although he considered "the relation of master and slave...the best that can exist between the white and black races while intermingled as at present in this country," Lincoln had long been using blacks to crush the Confederacy. Why should the Confederacy not use them in its defense? He advised Congress to authorize slave enlistments immediately and adopt a plan for "gradual and general emancipation."[65]

Over the next few weeks, soldiers in Lee's Army of Northern Virginia passed resolutions supporting their commander's position. General John B. Gordon of Georgia polled his entire corps and reported that it overwhelmingly favored enlisting blacks. The four regiments of Thomas's Georgia Brigade declared their support as well. General Howell Cobb found such expressions disgusting. He suggested that soldiers wanted more men in the army, even if they were black, mainly because they thought it might improve their chances of getting a furlough or discharge. To Cobb, the notion of arming slaves ran entirely counter to the Confederacy's founding principle of slavery. "You cannot make soldiers of slaves," he wrote to Secretary of War James Seddon in January 1865. "The day you make soldiers of them is the beginning of the end of the

---

[64]Mrs. C. J. Owen to Brown, 28 February 1862, Governor's Incoming Correspondence.

[65]Alan T. Nolan, *Lee Considered: General Robert E. Lee and Civil War History* (Chapel Hill: University of North Carolina Press, 1991) 175–77.

With desertion rampant, some officials began to consider asking enslaved Southerners to fight for the Confederacy. Already, close to 200,000 blacks were serving in Union armed forces, and doing so effectively. Still, most slaveholders opposed the idea. General Howell Cobb, commanding Georgia's state reserve force, thought the notion ridiculous. "You cannot make soldiers of slaves," he wrote January 1865. "If slaves will make good soldiers our whole theory of slavery is wrong." Image courtesy of the Hargrett Library, University of Georgia.

revolution. If slaves will make good soldiers our whole theory of slavery is wrong."[66]

William Scruggs, editor of the *Columbus Sun*, had little patience for slaveholders such as Cobb, whom he saw as concerned only for their own interests. On January 5, he published a strongly worded editorial in which he attacked Alexander Stephens's defense of slavery as the Confederacy's cornerstone. Scruggs called it a short-sighted policy and suggested that freeing the slaves "would excite the sympathy and secure the aid of the Christian world." By March, Scruggs had become more direct in his editorials. The Confederacy's fate, he said, was entirely in the hands of the slaves. "It is now evident that the negro slave is to be a sort of balance power in this contest, and that the side which succeeds in enlisting the feelings and in securing the active operation and services of the four millions of blacks, must ultimately triumph."[67] Lincoln, though belatedly, had already come to that conclusion.

The *Albany Patriot* suggested enticing blacks into the army by making them a better offer. Already the Union had promised them freedom and forty acres. Why not freedom and fifty acres? The editor was sure that slaves would never fight without such an incentive, writing, "Let those who fight truly, after the war, be owners of their own homes and fifty acres. Let the army negroes know that they are fighting for their own lands."[68]

---

[66]*OR*, series 1, vol. 51, part 2, 1063; Clarence L. Mohr, *On the Threshold of Freedom: Masters and Slaves in Civil War Georgia* (Athens: University of Georgia Press, 1986) 278, 362 n. 23; *OR*, series 4, vol. 3, 1009–10.

[67]Henry Cleveland, *Alexander H. Stephens in Public and Private* (Philadelphia: National Publishing, 1866) 721; *Columbus Sun*, 5 January and 22 March 1865.

[68]*Albany Patriot*, 23 February 1865. The assumption of a forty-acre promise originated with General William T. Sherman's Special Field Orders Number 15, issued in Savannah on 16 January 1865, which reserved tidewater areas between Hilton Head, South Carolina, and Jacksonville, Florida, for black settlement. Planters had largely abandoned that region in the war's early years, leaving it in the hands for former slaves. In May, upholding Lincoln's earlier amnesty decree, President Andrew Johnson's own Amnesty Proclamation restored those lands to their former owners. See Ira Berlin et al., eds., *Freedom: A Documentary*

Despite growing support for arming slaves, most slaveholders stubbornly resisted. They feared not only the loss of their "property" but also what black enlistment would mean for slavery's future. Slaveholders found strong support from Milledgeville. In a February 1865 message to the General Assembly, Governor Brown warned that arming slaves would be "a great error." Most Georgia legislators agreed. They rejected every resolution put forward for arming blacks. Proponents of slavery's status quo found supporters in the press as well. Athens's *Southern Watchman* saw abolishing slavery as "a base surrender—the most abject *submission* to the enemy!... the country was assured at the outset that the object was to prevent the abolition of slavery by the Lincoln party. If we abolish it now, have we not yielded all that our leaders in 1860–1861 said they demanded?" E. H. Grouby of the *Early County News* felt even more strongly about the matter. He called on his friends and neighbors to lynch anyone who dared "preach abolitionism."[69]

Samuel Boykin of Macon's *Christian Index* fell back on religious arguments to oppose abolition. "The institution of slavery as it exists among us is of Divine appointment," Boykin insisted. He called blacks "indolent, thriftless and incapable of self-government." Left to themselves, they would likely forget Christian virtues and drift into paganism. Freeing the slaves, warned Boykin, would be a rejection of God's "Divine appointment" and a threat to Christianity itself.[70]

Editor N. S. Morse of the *Augusta Chronicle* expressed his opposition to arming blacks in somewhat religious terms as well. Giving blacks freedom and rifles would simply transform them into "a race of de-

---

History of Emancipation, 1861–1867, series 1, vol. 3, *The Wartime Genesis of Free Labor: The Lower South* (New York: Cambridge University Press, 1990) 338–40; *Statutes at Large, Treaties, and Proclamations of the United States of America*, vol. 13 (Boston: Little, Brown, and Company, 1866) 737–39, 758–60.

[69]Allen D. Candler, comp., *The Confederate Records of Georgia*, 6 vols. (Atlanta: State Printing Office, 1909–1911) 2:832–35; Bryan, *Confederate Georgia*, 134; *Athens Southern Watchman*, 15 March 1865; *Early County News*, 18 January 1865.

[70]Bruce T. Gourley, *Diverging Loyalties: Baptists in Middle Georgia during the Civil War* (Macon, GA: Mercer University Press, 2011) 162–63.

mons…howling for blood." Rather than defending the Confederacy, armed blacks might turn against their former owners. *Columbus Times* editor J. W. Warren expressed the same fear. He was certain that slaves would never fight for the Confederacy even if it abolished slavery. Blacks would desert to federal lines as soon as they reached the front. If the slaves were armed, he warned, "we will ourselves, take the best in the country, drill and train them, and then hand them over—ready made warriors—to the enemy."[71]

Blacks by the hundreds that winter were already escaping to Savannah and Union-held areas of the coast, just as they had been since federal forces arrived. In early 1865, the General Assembly asked Governor Brown to stop the exodus by placing a line of troops between the Savannah and Ogeechee rivers. Much as he would have liked to, Brown could not comply. He did not have enough troops to do the job effectively.[72]

Those slaves remaining at home were largely doing as they pleased in any case. A report from Blakely told of "more *stealing,* and *rascality generally,* going on…for the past few months, than has ever been known…negroes are doing a great deal of this stealing." S. S. Massey of Chattahoochee County complained that slaves were "killing up the stock and stealing every thing they can put their hands on."[73] To the slaves, it seemed just compensation, and little enough at that, for the labor that had been stolen from them all their lives. For them, back pay was long overdue.

Despite the unlikely nature of the effort and the reality that blacks were already taking freedom for themselves, on March 13, 1865, Congress finally passed legislation authorizing Davis to recruit up to three hundred thousand blacks. There was, however, no promise of freedom for those who agreed to serve. Congress insisted that both the states and

---

[71]J. William Harris, *Plain Folk and Gentry in a Slave Society: White Liberty and Black Slavery in Augusta's Hinterlands* (Middletown, CT: Wesleyan University Press, 1985) 186; *Columbus Times*, 15 February 1865.

[72]Bryan, *Confederate Georgia*, 128.

[73]*Early County News*, 6 April 1864; Massey to Brown, 9 March 1865, Governor's Incoming Correspondence.

individual slaveholders must agree to any alteration in the legal standing of slave-soldiers. In his General Order No. 14 implementing the act, Davis went a step further, stating that "no slave will be accepted as a recruit unless with his own consent and with the approbation of his master by a written instrument conferring...the rights of a freedman."[74]

Reaction in Georgia was predictably mixed. Most slaveholders raised "a devil of a howl," denouncing the act as a direct threat to their property rights. To a "poor soldier" from near Augusta, on the other hand, slaveholders' refusal to support black enlistment was one more sign that the struggle was a rich man's war, carried out only to preserve their property in slaves. On April 5, 1865, T. E. Speight, who had replaced E. H. Grouby as editor of the *Early County News*, condemned the "starch-shirt gentry" who advocated military service for everyone except themselves and their slaves. Since they would not fight, Speight was glad to see that their slaves might have to.[75] It hardly mattered one way or the other. By then it was too late. On very rare occasions throughout the war, blacks were unofficially pressed into combat service with guns at their backs and their families held hostage in slavery. But the Confederacy formed no units of black troops. No blacks ever saw combat as congressionally authorized soldiers.

It Ain't Gonna Be Long Now

By mid-March 1865, Ulysses S. Grant, now general-in-chief of all federal armies, was planning a final blow to hasten Confederate collapse. He would send a large raiding party through the Deep South to strike at supply lines and manufacturing centers. To carry out the assignment, Grant chose Major General James Harrison Wilson, a twenty-seven-year-old cavalry officer. He would lead a mounted infantry

---

[74]Mohr, *On the Threshold of Freedom*, 283–84. An excellent study of how the issue of arming slaves developed in Georgia is Philip David Dillard, "Arming the Slaves: Transformation of the Public Mind" (master's thesis, University of Georgia, 1994).

[75]Mohr, *On the Threshold of Freedom*, 283–84; Harris, *Plain Folk and Gentry*, 186–87; *Early County News*, 5 April 1865.

corps through Alabama and Georgia to wipe out the Confederacy's remaining military production centers at Selma, Alabama, and Columbus, Georgia.[76]

On March 22, Wilson set out from his base on the Tennessee-Alabama border with more than thirteen thousand well-equipped troops. Wilson met little opposition in northern Alabama, but as he approached Selma on April 2, his corps ran into the remnants of Nathan Bedford Forrest's cavalry. Wilson's numerical advantage gave him a swift and thorough victory. With Forrest's defeat and Selma's subsequent destruction, Wilson was free to move against Montgomery. The undefended city did not resist, and Wilson quickly continued his advance toward Columbus.

At the same time, another column of four thousand Union cavalrymen set out from Mobile, Alabama, under command of Major General Benjamin H. Grierson. Their original target had been Montgomery, but when Grierson received news of the city's capture, he turned east at Greenville and headed for Georgia.[77]

Governor Brown responded to the threat by ordering non-engaged units to rendezvous at Columbus. Two regiments of the Georgia militia, two artillery batteries, and a few reserve units from surrounding Georgia and Alabama counties were all pressed into service, at least those willing to be pressed. War weariness had long since depleted their ranks. The Peace Society may also have discouraged men from answering the call and may even have helped the Federals. William Scott of the 4th Iowa wrote of one local man who revealed the location of Confederate defenses.[78]

---

[76]For an overview of Wilson's Raid see James Pickett Jones, *Yankee Blitzkrieg: Wilson's Raid through Alabama and Georgia* (Athens: University of Georgia Press, 1976). By far the most complete treatment of the Battle for Columbus is Charles A. Misulia, *Columbus, Georgia, 1865: The Last True Battle of the Civil War* (Tuscaloosa: University of Alabama Press, 2010).

[77]*OR*, series 1, vol. 49, part 1, 300.

[78]Candler, *Confederate Records of Georgia*, 3:712; Nancy Telfair, *A History of Columbus, Georgia* (Columbus, GA: Historical Publishing, 1929) 134; Bill Winn, "Columbus' Last Battle: Peace Society May Have Aided City's Fall,"

There were many in Columbus who questioned the wisdom of resistance. Armed opposition seemed not only useless, but it might place the city in even greater danger. Its few defenders could not hope to stop Wilson's battle-hardened veterans. They might delay the Federals for a short time, but such futile opposition could only antagonize them. The best course of action would be to form a delegation, meet the Yankees before they reached Columbus, and negotiate terms of surrender. But General Howell Cobb, the ranking military official at Columbus, refused to consider any such suggestions.[79]

As the Federals approached, Cobb and his assistant, Colonel Leon von Zinken, developed plans to defend Columbus. Even so, despite their refusal to negotiate a surrender, they knew that the fight would be in vain. On April 15, Zinken warned Columbus citizens to "make preparations for their safety."[80] Cobb had already prepared for his own safety. A train was standing by to speed him off at a moment's notice.

Upriver from Columbus, Troup County was also preparing to meet the Union threat. Wilson had sent a brigade under Colonel Oscar LaGrange up the rail line from Montgomery, and by nightfall on April 15 it had reached Auburn. Warned by that town's refugees of LaGrange's approach, one-legged general Robert C. Tyler quickly assembled a small force of convalescent soldiers, hospital employees, and local citizens. By morning on the sixteenth, Tyler had placed little more than a hundred men in a small earthen fort guarding the bridges into West Point on the Alabama side of the Chattahoochee River.[81]

Columbus Ledger-Enquirer, 19 April 1987; William Forse Scott, *The Story of a Cavalry Regiment: The Career of the Fourth Iowa Veteran Volunteers from Kansas to Georgia, 1861–1865* (New York: Knickerbocker Press, 1893) 492.

[79]See Winn, "Columbus' Last Battle."

[80]Leon von Zinken, "Notice to the Citizens of Columbus," 15 April 1865, Columbus State University Archives, Columbus, GA.

[81]Robert U. Johnson and Clarence C. Buel, *Battles and Leaders of the Civil War*, vol. 4 (New York: Century Co., 1888) 761; L. B. M'Farland, "The Battle of West Point," *Confederate Veteran* 23 (1915): 353; Clifford L. Smith, *History of Troup County* (Atlanta: Foote and Davies, 1933) 78.

Troup County's seat of LaGrange was defended almost solely by an unofficial company of well-to-do women, the "Nancy Harts," named after Georgia's legendary heroine of the War for Independence. Formed in 1863, it was mainly a social and service organization. Most of the women's time was spent ministering to wounded soldiers in area hospitals. Still, the women armed themselves with old muskets and hunting rifles, made their own ammunition, and held mock drills and target practice.[82]

On Easter Sunday, April 16, Wilson's troopers prepared for their assaults on Columbus and West Point. LaGrange's men reached Tyler's fort by mid-morning and shelled it before beginning their attack at 1:30. After chasing Rebel skirmishers into the fort, LaGrange left his main force to continue the assault while he led a detachment to capture the main bridge into West Point. He and his men had little difficulty driving off the bridge's few defenders. West Point, with its rail center and bridges, was now in Union hands.[83]

The main Federal force under Wilson arrived on the outskirts of Girard, now Phenix City, at 2:00 that Sunday afternoon. Wilson hoped that at least one of the three local Chattahoochee bridges could be taken intact. Clapp's Factory bridge, three miles north of Columbus, would be ideal. If the Federals crossed there, they could flank the Confederates and take Columbus from the rear. At Wilson's direction, General Emory Upton, commanding the lead column, ordered two hundred men of the 10th Missouri to take the bridge. Columbus defenders had anticipated this maneuver and had prepared the bridge for burning. As Upton's men approached, the Confederates ignited turpentine-soaked bales of cotton lining the wooden structure. Within seconds, flames engulfed the bridge.[84]

---

[82]Bryan, *Confederate Georgia*, 185; Forrest Clark Johnson, III, *Histories of LaGrange and Troup County, Georgia, Volume 1, A History of LaGrange, Georgia, 1828–1900* (LaGrange, GA: Family Tree, 1987) 71.

[83]*OR*, series 1, vol. 49, part 1, 428–29; Scott, *Story of a Cavalry Regiment*, 481; M'Farland, "Battle of West Point," 354; Robert C. Black, *Railroads of the Confederacy* (Chapel Hill: University of North Carolina Press, 1952) 287–90.

[84]*OR*, series 1, vol. 49, part 1, 480; Peter Michie, ed., *The Life and Letters of*

At the same time, Upton sent another force to capture the lower bridge at Dillingham Street, but Columbus defenders had already torn up the bridge's flooring planks, making a mounted advance impossible. As the Union troopers made ready for a dismounted assault, an over-anxious Confederate gunner set the bridge on fire. According to a Federal account, this premature burning of the bridge saved the Yankees from certain death. The flames spread too rapidly to have allowed escape. With the bridge at Dillingham Street now gone, only the upper bridge connecting Girard's Broadnax Street to Columbus's Franklin (later Fourteenth) Street was left intact.[85]

The Confederate defensive strategy had hinged on the destruction of the Clapp's Factory and Dillingham Street bridges. This done, the Confederates could now lure Wilson's men into a heavily protected area around the upper bridge using the bridge itself as bait. Once the Yankee cavalry was in range, Confederate batteries would turn loose a devastating artillery barrage. As a last-ditch defense, Confederates placed two cannons loaded with grapeshot on the Georgia side of the bridge in case the first line of artillery failed.

The temptation to take the remaining bridge was too great for Wilson, even though he had pontoon bridges and might have crossed the river at any point. He decided to aim his attack at the defenders entrenched along Summerville Road just north of Girard, break the Confederate line at that point, then make a rush on the bridge. Wilson told his troopers to make coffee, prepare their supper, and rest for the coming battle while he made final preparations.[86]

A Russell County man later recorded his reflections of that Easter Sunday. From his home just west of Girard, he could see smoke rising from the burning bridges and hear the thunder of artillery. "The day was filled with dread and terror," he recalled, "and was so long that it seemed

---

Emory Upton (New York: D. Appleton, 1885) 166.

[85]W. L. Curry, comp., *Four Years in the Saddle: History of the First Regiment, Ohio Volunteer Cavalry* (Jonesboro, GA: Freedom Hill Press, 1898) 223, 224.

[86]Curry, *Four Years in the Saddle*, 259, 261.

that Joshua had commanded the sun to stand still."[87] With Wilson planning to take the remaining bridge under cover of darkness, a rare tactic during the Civil War, the coming hours would seem even longer.

The night of April 16 was, in the words of one soldier, "black as pitch." The darkness of the moonless night heightened tensions on both sides. At 8:00 P.M., six dismounted companies of the 3rd Iowa Cavalry advanced on fortifications straddling Summerville Road. They approached with surprising stealth and managed to get within fifty yards of the Confederate works without firing a shot. When they finally saw the Federals coming, Rebel gunners opened fire. But their aim was high and did little to slow the Yankee advance. Within five minutes, Federals controlled that stretch of the road.[88]

Believing that he had broken the main Confederate line, Upton ordered the 10th Missouri Cavalry to make a dash for the bridge. In a headlong rush down Summerville Road, the troopers quickly found themselves nearing the bridge. To their astonishment, they also found themselves behind an unbroken Rebel line. They had met no resistance because they were mistaken for retreating Confederate pickets. The defenders soon realized their error and opened fire on the 10th Missouri. Close to being trapped, the cavalrymen wheeled around and rushed back through the Rebel lines.

Meanwhile, Upton had turned his remaining troops left in a drive against entrenchments on Ingersoll Hill. Their progress was slowed to a crawl by thick woods and muddy bogs at the foot of the hill. The Federals doggedly pushed forward but soon became disoriented in the darkness. A few of the advancing troopers yelled "Go to the right" while others cried out "Go to the left." Despite the confusion they made their way

[87]F. A. Ellison letter, Hurtsboro folder, Russell County clippings file, Alabama Department of Archives and History, Montgomery.

[88]*OR*, series 1, vol. 49, part 1, 474; James Harrison Wilson, *Under the Old Flag*, vol. 2 (New York: D. Appleton, 1912) 261; *OR*, series 1, vol. 49, part 1, 481.

through the underbrush, overwhelmed the outnumbered Confederates and sent them running for the upper bridge.[89]

Wilson's men now regrouped for a final assault on the prized bridge. They hurried over the top of Ingersoll Hill and rushed down toward Broadnax Street. Near Jackson Street, the 4th Iowa turned right and captured Confederate artillery on Red Hill.[90]

The path to the bridge was now clear, and Federal troops swarmed through the streets of Girard. As they neared their objective, the enthusiastic Federals shouted "Go for the bridge! Waste no time with prisoners!" They quickly became entangled with a throng of retreating Confederates, and for a short time confusion reigned. One observer recalled that "horsemen and footmen, artillery wagons and ambulances were crowded and jammed together in the narrow avenue, which was 'dark as Egypt'...for that bridge had no gas fixtures and was never lighted. How it was that many were not crushed to death in the tumultuous transit of the Chattahoochee seems incomprehensible." The Federals pressed on and, to their amazement, managed to cross the bridge without sustaining a single casualty. Confederates guarding the eastern end of the bridge had refused to fire their two canister-loaded howitzers for fear that the spray of lead would kill friend as well as foe.[91]

The 4th Iowa was first across the bridge. It fanned out to through Columbus and moved downstream to capture the guns guarding Dillingham Street Bridge. One detachment rushed to the depot. By the time they arrived, an entire trainload of officers and prominent citizens was already gone. General Cobb missed the train but escaped on horseback. Though top Confederate officials eluded capture, Columbus was now in Union hands. The city's capture had taken little more than an hour.

Residents panicked as federal troops swarmed the city. One eyewitness recalled that "women and children were running through the streets like people deranged, and men, with mules and wagons, [were] driving in every direction." Roads leading eastward out of town were packed with

---

[89]Jones, *Yankee Blitzkrieg*, 136–37; *OR*, series 1, vol. 49, part 1, 493–94.
[90]*OR*, series 1, vol. 49, part 1, 481.
[91]Wilson, *Under the Old Flag*, 264; Jones, *Yankee Blitzkrieg*, 138.

soldiers and civilians alike. One who remained was Randolph Mott, a longtime Union man. He offered his home to Wilson as a temporary headquarters.[92]

Mayor F. G. Wilkins also stayed behind. Early the next morning, he issued a statement to his constituents:

> The Federals under command of Major Gen. Wilson, having captured our city, I am assured by him that private property will be protected. It is ordered that all citizens remain on their premises until he can have a proper guard for our defense detailed. The Major General further requires of the citizens 30,000 rations, which must be furnished by 12 o'clock noon.[93]

Wilson ordered the destruction of "everything within reach that could be made useful for the continuance of the Rebellion." He placed General Edward Winslow in charge of burning Columbus warehouses and factories. Winslow's brigade also put 125,000 bales of cotton to the torch. Quartermaster stores that had not already been pillaged were opened to city residents.[94]

Hardest hit by Union occupation were the navy yard and naval iron works. The Federals wrecked or dismantled machinery and burned the ironclad CSS *Jackson* to the water line. The vessel, 250 feet long and boasting six seven-inch guns, had nearly been ready for its maiden voyage. The journey did occur, though not in quite the way intended by its builders. After being set afire, the burning hulk drifted thirty miles downriver before sinking. The gunboat *Chattahoochee* suffered a similar fate though not at the hands of the Federals. It had already been set afire and adrift by navy yard officials to keep it out of enemy hands. It ran aground twelve miles south of Columbus.[95]

---

[92]Jones, *Yankee Blitzkrieg*, 139; Charles Jewett Swift, *The Last Battle of the Civil War* (Columbus, GA: Gilbert Printing, 1915) 27.

[93]Original held by Mrs. Lee Sloan, Harris County, GA. Photocopy on file at Georgia Department of Archives and History.

[94]Wilson, *Under the Old Flag*, 266; Swift, *Last Battle of the Civil War*, 31; *OR*, series 1, vol. 49, part 1, 487.

[95]*OR*, series 1, vol. 49, part 1, 485; William Watts Carnes Memoirs, 204–

The demolition of Columbus industries continued throughout the day on April 17. Almost all the mills and factories were damaged, including the textile and paper mills. But food-processing mills, such as those of the Empire grist operations, were spared at Wilson's order. Facilities of military value—the quartermaster depot, navy yard, naval iron works, arsenal, and Haiman's sword factory—were his primary targets. Kate Cumming, then serving as a nurse in Columbus, recalled that Wilson's men did little damage to nonmilitary private property.[96] Most of that was done by the people of Columbus themselves. Even before the Federals left, mobs began to roam the streets looting businesses and storehouses that had anything of value. One eyewitness noted that many well-dressed women, by all appearances affluent, were eager for their share of the spoils. "They frantically join and jostle in the chaos, and seem crazy for plunder."[97]

By the morning of April 18, the industrial sections of Columbus lay in ruins. While parts of the city were "still a mass of flame and coals," Wilson and his troops headed out on their way to Macon.[98]

The town of LaGrange suffered its own Federal occupation, though destruction was much more limited. On the morning of April 17, as Colonel LaGrange approached the town, which coincidentally bore his name, the Nancy Harts gathered two blocks west of the town square. From there they moved toward the Female College and met the Yankees

---

205, National Civil War Naval Museum, Columbus, GA; Augustus McLaughlin Letterbook and Confederate Navy Yard Log and Accounts, 16 April 1865, National Civil War Naval Museum, Columbus, Georgia; Lynn Willoughby Ware, "Enchantment and Ennui: The Experiences of the Crew of the CSS *Chattahoochee*," *Georgia Historical Quarterly* 70 (1986): 431–32; Maxine Turner, *Navy Gray: A Story of the Confederate Navy on the Chattahoochee and Apalachicola Rivers* (Tuscaloosa: University of Alabama Press, 1988) 233–34, 142–45.

[96]Cumming, *Journal of Kate Cumming*, 279.

[97]Jones, *Yankee Blitzkrieg*, 142–43; Mary DeCredico, *Patriotism for Profit: Georgia's Urban Entrepreneurs and the Confederate War Effort* (Chapel Hill: University of North Carolina Press, 1990) 114–15.

[98]Lurton Dunham Ingersoll, *Iowa and the Rebellion* (Philadelphia: J. B. Lippincott, 1866) 438.

in front of campus. The women agreed to surrender and disperse only after Colonel LaGrange promised not to destroy private homes, which he did not intend to target anyway. That evening the ladies entertained LaGrange and his officers. Next morning, the Federals tore up track and destroyed the depot, but, true to their commander's word, they stayed out of private dwellings. Their work completed, LaGrange and his men turned east to rendezvous with the rest of Wilson's command.[99]

Two days later, on April 20, Wilson arrived in Macon. There, much to his surprise, he learned that Lee had surrendered more than a week earlier in Virginia and that Abraham Lincoln was dead. For all practical purposes, the war had been over several days before the raids on West Point, LaGrange, and Columbus. Wilson later wrote, "Had we but known what had taken place in Virginia...we should certainly have not...participated in the injury which was inflicted upon [Columbus] industries." Fortunately, before General Grierson could do any damage in the state, he also received news of the war's end as his men camped astride the Chattahoochee River at Georgetown in Quitman County.[100]

Although Georgia slaveholders greeted the Federals with apprehension, not everyone was sorry to see them come. For many poor whites, it was a sure sign that the war was finally over. Some even profited from Wilson's raid. One former slave recalled that as Union soldiers moved through Troup County, they drove off all the mules on his owner's plantation. The animals wandered into neighboring Harris County and, as the old man said, "there was lots of white folks what never had owned nothin' went over there and got theirselves a mule."[101]

---

[99]Bryan, *Confederate Georgia*, 185; Johnson, *Histories of LaGrange and Troup County*, 73; *Augusta Chronicle and Sentinel*, 10 May 1865; Mrs. Thaddeus Horton, "The Story of the Nancy Harts," *Ladies Home Journal* (November 1904): 14. For a firsthand account of LaGrange's occupation and the role of the Nancy Harts see Leila C. Morris, "Personal Recollections of the War," Nancy Harts folder, Troup County Archives, LaGrange, GA.

[100]Jones, *Yankee Blitzkrieg*, 144, *OR*, series 1, vol. 49, part 1, 300.

[101]"Uncle Lon" Winston interview (c. 1940) in "Little Valley Stories: Slavery Days," Margaret Parker Milford Collection, Cobb Memorial Archives, Valley, AL.

For slaves, Wilson's coming was a long-anticipated guarantee of freedom. When news of the Columbus raid reached slaves on one Stewart County plantation, they spoke for many thousands of Georgians, black and white, when they rejoiced, "It ain't gonna be long now!"[102] And it was not. On May 10, Wilson's men captured Jefferson Davis in Irwin County as he fled south in a vain effort to get out of the country and establish a Confederate government-in-exile. Vice President Stephens and Governor Brown were also arrested, as was Senator Benjamin Hill at his home in Troup County. Other Confederate officials were soon in custody, and the Confederate nation ceased to be.

Don't Think There Is Much Regret for the Loss

In a way, the Confederacy as a nation, with all the emotional attachments and widespread support that the term suggests, never existed at all. More than half a century ago, eminent Georgia historian E. Merton Coulter, enamored as he was with the Confederacy, still recognized that it "was not blessed with a 'one for all and all for one' patriotism with which future generations of sentimental romancers were to endow it. Had it been so, this new-born nation might well have established its independence." The Confederacy, Coulter knew, never became an "emotional reality" to most Southern whites until after Reconstruction, when the Lost Cause became a euphemism for white supremacy and united Southern whites like secession never could.[103]

From its beginnings, the Lost Cause's lack of firm support from most Southerners largely explains why it was lost. Most Southern whites had opposed secession to begin with. Even a slight majority of Georgia voters likely rejected it. As for black Southerners, they could hardly have

---

[102]Rhodus Walton, *Georgia Narratives*, part 4, 126, in *Slave Narratives: A Folk History of Slavery in the United States from Interviews with Former Slaves*, Manuscript Division, Library of Congress, Washington, DC.

[103]E. Merton Coulter, *Confederate States of America, 1861–1865* (Baton Rouge: Louisiana State University Press, 1950) 374, 105. An adherent of white supremacy himself, Coulter recognized it as the one force behind which nearly all white Southerners could, and did, unite.

felt much enthusiasm for a government that considered slavery their "natural and normal condition." What early support the Confederacy did have eroded steadily as the passions of 1861 died away.[104]

From 1862 on, conscription accelerated declining Confederate support. Devastating as well were attitudes of planters and the privileges granted them by the government. They were not only exempt from the draft but also continued to grow too much cotton while soldiers and their families went hungry. In doing so, planters helped starve the Confederacy out of existence.

Hunger in the army and at home contributed to a desertion rate that crippled the war effort early on. Robert E. Lee wrote in fall 1862 that desertion and straggling were the main reasons for his army's defeat at Antietam. That loss had far reaching effects. It spurred Lincoln to announce the Emancipation Proclamation, which made diplomatic recognition for the Confederacy by Britain or France impossible. And it drew roughly two hundred thousand African Americans, most of them Southerners, into the Union army and navy. Lincoln himself admitted that the Union could not have prevailed without their help.[105]

Typically in American history text books, the Union's victory is attributed to Northern population and industry. Although it is true that the North had more people and more factories than the South, assuming these were overriding reasons for Confederate defeat ignores more decisive realities of the battlefield and home front. Despite the North's population advantage of two to one, only half of the Union's armed forces

---

[104]Cleveland, *Alexander H. Stephens*, 721.

[105]*OR*, series 1, vol. 19, part 2, 622; Michael P. Johnson, ed., *Abraham Lincoln, Slavery, and the Civil War: Selected Writings and Speeches* (Boston: Bedford/St. Martin's, 2001) 302–303. Blacks in the Union army totaled almost 179,000. Figures for those in the Union navy, according to Howard University's Black Sailors Project, show that approximately 18,000 served, though some sources give higher estimates. See John David Smith, ed., *Black Soldiers in Blue: African American Troops in the Civil War Era* (Chapel Hill: University of North Carolina Press, 2002) xiii; Barbara Brooks Tomblin, *Bluejackets and Contrabands: African Americans and the Union Navy* (Lexington: University Press of Kentucky, 2009) 188.

were made up of native-born Northerners, about a million of them—little more than the number of Southerners who served the Confederacy. A fourth of the Union's two million servicemen were immigrants, and almost another fourth, nearly a half million, were Southerners, black and white, thousands of Georgians among them.[106]

It was, in the end, Southerners who gave Union forces their numerical superiority. Given the limits of support Lincoln was able to muster in the North, the war's resolution came down to Southerners themselves. Had all soldiers *from* the South fought *for* the South, or more precisely for the Confederacy, the result would have been parity on the battlefield and perhaps Confederate victory.

As for the North's industrial advantage, its impact was significant but not decisive. So successful was the Confederacy's war materiel production program that never did its forces lose a major battle for lack of munitions. What Confederates did constantly lack, unlike their Union counterparts, was food. Cotton production was, for the most part, responsible for that. It was equally responsible for home-front food shortages that contributed to inflation, speculation, women rioting, and, worst of all for the Confederate cause, soldiers deserting. Ultimately, as historian Paul Escott put it, "the decision which common soldiers made with their feet sealed the fate of the Confederacy."[107]

---

[106]William W. Freehling, *The South vs. the South: How Anti-Confederate Southerners Shaped the Course of the Civil War* (New York: Oxford University Press, 2001) xiii; Richard N. Current, *Lincoln's Loyalists: Union Soldiers from the Confederacy* (New York: Oxford University Press, 1994) 218; Ella Lonn, *Foreigners in the Union Army and Navy* (New York: Greenwood, 1969) 582. Roughly 100,000 white Southerners who served in the Union military were from the eleven Confederate states. Another approximately 200,000 were from the Border South slave states of Missouri and Kentucky (both claimed by the Confederacy), Maryland, and Delaware. Border South states, with the exception of Delaware, fielded regiments for both the Union and Confederate armies, as did nearly every Southern state.

[107]Richard E. Beringer, Herman Hattaway, Archer Jones, and William N. Still, *Why the South Lost the Civil War* (Athens: University of Georgia Press, 1986) 13; *OR*, series 1, vol. 30, part 4 180; Paul Escott, *After Secession: Jefferson Davis and the Failure of Confederate Nationalism* (Baton Rouge: Louisiana State

For most soldiers, that decision came much earlier and had its impact much sooner than historians have traditionally acknowledged. Some have argued that the fall of Atlanta and Sherman's March to the Sea, along with Lincoln's reelection in late 1864, were the key events leading to Southern loss of will and Confederate defeat. Others see July 1863 as the turning point, with Confederate defeats at Gettysburg and Vicksburg. In any case, so the argument goes, it was military defeat that brought a loss of will and doomed the Confederacy.[108]

Certainly defeats on the battlefield sapped the Confederacy's will to fight, but those defeats came largely because so many soldiers had already lost their will to fight and deserted the army. Many, perhaps most, had never had much will to fight in the first place. Had the Confederacy had enough willing soldiers to sustain itself, conscription would never have been necessary.

By the time Atlanta was in Union hands, and well before Sherman's March, two-thirds of the Confederate army was absent, "most of them," as Jefferson Davis admitted, "absent without leave."[109] Desertion was at the root of Confederate failures even before the summer 1863 defeats at Gettysburg and Vicksburg, as Robert E. Lee himself wrote just after his September 1862 retreat from Antietam. Soldiers were, in fact, leaving before the war's first year was out, which in large part led to conscription in April 1862.[110] Some left because the army could not feed them. Some

---

University Press, 1978) 128.

[108]Perhaps foremost among those who, in my view, put the cart before the horse when discussing Confederate defeat is Gary Gallagher. In his book *The Confederate War* (Cambridge, MA: Harvard University Press, 1997), Gallagher maintains that we hardly need look any further than the battlefield to understand the war's outcome. The Confederacy was whipped—that's why it lost. One might forgive Gallagher his narrow, circular reasoning since he rarely glanced beyond the battlefield in his prior scholarly works. *The Confederate War*, Gallagher's first venture behind the lines, is itself largely a commentary on existing literature rather than original research.

[109]*Macon Telegraph*, 24 September 1864.

[110]Escott, *After Secession*, 219; *OR*, series 1, vol. 19, part 2, 622. Beginning spring 1862, with conscription bearing down, what volunteering there was reflected more a will to avoid being drafted, losing the fifty-dollar enlistment bo-

left because their families were not being fed. What little food soldiers' families had was often hauled away by impressment and commissary agents, who frequently lined their pockets with ill-gotten gains.

Soldiers left because speculators preyed on their families, sometimes in cooperation with corrupt civil and military officials. Some left because the Confederacy did little to encourage food production. Others left because they had never wanted secession in the first place. Some left because they decided that the cause was not worthy of their sacrifice, much less that of their families. And, finally, they left because they were tired of fighting a rich man's war. That point was stressed in early April 1865, only days before the war's end, when the *Early County News* expressed a widespread and long-standing frustration among plain folk.

> This has been a "rich man's war and a poor man's fight." It is true that there are a few wealthy men in the army, but nine tenths of them hold positions, always get out of the way when they think a fight is coming on, and treat the privates like dogs.... there seems to be no chance to get this class to carry muskets.[111]

There was little love left for the Confederacy even among those who had never wavered. What loyalty they still felt was more for their comrades than anyone or anything else. Sergeant William Andrews of the 1st Georgia Regiment enlisted in February 1861 and remained through the entire war. Few could match his service to the cause of Southern independence. Still, only a few weeks after the war's end he wrote, "While it is a bitter pill to have to come back into the Union, don't think there is much regret for the loss of the Confederacy. The treatment the soldiers have received from the government in various ways put them against

---

nus, and being denigrated as a "conscript." While more than half of those who volunteered in the war's first year expressed pro-Confederate motives, only 14 percent of those who enlisted after spring 1862 did so. See J. William Harris, *The Making of the American South: A Short History, 1500–1877* (Malden, MA: Blackwell Publishing, 2006) 201.

[111]*Early County News*, 5 April 1865.

it."[112] That was just as true of the civilian population and says much about why the Confederacy failed.

[112]William H. Andrews, *Footprints of a Regiment: A Recollection of the First Georgia Regulars, 1861–1865*, annotated and introduction by Richard M. McMurry (Atlanta: Longstreet Press, 1992) 184.

Although most soldiers abandoned their ranks long before the Confederacy's surrender, those who stayed often did so with little enthusiasm. What loyalty they felt was more for their comrades than the government. Sergeant William Andrews of Clay County, a four-year veteran, wrote in May 1865, "While it is a bitter pill to have to come back into the Union, don't think there is much regret for the loss of the Confederacy. The treatment the soldiers have received from the government in various ways put them against it." Image courtesy of Longstreet Press.

Epilogue

The New Slavery and Georgia's Ongoing Civil War

Shortly after he passed through the Deep South at war's end, Union general Benjamin Grierson recorded his impressions of the region's people.

> The country was filled with armed marauders, composed mostly of deserters from the late rebel armies, who have returned to find their families suffering from the neglect and persecution of the wealthy leaders, at whose instigation they joined the rebel ranks. The poor people, including the returned Confederate private soldiers, are, as a general thing, now loyal, but the far greater portion of the wealthy classes are still very bitter in their sentiments against the Government, and clutch onto slavery with a lingering hope to save at least a relic of their favorite yet barbarous institution for the future.

Grierson recommended leniency for poorer folk. They had suffered too much already in a war not of their making. But the "spirit of resistance" among former slaveholders would have to be broken down completely if black folk were ever to be truly free.[1]

Planter resistance to emancipation was nowhere more evident than in Georgia. Writing from Macon in June 1865, a federal officer reported that he had "the greatest trouble" convincing planters that they were no longer slaveholders. They desperately held to "a hope that something will yet turn up which will give them at least a life lease of slavery." He heard one member of the old slaveocracy comment that "if we cannot whip the

[1] *War of the Rebellion: A Compilation of the Official Records of the Union and Confederate Armies* (Washington, DC: Government Printing Office, 1880–1901) series 1, vol. 49, part 1, 301 (hereafter cited as *OR*).

Negro, they and I cannot live in the same country." That feeling, he noted, was common among former slaveholders.[2]

Whites who held to their old attitudes had a firm friend in the White House. Andrew Johnson, who ascended to the presidency in April 1865 after Lincoln's assassination, was a former slaveholder from Tennessee who had no wish to bestow civil rights on former slaves. His only condition for a state's readmission to the Union was ratification of the Thirteenth Amendment abolishing chattel slavery. Aside from that, Johnson was content to leave Southern state governments in the hands of former slaveholders. They took full advantage of the opportunity.

In October 1865, at the urging of Provisional Governor James Johnson, delegates to Georgia's constitutional convention reluctantly accepted slavery's demise. For some months Governor Johnson, a Columbus native and long-time Union man, had been encouraging planters to acknowledge that fact. In plain language, he publicly stated that "slavery is extinguished. It is gone—it is gone forever." Nonetheless, the convention's resolution accepting slavery's end also defended the institution as "consistent with the dictates of humanity and the strictest principles of morality and religion." The new constitution, like its predecessors, left control of the General Assembly to Black Belt planters. And it denied blacks access to the ballot box.[3]

Restricting the franchise was only the first step in maintaining virtual enslavement. Under a series of Black Codes, which closely resembled the old slave codes, freedom for black folk was made little more than nominal. Blacks could not serve on juries, hold public office, or quit jobs at will. Most oppressive was the vagrancy law. Blacks found "wandering or strolling about in idleness, who are able to work and who have not property to support them," and most did not, could be arrested and sold off, usually to large landholders, for the price of their fine. They were supposed to be held only until they worked off their fine, but with the

---

[2]*OR*, series 1, vol. 49, part 2, 1041–42.

[3]*Macon Telegraph*, 18 July 1865; Lewis Nicholas Wynne, *The Continuity of Cotton: Planter Politics in Georgia 1865–1892* (Macon, GA: Mercer University Press, 1986) 2–4.

costs of food, clothing, and shelter added to their debt, blacks arrested for vagrancy could remain in bondage for years if not for life. Since few blacks owned property of any kind, most were in very real danger of being re-enslaved under the vagrancy law.[4]

If President Johnson and Southern state legislatures cared nothing for black rights, Congress's Republican majority certainly did, at least as far as voting rights went. Knowing that black men would likely vote against the planter-dominated Democrats, congressional Republicans took steps to shore up their base in the South with a series of Reconstruction Acts. Beginning in 1867, over Johnson's veto, Congress divided most of the old Confederacy into five districts, put military governors in place, and charged them with guaranteeing voting rights, black and white. The next year saw ratification of the Fourteenth Amendment granting citizenship to "all persons born or naturalized in the United States" and promising them "equal protection of the laws." Finally, with the Fifteenth Amendment, the Constitution guaranteed voting rights to all citizens regardless "of race, color, or previous condition of servitude."[5]

Congressional Reconstruction did succeed for a time in extending political rights to black men. They voted in large numbers and won seats in Southern state legislatures and even in Congress on the Republican ticket. But electoral supervision was so weak that the planter power structure soon found ways to suppress both the black vote and the vote of those few whites who dared cast Republican ballots. It was not difficult to know who voted for whom in an era before the secret ballot was in common use. John Cobb of Sumter County, a planter and Democratic legislator, wrote in 1868 that "every man who voted the Radical [Repub-

---

[4]Donald L. Grant, *The Way It Was in the South: The Black Experience in Georgia*, ed. Jonathan Grant (New York: Birch Lane Press, 1993) 95–96; Charles L. Flynn, Jr., *White Land, Black Labor: Caste and Class in Late Nineteenth-Century Georgia* (Baton Rouge: Louisiana State University Press, 1983) 35–37.

[5]Both the federal and state judiciaries understood and interpreted the amendment to apply only to males. Voting rights for women, black or white, were not admitted nationally until 1920 when the Nineteenth Amendment went into effect.

lican] ticket in this county was watched and his ticket marked and all are now known and they will never cease to regret it as long as they live." Various terrorist organizations, nearly all eventually associated with the Ku Klux Klan, would see to that.[6]

Operating as the terrorist arm of the Democratic Party, bands of hooded night riders attacked both blacks and whites who openly sided with Republicans. They broke up prayer meetings, burned homes and churches, and beat or killed their victims. Black officeholders became special Klan targets. One evening forty Klansmen broke into the home of Alfred Richardson, a black member of the Georgia legislature, and shot him nearly to death. Another black Georgia legislator, Abram Colby, was given one thousand lashes after turning down a bribe to cease his political activity.[7]

White Republicans died as well. In southwestern Georgia, blacks and some of their local white allies were massacred during a Republican rally at Camilla in 1868. That same year George Ashburn, a white native Georgian and Republican politician, was murdered following a rally in Columbus. Shortly after midnight, several well-dressed, masked men broke into Ashburn's bedroom and shot him dead.[8]

Lacking effective protection from both local authorities and Reconstruction governments, black folk were most often left to defend themselves. As early as 1865, blacks formed armed militias for self-protection. That year black activist Tunis Campbell organized unofficial militias

---

[6]Edmund L. Drago, *Black Politicians and Reconstruction in Georgia: A Splendid Failure* (Baton Rouge: Louisiana State University Press, 1982) 148.

[7]Ibid., 146–47.

[8]Lee W. Formwalt, "The Camilla Massacre of 1868: Racial Violence as Political Propaganda," *Georgia Historical Quarterly* 71 (1987): 399–426; Elizabeth Otto Daniell, "The Ashburn Murder Case in Georgia Reconstruction, 1868," *Georgia Historical Quarterly* 59 (1975): 296–312. For more on the Camilla Massacre see Joshua William Butler, "Almost Too Terrible to Believe: The Camilla, Georgia, Race Riot and Massacre" (master's thesis, Valdosta State University, 2012). For further details of the Ashburn murder see William A. Link, *Atlanta, Cradle of the New South: Race and Remembering in the Civil War's Aftermath* (Chapel Hill: University of North Carolina Press, 2013) 93–108.

along the Georgia coast. Freedmen in southwest Georgia drilled nightly on the outskirts of Bainbridge and Albany. In Stewart County, they fought off night riders, killing three, and forced the release of a prisoner in the Lumpkin jail by threatening to set the town on fire. In Hancock County, blacks ambushed Klan riders as they crossed a bridge. Firing from both ends, they forced the Klansmen into the river. For the time being at least, that ended Klan activity in Hancock County.[9]

Though sometimes effective, black militias had no backing from Reconstruction governments. Nor did they hold any force in law. That placed them on legal ground every bit as shaky as that of the Klan but without the accompanying political protection. It meant open season on blacks whenever whites were inclined to engage in the hunt. Klan terrorism had its effect on suppressing Republican voters in the elections of 1868. In Stewart County, where 752 had voted for the Republican gubernatorial candidate in April, the party's candidate for president, Ulysses S. Grant, received only 63 votes that November. More than 1,500 blacks were registered to vote in the county. White voters numbered less than a thousand. Just to the south in Randolph County, with nearly 1,200 blacks and fewer than a thousand whites registered, Republicans returned nearly seven hundred ballots for their candidate in April. By November, only one man in the whole county voted the Republican ticket.[10]

Threats of violence were so widespread that few blacks dared vote alone. One hundred blacks in Columbia County armed themselves and assembled twelve miles from the county seat before setting out to vote. Abram Colby of Greene County organized local blacks into armed com-

---

[9]Russell Duncan, *Freedom's Shore: Tunis Campbell and the Georgia Freedmen* (Athens: University of Georgia Press, 1986) 25, 30; Susan E. O'Donovan, *Becoming Free in the Cotton South* (Cambridge, MA: Harvard University Press, 2007) 230, 223–24; Paul A. Cimbala, *Under the Guardianship of the Nation: The Freedmen's Bureau and the Reconstruction of Georgia, 1865–1870* (Athens: University of Georgia Press, 1997) 210; Bryant Huff, *Georgia Narratives*, part 2, 242, in *Slave Narratives: A Folk History of Slavery in the United States from Interviews with Former Slaves*, Manuscript Division, Library of Congress, Washington, DC; Claiborne Moss, *Arkansas Narratives*, part 5, 164.

[10]Drago, *Black Politicians and Reconstruction in Georgia*, 149.

Leading up to the 1868 elections, black voter registration drives signed up more than 90 percent of eligible black men in every state except Mississippi, where the rate was 83 percent. Threats of ambush by white vigilantes were so serious that few blacks dared vote alone. Many formed militias for self-protection. In this scene, armed Georgia freedmen wade a creek on their way to vote in Appling, the seat of Columbia County. Image from Charles Sterns, *The Black Man of the South, and the Rebels* (1872).

panies, marched them to the polls, and carried local elections for the Republicans.[11] But such successes were less and less frequent as Klan violence increasingly took its toll.

Continuing low Republican turnout over the next few years reflected not only Klan violence but also a waning commitment by Congress to secure black civil rights. Certainly blacks could provide Republicans with votes, but Southern planters, the South's largest landholders, could provide something much more important—the very thing Northern elites had gone to war for in the first place—access to cheap natural resources. All Congress had to do was give its former adversaries a free hand to deal with the South's labor force as they saw fit, and riches in the form of lumber, iron, oil, and, most importantly, cotton would flow north. This economic alliance with planters was much more valuable to Northern industrialists than any political alliance they could ever have with Southern blacks. Never enthusiastic about a war to end slavery to begin with, much less equal rights for black folk, Northerners found the arrangement comfortable. They withdrew their largely ineffective army of occupation and left blacks at the mercy of former slaveholders.

With planters back in control both politically and economically, they moved quickly to reestablish the old order. Southern state governments enacted a series of "Jim Crow" laws firmly establishing social segregation. Blacks were barred from voting by such measures as literacy tests and poll taxes, which often kept poor whites from voting as well. And, despite lip-service to the idea of a "New South" with a diversified economy modeled after that of the North, agriculture remained the region's leading economic activity and cotton remained king. It suited those in power even if it kept most Southerners, black and white, in poverty.[12]

---

[11]Charles Stearns, *The Black Man of the South, and the Rebels; or, The Characteristics of the Former and the Recent Outrages of the Latter* (New York: American News Co., 1872) 208; Jonathan M. Bryant, *How Curious a Land: Conflict and Change in Greene County, Georgia, 1850–1885* (Chapel Hill: University of North Carolina Press, 1996) 127.

[12]One of the best overviews of how and to what extent planters regained power in Georgia is Lewis Nicholas Wynne's *The Continuity of Cotton: Planter*

Poverty was a key element in planter efforts to regain and maintain control. Shortly before the war's end, some slaves had been promised forty acres once they became free. It would have been little enough compensation for people who had labored all their lives and never received a cent in pay.[13] But the promise was a hollow one. In December 1865, a former Confederate general offered this explanation for poverty among Southern blacks: "The emancipated slaves own nothing, because nothing but freedom has been given to them."[14] It was a remarkably candid admission of the link between freedom and financial security.

A growing number of landless whites joined the property-less freedmen throughout the late nineteenth century. Many had owned no land before the war. Others lost their holdings to neighboring planters during or after the war for lack of ability to pay off debt. Still others moved down from the hill country looking for economic opportunity. They found little or none. With few skills other than farming and no land of their own to farm, most blacks and many whites slipped into tenancy, or, as one Georgia historian called it, "the new slavery."[15]

Tenant farming was certainly a kind of slavery. Farmers worked for a share of the crop, borrowed against expected earnings, and were extended credit for rent on land and equipment. They had little choice but to deal in credit following the war. If they had any money at all, it was in worthless Confederate notes. Once caught in the cycle of debt, tenants

---

Politics in Georgia, 1865–1892. For an excellent local study see Lee W. Formwalt, "Planter Persistence in Southwest Georgia, 1850–1870," *Journal of Southwest Georgia History* 2 (1984): 40–58.

[13]Well into the twentieth century there were former slaves who still felt the injustice of having worked for so long, they and their ancestors, without pay. In 1936, Mary Carpenter of Harris County asked one special favor of the person interviewing her for the Federal Writers Project. "All us old slave-time darkies oughta be pensioned, and I wish you'd tell Governor [Eugene] Talmadge that I said that." See George P. Rawick et al., comp., *The American Slave: A Composite Autobiography* (Westport, CT: Greenwood Press, 1972 and 1977) supplement, series 1, vol. 3, part 1, 145.

[14]Eric Foner, *Nothing but Freedom: Emancipation and Its Legacy* (Baton Rouge: Louisiana State University Press, 1983) 6.

[15]Grant, *The Way It Was in the South*, 137.

were usually trapped for life. With local landholders and merchants, who were often the same people, keeping the books, tenants' annual incomes almost never covered their previous year's debt. They were tied to the land until they could pay off their debt, which was nearly impossible under the circumstances.

Even those farmers who worked their own small landholdings became trapped in a kind of debt slavery under the oppressive crop-lien system. Local planter-merchants forced farmers to put up their next year's crop as collateral in exchange for supplies. Interest rates were so high, up to 75 percent in some cases, that, like their tenant neighbors, small landholders ended up further in debt than they had been the year before. Many found it impossible to pay off their debt from one year to the next. These people often fell into tenant farming and lost their land to those who already had large holdings. By the turn of the century, two-thirds of all Georgia farmers were tenants, and tenancy rates continued to rise well into the twentieth century.[16]

Debt slavery was also common among mill workers in company towns such as those in Atlanta, Marietta, Augusta, Columbus, West Point, and LaGrange. Employees, most of whom were customarily white, worked for company wages, lived in company housing, and were most often paid not in cash but in company scrip that could be spent only at the company store. With the company controlling their salaries, rents, and commodity prices, it is hardly surprising that no matter what their income, their cost of living was always higher. As a result, they were perpetually indebted to the company.

Even in the face of overwhelming poverty, most whites who bothered to vote at all consistently cast their ballots for the very men who kept them poor. To vote otherwise, they were told by the planter-dominated Democrats, would mean white subordination to "negro rule." Though poor whites had no great love for planters, they were as dedicated as ever to white supremacy. If nothing else, it gave them an artificial status that the reality of their impoverishment denied.

---

[16]Kenneth Coleman, ed., *A History of Georgia* (Athens: University of Georgia Press, 1977) 259.

There were those who challenged planter dominance. The most serious threat came in the 1890s from the newly formed Populist Party. With its focus on reforming the credit and tax systems, the party was designed to appeal to small farmers and tenants alike. Of course, the Populists had no financial backing from Southern economic elites. If they were to have any chance for success, they had to have maximum support from lower class folk to offset the economic advantage of their political opponents. And for that, they needed poor blacks as well as whites.

Georgia Populist Tom Watson was the party's most vocal advocate of cooperation between blacks and whites in facing their common economic problems. Time and time again, he pointed out that "the accident of color can make no difference in the interests of farmers, croppers, and laborers." Watson often addressed groups of black and white farmers, always hammering home the message of their shared plight. In 1892, Watson told his audience, "You are kept apart that you may be separately fleeced of your earnings. You are made to hate each other because upon that hatred is rested the keystone of the arch of financial despotism which enslaves you both. You are deceived and blinded that you may not see how this race antagonism perpetuates a monetary system which beggars both."[17]

Try as they might, Populists found it impossible to suppress generations of socially ingrained racism. Watson himself recognized the limitations of the Populist approach but could find no way to overcome it. One could get a white farmer's attention, said Watson, with promises to abolish the crop-lien system, provide for more reasonable credit, and reform the regressive tax system. But at the first cry of "Negro rule!", Watson wrote with regret, "the entire fabric of reason and common sense which you had patiently constructed would fall."[18]

---

[17]C. Vann Woodward, *Tom Watson* (Savannah, GA: Beehive Press, 1973) 190. Watson later adopted an "if you can't beat them, join them" strategy, becoming one of the most racist campaigners in Georgia's political history. In 1920, Watson was elected to the U.S. Senate.

[18]Ibid., 191.

The literary and cultural Lost Cause movement played on that lack of reason and contributed much to it. With white supremacy its creed—and Robert E. Lee its Christ—the Lost Cause became something of a religion for most white Southerners, who romanticized the South's Confederate past and encouraged a racist future. That white Southerners had once called the sectional conflict a "rich man's war" and had fought each other "harder than we have ever fought the enemy"—that even Confederate veterans had little regret for the Confederacy's loss—all mattered little in the postwar era.[19] What mattered was that the fiction of kind masters, contented slaves, and happily supportive plain folk vindicated the Confederacy and bolstered white supremacy. It was this newly idealized Confederate South, not the Confederacy as it had been, that was firmly planted in the popular mind and became both a justification and a euphemism for white supremacy.

Lost Causers went to great lengths to preserve their rosy image of the past. They erected Confederate monuments all over the South. They named parks, roads, buildings, towns, and counties after leading Confederates. They enshrined Confederate ideology and icons in novels, in movies, at public events, and on Southern state flags. The Lost Cause and its myth of Southern unity were perhaps most firmly cemented with the 1939 movie *Gone with the Wind*, set in Georgia and based on the novel by Atlanta writer Margaret Mitchell. The film won ten Academy Awards and became one of the most widely viewed motion pictures in cinema history. Though it contains no hint of the internal divisions that fatally undermined the Confederate war effort, *Gone with the Wind* largely defines the Civil War South in the public's imagination to this day.

For generations, the Lost Cause called white Southerners to an ongoing war for white supremacy in which it was all too easy for vices to become virtues and the other way around. Elevating whites meant sup-

---

[19]*Early County News*, 5 April 1865; *Milledgeville Confederate Union*, 24 November 1863; William H. Andrews, *Footprints of a Regiment: A Recollection of the First Georgia Regulars, 1861–1865*, annotated and introduction by Richard M. McMurry (Atlanta: Longstreet Press, 1992) 184.

pressing blacks. Defending white women required lynching black men. Beating nonviolent black students sitting at public lunch counters made one a latter-day Johnny Reb. So did throwing insults, or worse, at black children on their way to formerly all-white schools. Flying the Confederate battle flag in the face of those who might have been perpetually enslaved under it became honoring one's heritage. Doing unto others as you would have them do unto you made one, in the parlance of the day, a "nigger lover" and race traitor. For most white Southerners, their Confederate heritage far outweighed their Christian heritage. In fact, for a century or more after the Civil War, the Lost Cause *was* the white South's dominant religion. For some deluded fanatics, it still is.

Most Southern whites never lynched black folk, never beat black students, never accosted or assaulted black children. But they did cling to a social system that made such atrocities acceptable, even applauded. Out of irrational fear, prejudicial pride, and a misremembered history, they latched onto the Lost Cause and its assurance of white supremacy. In doing so, to their own detriment, they helped sustain a system of class and race oppression that for decades made the New South much like the Old South.

Significant change began only in the early twentieth century after the boll weevil wiped out the South's cotton crop. No longer needed to pick cotton, millions of tenant farmers, black and white, were turned off the land and released from their debt slavery. In a way, the tiny boll weevil freed more slaves in a few seasons of pestilence than Lincoln and the Union army did in four years of war. Over the next few decades, New Deal programs, farm mechanization, expanding markets, education reform, and the Civil Rights movement propelled the region toward becoming a truly New South. Still, strong elements of the Old South remain, often expressed as a romanticized Confederate South.

Southern whites of a century and a half ago could not so easily romanticize the Confederacy. Most eventually came to withhold support from the Richmond regime or oppose it outright. Their attitudes and actions, along with slave resistance, contributed decisively to the Confederacy's downfall. Although few seem aware of it today, that fact was well known to Georgians at war's end. Some had even predicted it. In fall 1862, an Atlanta newspaper went straight to the point: "If we are defeated, it will be by the people at home."[20] And so the Confederacy was defeated, not only by Union armed forces—in which close to half a million Southerners served—but also by widespread and often violent resistance on the home front.

[20]*Atlanta Southern Confederacy*, 25 October 1862.

Bibliography

Primary Sources

Archival Collections

Adjutant and Inspector General's Incoming Correspondence. Georgia Department of Archives and History, Morrow.

Adjutant General's Letter Books. Georgia Department of Archives and History, Morrow.

Barnsley, Godfrey, Papers. Felix Hargrett Rare Book and Manuscript Library, University of Georgia, Athens.

Berrien County Inferior Court Minutes, 1865. Georgia Department of Archives and History, Morrow.

Boyd Letters. Columbus State University Archives, Columbus, GA.

Brooks, William, Civil War Letter. Georgia Department of Archives and History, Morrow.

Brown, Joseph E., Papers. Felix Hargrett Rare Book and Manuscript Library, University of Georgia, Athens.

Brown, Joseph E., Papers. Library of Congress, Washington, DC.

Carnes, William Watts, Memoirs. National Civil War Naval Museum, Columbus, GA

Civil War Miscellany. Georgia Department of Archives and History, Morrow.

Cobb, Howell, Papers. Felix Hargrett Rare Book and Manuscript Library, University of Georgia, Athens.

Comer, Laura Beecher, Papers. Southern Historical Collection. University of North Carolina at Chapel Hill.

Compiled Service Records of the Confederate Soldiers Who Served in Organizations from the State of Georgia. National Archives, Washington, DC.

Confederate Bible Records. United Daughters of the Confederacy. Georgia Department of Archives and History, Morrow.

Confederate Letters Collection. United Daughters of the Confederacy. Georgia Department of Archives and History, Morrow.

Curry Hill Plantation Records. Georgia Department of Archives and History, Morrow.

Governor's Incoming Correspondence. Georgia Department of Archives and History, Morrow.

Governor's Letter Book. Georgia Department of Archives and History, Morrow.

Governor's Petitions. Georgia Department of Archives and History, Morrow.

Hurtsboro folder. Russell County clippings file. Alabama Department of Archives and History, Montgomery.

Jenkins, Cyrus F., Diary. Troup County Archives, LaGrange, GA.

Letters Received. Confederate Secretary of War. National Archives, Washington, DC.

"Little Valley Stories: Slavery Days." Margaret Parker Milford Collection. Cobb Memorial Archives, Valley, AL.

Mann Civil War Papers. Georgia Department of Archives and History, Morrow.
McLaughlin, Augustus. Letterbook and Confederate Navy Yard Log and Accounts. National Civil War Naval Museum, Columbus, GA.
Morris, Leila C. "Personal Recollections of the War." Nancy Harts folder. Troup County Archives, LaGrange, GA.
Prescott, Emma J. Slade, Reminiscences. Atlanta Historical Society Archives.
Savannah City Council Minutes, 1864. Georgia Department of Archives and History, Morrow.
Small Print Collection. Georgia Department of Archives and History, Morrow.
Southern Claims Commission Reports. National Archives, Washington, DC.
Sumter County Superior Court Records. Georgia Department of Archives and History, Morrow.
Talemon Cuyler Collection. Felix Hargrett Rare Book and Manuscript Library, University of Georgia, Athens.
Thomas County Superior Court. Minute Book, 1858-1865. Thomasville, GA.
Turner, William Weaver, Letters. Troup County Archives, LaGrange, GA.
Wisenbaker, Thannie, Reminiscences. South Georgia Regional Library, Valdosta, GA.
Zinken, Leon von. "Notice to the Citizens of Columbus." Columbus State University Archives, Columbus, GA.

Government Publications

Acts of the General Assembly of Georgia, 1861. Milledgeville, GA: Boughton, Nisbet, and Barnes, 1862.
Acts of the General Assembly of Georgia, 1862. Milledgeville, GA: Boughton, Nisbet, and Barnes, 1863.
Candler, Allen D., comp. *The Confederate Records of Georgia*. 6 vols. Atlanta: State Printing Office, 1909-1911.
Cobb, Thomas R. R., comp. *A Digest of the Statutes of the State of Georgia in Force Prior to Session of the General Assembly of 1851*. Vol. 2. Athens, GA: Christy, Kelsea, and Burke, 1851.
Cobb, Thomas R. R., comp. *Reports of Cases in Law and Equity, Argued and Determined in the Supreme Court of the State of Georgia*. Athens, GA: Reynolds and Bro., 1855.
Journal of the House of Representatives of the United States. 37th Congress, 1st session. Washington, DC: Government Printing Office, 1861.
Journal of the Public and Secret Proceedings of the Convention of the People of Georgia, 1861. Milledgeville, GA: Boughton, Nisbet, and Barnes, 1861.
Journal of the Senate of the United States. 37th Congress, 1st session. Washington, DC: Government Printing Office, 1861.
Lester, George N., comp. *Cases in Law and Equity Argued and Determined in the Supreme Court of the State of Georgia*. Vol. 33. Atlanta: Franklin-Turner, 1907.
Official Records of the Union and Confederate Navies in the War of the Rebellion. 31 vols. Washington, DC: Government Printing Office, 1894-1927.
Statutes at Large, Treaties, and Proclamations of the United States of America. Vol. 13. Boston: Little, Brown, and Company, 1866.
United States. *Eighth Census of the United States, 1860*. Washington, DC: Government

Printing Office, 1864.

War of the Rebellion: A Compilation of the Official Records of the Union and Confederate Armies. 128 parts in 70 vols. and atlas. Washington, DC: Government Printing Office, 1880-1901.

Newspapers and Periodicals

Albany (GA) Patriot
Albany (NY) Evening Journal
Athens (GA) Southern Watchman
Atlanta (GA) Intelligencer
Atlanta (GA) Southern Confederacy
Augusta (GA) Chronicle and Sentinel
Augusta (GA) Constitutionalist
Boston (MA) Commonwealth
Boston (MA) Herald
Charleston (SC) Mercury
Columbus (GA) Sun
Columbus (GA) Enquirer
Columbus (GA) Times
Congressional Globe (Washington, DC)
Cuthbert (GA) Reporter
De Bow's Review (New Orleans, LA)
Early County News (Blakely, GA)
Eufaula (AL) Express
Georgia Journal and Messenger (Milledgeville)
Griffin (GA) American Union
Harper's Weekly (New York)
Harris County Enterprise (Hamilton, GA)
Indianapolis (IN) Daily Journal
Leslie's Illustrated Newspaper (New York)
Liberator (Boston, MA)
Macon (GA) Telegraph
Milledgeville (GA) Confederate Union
Milledgeville (GA) Southern Federal Union
Milledgeville (GA) Southern Recorder
New York (NY) Herald
New York (NY) Tribune
Opelika (AL) Southern Republic
Philadelphia (PA) Inquirer
Rome (GA) Tri-Weekly Courier
Rome (GA) Weekly Courier
Salem (MA) Register
Savannah (GA) Morning News
Savannah (GA) Republican
Selma (AL) Morning Reporter

Sumter Republican (Americus, GA)
Thomaston (GA) Upson Pilot
Thomasville (GA) Southern Enterprise
Troy (AL) Southern Advertiser
Turnwold Countryman (Eatonton, GA)
Washington (DC) Daily National Intelligencer

Web Sites

Slave Narratives: A Folk History of Slavery in the United States from Interviews with Former Slaves. Manuscript Division, Library of Congress. Washington, DC. Available on line as *Born in Slavery: Slave Narratives from the Federal Writers' Project, 1936-1938* (https://www.loc.gov/collections/slave-narratives-from-the-federal-writers-project-1936-to-1938)

Published Documentary Sources

American Annual Cyclopedia and Register of Important Events of the Year 1863. New York: D. Appleton, 1864.

Andrews, Eliza Frances. *The War-Time Journal of a Georgia Girl*. New York: D. Appleton, 1908.

Andrews, William H. *Footprints of a Regiment: A Recollection of the First Georgia Regulars, 1861-1865*. Introduction by Richard M. McMurry. Atlanta: Longstreet Press, 1992.

Basler, Roy P., Marion Dolores Pratt, and Lloyd A. Dunlap, eds. *The Collected Works of Abraham Lincoln*. 9 vols. New Brunswick, NJ: Rutgers University Press, 1953-55.

Berlin, Ira, et al., eds. *Freedom: A Documentary History of Emancipation, 1861-1867*. Series 1, vol. 1, *The Destruction of Slavery*. New York: Cambridge University Press, 1985.

______, et al., eds. *Freedom: A Documentary History of Emancipation, 1861-1867*. Series 1, vol. 3, *The Wartime Genesis of Free Labor: The Lower South*. New York: Cambridge University Press, 1990.

Berlin, Ira, Joseph P. Reidy, and Leslie S. Rowland, eds. *Freedom: A Documentary History of Emancipation, 1861-1867*. Series 2, *The Black Military Experience*. New York: Cambridge University Press, 1982.

Boyle, John Richards. *Soldiers True: The Story of the One Hundred and Eleventh Regiment Pennsylvania Veteran Volunteers*. New York: Eaton and Mains, 1903.

Brooks, R. P., ed. "Howell Cobb Papers." *Georgia Historical Quarterly* 6 (1922): 355-94.

Brown, John Fulton. *The Bushwhackers: The Story of a Reluctant Rebel During the Civil War*. Bloomington, IN: iUniverse Inc., 2009.

Browne, Junius Henri. *Four Years in Secessia: Adventures Within and Beyond the Union Lines*. Hartford, CT: O. D. Case and Co., 1865.

Buckingham, James Silk. *The Slave States of America*. 2 vols. London: Fisher, Son, and Co., 1842.

Burnett, Edmund Cody, ed. "Letters of Barnett Hardeman Cody and Others, 1861-1864." *Georgia Historical Quarterly* 23 (1939): 265-99, 362-80.

_____, ed. "Letters of Three Lightfoot Brothers, 1861-1864." *Georgia Historical Quarterly*

25 (1941): 371-400; 26 (1942): 65-90.

_____, ed. "Letters of Three Lightfoot Brothers, 1861-1864." *Georgia Historical Quarterly* 26 (1942): 65-90.

Chapman, R. D. *A Georgia Soldier in the Civil War, 1861-1865*. Houston, TX: n.p., 1923.

Cleveland, Henry. *Alexander H. Stephens in Public and Private*. Philadelphia: National Publishing, 1866.

Confederate Reminiscences and Letters. 7 vols. Atlanta: United Daughters of the Confederacy, 1997.

Coyngham, David Power. *Sherman's March Through the South, with Sketches and Incidents of the Campaign*. New York: Sheldon and Co., 1865.

Craft, William. *Running a Thousand Miles for Freedom; or, The Escape of William and Ellen Craft from Slavery*. London: William Tweedie, 1860.

Crist, Lynda Lasswell, and Mary Seaton Dix, eds. *The Papers of Jefferson Davis*. Vol. 7. Baton Rouge: Louisiana State University Press, 1992.

Cumming, Kate. *Gleanings From Southland*. Birmingham, AL: Roberts and Son, 1895.

_____. *The Journal of Kate Cumming, A Confederate Nurse, 1862-1865*. Edited by Richard Harwell. Savannah: Beehive Press, 1975.

Curry, W. L., comp. *Four Years in the Saddle: History of the First Regiment, Ohio Volunteer Cavalry*. Jonesboro, GA: Freedom Hill Press, 1898.

Devens, R. M. *Pictorial Book of Anecdotes and Incidents of the War of the Rebellion*. Hartford, CT: Hartford Publishing, 1866.

Duncan, Russell, ed. *Blue-Eyed Child of Fortune: The Civil War Letters of Colonel Robert Gould Shaw*. Athens: University of Georgia Press, 1992.

Ellis, Daniel. *The Thrilling Adventures of Daniel Ellis*. New York: Harper and Brothers, 1867.

Fitzhugh, George. *Sociology for the South, or The Failure of Free Society*. Richmond: A. Morris, 1854.

Hague, Parthenia A. *A Blockaded Family: Life in Southern Alabama during the Civil War*. 1888. Reprint, Freeport, NY: Books for Libraries Press, 1971.

Helper, Hinton Rowan. *The Impending Crisis of the South*. New York: Burdick Brothers, 1857.

Higginson, Thomas Wentworth. *Army Life in a Black Regiment*. Boston: Fields, Osgood, and Co., 1870.

Hill, Benjamin H., Jr. *Senator Benjamin H. Hill of Georgia: His Life, Speeches, and Writings*. Atlanta: H. C. Hudgins, 1891.

Hopley, Catherine C. *Life in the South; From the Commencement of the War*. Vol. 2. London: Chapman and Hall, 1863.

Horton, Mrs. Thaddeus. "The Story of the Nancy Harts." *Ladies Home Journal* (Nov. 1904): 14.

Houghton, W. R., and M. B. Houghton. *Two Boys in the Civil War and After*. Montgomery, AL: Paragon Press, 1912.

Ingersoll, Lurton Dunham. *Iowa and the Rebellion*. Philadelphia: J. B. Lippincott, 1866.

Johnson, Michael P., ed. *Abraham Lincoln, Slavery, and the Civil War: Selected Writings and Speeches*. Boston: Bedford/St. Martin's, 2001.

Johnson, Robert U., and Clarence C. Buel, eds. *Battles and Leaders of the Civil War*. Vol. 4. New York: Century Co., 1888.

Kellogg, John Azor. *Capture and Escape: A Narrative of Army and Prison Life*. Wisconsin Historical Commission, 1908.
Kemble, Frances Anne. *Journal of a Residence on a Georgian Plantation in 1838-1839*. New York: Harper and Brothers, 1863.
Lane, Mills, ed. *Times That Prove People's Principles: Civil War in Georgia – A Documentary History*. Savannah: Beehive Press, 1993.
Lokey, J. W. *My Experiences in the War Between the States*. Tishomingo, OK: n.p., 1959.
Longstreet, James. *From Manassas to Appomattox: Memoirs of the Civil War in America*. Philadelphia: J. B. Lippincott, 1896.
M'Farland, L. B. "The Battle of West Point." *Confederate Veteran* 23 (1915): 353-55.
Merz, Louis. "Diary of Private Louis Merz, C.S.A., of the West Point Guards, 1862." *Chattahoochee Valley Historical Society Bulletin* 4 (1959): 17-45.
Meyers, Christopher C., ed. *Empire State of the South: Georgia History in Documents and Essays*. Macon, GA: Mercer University Press, 2008.
Michie, Peter, ed. *The Life and Letters of Emory Upton*. New York: D. Appleton, 1885.
Moore, Frank, ed. *The Rebellion Record: A Diary of American Events*. Vol. 1. New York: G. P. Putnam, 1861.
Moses, Jacob Raphael. "A Southern Romantic." In *Memoirs of American Jews, 1775-1865*, compiled by Jacob Rader Marcus. Vol. 1. Philadelphia: Jewish Publication Society of America, 1955.
Nichols, George Ward. *The Story of the Great March, From the Diary of a Staff Officer*. New York: Harper, 1865.
Olmsted, Frederick Law. *The Cotton Kingdom*. 2 vols. New York: Mason Brothers, 1861-1862.
Phillips, Ulrich Bonnell, ed. *Correspondence of Robert Toombs, Alexander H. Stephens, and Howell Cobb*. Washington, DC: Government Printing Office, 1913.
Plumley, G. S. "In Dixie." *Harper's New Monthly Magazine* 29 (July 1864): 232-35.
Rawick, George P., et al., comp. *The American Slave: A Composite Autobiography*. Series 1 and 2, and supplement, Series 1. Westport, CT: Greenwood Press, 1972 and 1977.
Richardson, Albert D. *The Secret Service, the Field, the Dungeon, and the Escape*. Hartford, CT: American Publishing, 1866.
"Samuel Henderson Frier, 1833-1863: AWOL from the Confederate Army." *Huxford Genealogical Society Magazine* 26 (1999): 81-83.
Scott, William Forse. *The Story of a Cavalry Regiment: The Career of the Fourth Iowa Veteran Volunteers from Kansas to Georgia, 1861-1865*. New York: Knickerbocker Press, 1893.
Sherman, William T. *Memoirs of W. T. Sherman*. Vol. 2. New York: Charles L. Webster, 1891.
Simms, James M. *The First Colored Baptist Church in North America*. Philadelphia: J. B. Lippincott, 1888.
Stearns, Charles. *The Black Man of the South, and the Rebels; or, The Characteristics of the Former and the Recent Outrages of the Latter*. New York: American News Co., 1872.
Still, William. *The Underground Rail Road*. Philadelphia: Porter and Coates, 1872.
Stirling, James. *Letters from the Slave States*. London: Parker and Son, 1857.
Stuart, James. *Three Years in North America*. Edinburgh, Scotland: Robert Cadell, 1833.
Taylor, Susie King. *Reminiscences of My Life in Camp*. 1902. Reprint, with new introduc-

tion by Catherine Clinton, Athens: University of Georgia Press, 2006.
Twenty-Eighth Annual Report of the American Anti-Slavery Society. New York: American Anti-Slavery Society, 1861.
Upson, Theodore F. *With Sherman to the Sea*. Bloomington: Indiana University Press, 1958.
Watkins, Sam R. *Co. Aytch*. 1882. Reprint, Wilmington, NC: Broadfoot Publishing, 1987.
Wesley, John. *The Works of the Reverend John Wesley*. Vol. 6. New York: Emory and Waugh, 1831.
Wiley, Bell Irvin, ed. "The Confederate Letters of John W. Hagan." *Georgia Historical Quarterly* 38 (1954): 170-200, 268-89.
Wilson, James Harrison. *Under the Old Flag*. Vol. 2. New York: D. Appleton, 1912.
Wynne, Lewis N., and Guy Porcher Harrison, eds. "'Plain Folk' Coping in the Confederacy: The Garrett-Asbell Letters." *Georgia Historical Quarterly* 72 (1988): 102-18.

Secondary Sources

Amos, Harriet E. "'All Absorbing Topics': Food and Clothing in Confederate Mobile." *Atlanta Historical Journal* 22 (1978): 17-28.
Avery, I. W. *History of the State of Georgia*. New York: Brown and Derby, 1881.
Bailey, Anne J. *The Chessboard of War: Sherman and Hood in the Autumn Campaigns of 1864*. Lincoln: University of Nebraska Press, 2000.
_____. *War and Ruin: William T. Sherman and the Savannah Campaign*. Lanham, MD: Rowman and Littlefield, 1992.
Bailey, Anne J., and Walter J. Fraser. *Portraits of Conflict: A Photographic History of Georgia in the Civil War*. Fayetteville: University of Arkansas Press, 1996.
Barfield, Louise Calhoun. *History of Harris County, Georgia, 1827-1961*. Columbus, GA: Columbus Office Supply Co., 1961.
Barnard, George N. *Photographic Views of Sherman's Campaign*. New York: Dover Publications, 1977.
Barney, William L. *The Road to Secession: A New Perspective on the Old South*. New York: Praeger, 1972.
_____. *The Secessionist Impulse: Alabama and Mississippi in 1860*. Princeton, NJ: Princeton University Press, 1974.
Bartley, Numan. *The Creation of Modern Georgia*. Athens: University of Georgia Press, 1990.
Beringer, Richard E., Herman Hattaway, Archer Jones, and William N. Still. *Why the South Lost the Civil War*. Athens: University of Georgia Press, 1986.
Berlin, Ira. "Who Freed the Slaves? Emancipation and Its Meaning." In *Union and Emancipation: Essays on Politics and Race in the Civil War Era*, edited by David W. Blight and Brooks D. Simpson. Kent, OH: Kent State University Press, 1997.
Black, Robert C. *Railroads of the Confederacy*. Chapel Hill: University of North Carolina Press, 1952.
_____. "The Railroads of Georgia in the Confederate War Effort." *Journal of Southern History* 18 (1947): 511-34.

Bohannon, Keith S. "They Had Determined to Root Us Out: Dual Memoirs by a Unionist Couple in Blue Ridge, Georgia." In *Enemies of the Country: New Perspectives on Unionists in the Civil War South*, edited by John C. Inscoe and Robert C. Kenzer. Athens: University of Georgia Press, 2001.

Bonds, Russell S. *Stealing the General: The Great Locomotive Chase and the First Medal of Honor*. Yardley, PA: Westholme Publishing, 2006.

Bonner, James C. "David R. Snelling: A Story of Desertion and Defection in the Civil War." *Georgia Review* 10 (1955): 275-82.

Bragg, C. L., et al. *Never for Want of Powder: The Confederate Powder Works in Augusta, Georgia*. Columbia: University of South Carolina Press, 2007.

Bragg, William Harris. *Joe Brown's Army: The Georgia State Line, 1862-1865*. Macon, GA: Mercer University Press, 1987.

Bryan, T. Conn. "The Churches in Georgia During the Civil War." *Georgia Historical Quarterly* 33 (1949): 283-302.

_____. *Confederate Georgia*. Athens: University of Georgia Press, 1953.

Bryant, Jonathan M. *How Curious a Land: Conflict and Change in Greene County, Georgia, 1850-1885*. Chapel Hill: University of North Carolina Press, 1996.

Burchard, Peter. *One Gallant Rush: Robert Gould Shaw and His Brave Black Regiment*. New York: St. Martin's Press, 1965.

Butler, Joshua William. "Almost Too Terrible to Believe: The Camilla, Georgia, Race Riot and Massacre." Master's thesis, Valdosta State University, 2012.

Cain, Andrew W. *History of Lumpkin County for the First Hundred Years, 1832-1932*. Atlanta: Stein Printing, 1932.

Carlson, David. "'The Distemper of the Time': Conscription, the Courts, and Planter Privilege in Civil War South Georgia." *Journal of Southwest Georgia History* 14 (1999): 1-24.

_____. "The 'Loanly Runagee': Draft Evaders in Confederate South Georgia." *Georgia Historical Quarterly* 84 (2000): 589-615.

_____. "'Remember thy Pledge!': Religious and Reformist Influences on Joseph E. Brown's Opposition to Confederate Conscription." *Georgia Historical Quarterly* 98 (2014): 26-49.

Carlson, Robert David. "Breach of Faith: Conscription in Confederate Georgia." Ph.D. dissertation, Emory University, 2009.

_____. "Wiregrass Runners: Conscription, Desertion, and the Origins of Discontent in Civil War South Georgia." Master's thesis, Valdosta State University, 1999.

Chesson, Michael B. "Harlots or Heroines? A New Look at the Richmond Bread Riot." *Virginia Magazine of History and Biography* 92 (1984): 131-75.

Christian, Rebecca. "Georgia and the Confederate Policy of Impressing Supplies." *Georgia Historical Quarterly* 28 (1944): 1-33.

Cimbala, Paul A. *Under the Guardianship of the Nation: The Freedmen's Bureau and the Reconstruction of Georgia, 1865-1870*. Athens: University of Georgia Press, 1997.

Coleman, Kenneth, ed. *A History of Georgia*. Athens: University of Georgia Press, 1977.

Coulter, E. Merton. *Confederate States of America, 1861-1865*. Baton Rouge: Louisiana State University Press, 1950.

Covington, W. A. *History of Colquitt County*. Atlanta: Foote and Davies, 1937.

Cozzens, Peter. *The Shipwreck of Their Hopes: The Battles for Chattanooga*. Champaign:

University of Illinois Press, 1998.
_____. *This Terrible Sound: The Battle of Chickamauga*. Champaign: University of Illinois Press, 1992.
Crawford, George B. "Cotton, Land, and Sustenance: Toward the Limits of Abundance in Late Antebellum Georgia." *Georgia Historical Quarterly* 72 (1988): 215-47.
Crowley, John G. *Primitive Baptists of the Wiregrass South: 1815 to the Present*. Gainesville: University Press of Florida, 1998.
Current, Richard N. *Lincoln's Loyalists: Union Soldiers from the Confederacy*. New York: Oxford University Press, 1994.
Daniell, Elizabeth. "The Ashburn Murder Case in Georgia Reconstruction, 1868." *Georgia Historical Quarterly* 59 (1975): 296-312.
Davidson, William H. *Brooks of Honey and Butter: Plantations and People of Meriwether County, Georgia*. 2 vols. Alexander City, AL: Outlook, 1971.
Davis, Robert S. "Forgotten Union Guerrilla Fighters from the North Georgia Mountains." *North Georgia Journal* 5 (Summer 1988): 30-40.
_____, ed. "Memoirs of a Partisan War: Sion Darnell Remembers North Georgia." *Georgia Historical Quarterly* 80 (1996): 93-116.
_____. "White and Black in Blue: The Recruitment of Federal Units in Civil War North Georgia." *Georgia Historical Quarterly* 85 (2001): 347-74.
Davis, Stephen. *Atlanta Will Fall: Sherman, Joe Johnston, and the Yankee Heavy Battalions*. Lanham, MD: Rowman and Littlefield, 2001.
_____. *What the Yankees Did to Us: Sherman's Bombardment and Wrecking of Atlanta*. Macon, GA: Mercer University Press, 2012.
DeBats, Donald A. *Elites and Masses: Political Structure, Communication, and Behavior in Ante-Bellum Georgia*. New York: Garland Publishing, 1990.
DeCredico, Mary A. *Patriotism for Profit: Georgia's Urban Entrepreneurs and the Confederate War Effort*. Chapel Hill: University of North Carolina Press, 1990.
Dillard, Philip David. "Arming the Slaves: Transformation of the Public Mind." Master's thesis, University of Georgia, 1994.
Drago, Edmund L. *Black Politicians and Reconstruction in Georgia: A Splendid Failure*. Baton Rouge: Louisiana State University Press, 1982.
Du Bois, W. E. B. *Black Reconstruction: An Essay Toward a History of the Part which Black Folk Played in the Attempt to Reconstruct Democracy in America, 1860-1880*. New York: Harcourt, Brace, and Co., 1935.
Duncan, Russell. *Freedom's Shore: Tunis Campbell and the Georgia Freedmen*. Athens: University of Georgia Press, 1986.
Dyer, Thomas G. *Secret Yankees: The Union Circle in Confederate Atlanta*. Baltimore: Johns Hopkins University Press, 1999.
Edwards, Laura F. *Scarlett Doesn't Live Here Any More: Southern Women in the Civil War Era*. Urbana: University of Illinois Press, 2000.
Escott, Paul D. *After Secession: Jefferson Davis and the Failure of Confederate Nationalism*. Baton Rouge: Louisiana State Unviersity Press, 1978.
_____. "The Context of Freedom: Georgia's Slaves during the Civil War." *Georgia Historical Quarterly* 58 (1974): 79-104.
_____. "Joseph E. Brown, Jefferson Davis, and the Problem of Poverty in the Confederacy." *Georgia Historical Quarterly* 61 (1977): 59-71.

_____. *Many Excellent People: Power and Privilege in North Carolina, 1850-1900*. Chapel Hill: University of North Carolina Press, 1985.

Flynn, Charles L., Jr. *White Land, Black Labor: Caste and Class in Late Nineteenth-Century Georgia*. Baton Rouge: Louisiana State University Press, 1983.

Flynt, Wayne. *Poor but Proud: Alabama's Poor Whites*. Tuscaloosa: University of Alabama Press, 1989.

Foner, Eric. *Nothing but Freedom: Emancipation and Its Legacy*. Baton Rouge: Louisiana State University Press, 1983.

Formwalt, Lee W. "The Camilla Massacre of 1868: Racial Violence as Political Propaganda." *Georgia Historical Quarterly* 71 (1987): 399-426.

_____. "Planter Persistence in Southwest Georgia, 1850-1870." *Journal of Southwest Georgia History* 2 (1984): 40-58.

_____. "Planters and Cotton Production as a Cause of Confederate Defeat: Evidence from Southwest Georgia." *Georgia Historical Quarterly* 74 (1990): 269-76.

Fowler, John D., and David B. Parker, eds. *Breaking the Heartland: The Civil War in Georgia*. Macon, GA: Mercer University Press, 2011.

Franklin, John Hope, and Loren Schweninger. "The Quest for Freedom: Runaway Slaves and the Plantation South." In *Slavery, Resistance, Freedom*, edited by Gabor Boritt and Scott Hancock. New York: Oxford University Press, 2007.

Freehling, William W. *The South vs. the South: How Anti-Confederate Southerners Shaped the Course of the Civil War*. New York: Oxford University Press, 2001.

Freehling, William W., and Craig M. Simpson, eds. *Secession Debated: Georgia's Showdown in 1860*. New York: Oxford University Press, 1992.

French, Thomas L., Jr., and Edward L. French. "The Horace King Story: Building Bridges across Rivers and between Cultures." *Columbus and the Valley Magazine* (Spring 1994): 34-40.

Glatthaar, Joseph T. *The March to the Sea and Beyond: Sherman's Troops in the Savannah and Carolinas Campaigns*. New York: New York University Press, 1985.

Gould, Stephen Jay. *The Mismeasure of Man*. New York: Norton, 1981.

Gourley, Bruce T. *Diverging Loyalties: Baptists in Middle Georgia during the Civil War*. Macon, GA: Mercer University Press, 2011.

Graham, Christopher A. "Women's Revolt in Rowan County." *Columbiad* 3 (1999): 131-47.

Grant, Donald L. *The Way it Was in the South: The Black Experience in Georgia*. Edited with introduction by Jonathan Grant. New York: Birch Lane Press, 1993.

Grice, Warren. "The Confederate States Court for Georgia." *Georgia Historical Quarterly* 9 (1925): 131-58.

Hadden, Sally E. *Slave Patrols: Law and Violence in Virginia and the Carolinas*. Cambridge, MA: Harvard University Press, 2001.

Hamilton, J. G. De Roulhac. "The State Courts and the Confederate Constitution." *Journal of Southern History* 4 (1938): 425-48.

Harris, J. William. *The Making of the American South: A Short History, 1500-1877*. Malden, MA: Blackwell Publishing, 2006.

_____. *Plain Folk and Gentry in a Slave Society: White Liberty and Black Slavery in Augusta's Hinterlands*. Middletown, CT: Wesleyan University Press, 1985.

Henderson, Lillian, comp. *Roster of the Confederate Soldiers of Georgia, 1861-1865*. 6 vols.

Hapeville, GA: Longina and Porter, 1959-64.
Hess, Earl J. *Kennesaw Mountain: Sherman, Johnston, and the Atlanta Campaign*. Chapel Hill: University of North Carolina Press, 2013.
Hofstadter, Richard. *The American Political Tradition and the Men Who Made It*. New York: Vintage, 1948.
Horigan, Michael. *Elmira: Death Camp of the North*. Mechanicsburg, PA: Stackpole Books, 2002.
Hufton, Olwen. *The Prospect Before Her: A History of Women in Western Europe*. Vol. 1. New York: Alfred A. Knopf, 1996.
Inscoe, John C., ed. *The Civil War in Georgia: A New Georgia Encyclopedia Companion*. Athens: University of Georgia Press, 2011.
_____. "Moving Through Deserter County: Fugitive Accounts of the Inner Civil War in Southern Appalachia." In *The Civil War in Appalachia: Collected Essays*, edited by Kenneth W. Noe and Shannon H. Wilson. Knoxville: University of Tennessee Press, 1997.
Iobst, Richard W. *Civil War Macon: The History of a Confederate City*. Macon, GA: Mercer University Press, 1999.
Johnson, Forrest Clark, III. *Histories of LaGrange and Troup County, Georgia*. Vol. 1, *A History of LaGrange, Georgia, 1828-1900*. LaGrange, GA: Family Tree, 1987.
Johnson, Joseph Paul. "Southwest Georgia: A Case Study in Confederate Agriculture." Master's thesis, University of Georgia, 1992.
Johnson, Michael P. "A New Look at the Popular Vote for Delegates to the Georgia Secession Convention." *Georgia Historical Quarterly* 56 (1972): 259-75.
_____. *Toward a Patriarchal Republic: The Secession of Georgia*. Baton Rouge: Louisiana State University Press, 1977.
Johnston, Richard Malcolm, and William Hand Browne. *The Life of Alexander H. Stephens*. Philadelphia: J. B. Lippincott, 1883.
Jones, Jacqueline. "Georgia Lowcountry Battlegrounds during the Civil War." In *Breaking the Heartland: The Civil War in Georgia*, edited by John D. Fowler and David B. Parker. Macon, GA: Mercer University Press, 2011.
_____. *Saving Savannah: The City and the Civil War*. New York: Alfred A. Knopf, 2008.
Jones, James P. *Yankee Blitzkrieg: Wilson's Raid through Alabama and Georgia*. Athens: University of Georgia Press, 1976.
King, Spencer B., Jr. *Darien: The Death and Rebirth of a Southern Town*. Macon, GA: Mercer University Press, 1981.
Krakow, Kenneth K. *Georgia Place-Names*. Macon, GA: Winship Press, 1975.
Lebergott, Stanley. "Through the Blockade: The Profitability and Extent of Cotton Smuggling, 1861-1865." *Journal of Economic History* 41 (1981): 867-88.
_____. "Why the South Lost: Commercial Purpose in the Confederacy." *Journal of American History* 70 (1983): 58-74.
Levine, Bruce. *Confederate Emancipation: Southern Plans to Free and Arm Slaves During the Civil War*. New York: Oxford University Press, 2006.
Linderman, Gerald F. *Embattled Courage: The Experience of Combat in the American Civil War*. New York: Free Press, 1987.
Lockley, Timothy James. *Lines in the Sand: Race and Class in Lowcountry Georgia, 1750-1860*. Athens: University of Georgia Press, 2001.

Lonn, Ella. *Desertion During the Civil War*. New York: Century Co., 1928.
_____. *Foreigners in the Union Army and Navy*. New York: Greenwood, 1969.
Martis, Kenneth C. *The Atlas of the Congresses of the Confederate States of America, 1861-1865*. New York: Simon and Schuster, 1994.
Marvel, William. *Andersonville: The Last Depot*. Chapel Hill: University of North Carolina Press, 1994.
McGee, Val L. *Claybank Memories: A History of Dale County, Alabama*. Ozark, AL: Dale County Historical Society, 1989.
McMurry, Richard M. *Atlanta 1864: Last Chance for the Confederacy*. Lincoln: University of Nebraska Press, 2000.
Meyers, Christopher C. "'The Wretch Vickery' and the Brooks County Civil War Slave Conspiracy." *Journal of Southwest Georgia History* 12 (1997): 27-38.
Meyers, Christopher C., and David Williams. *Georgia: A Brief History*. Macon, GA: Mercer University Press, 2012.
Miller, Marion Mills, ed. *Great Debates in American History*. Vol. 4. New York: Current Literature Publishing, 1913.
Misulia, Charles A. *Columbus, Georgia, 1865: The Last True Battle of the Civil War*. Tuscaloosa: University of Alabama Press, 2010.
Mohr, Clarence L. *On the Threshold of Freedom: Masters and Slaves in Civil War Georgia*. Athens: University of Georgia Press, 1986.
_____. "Slavery and Class Tensions in Confederate Georgia." *Gulf Coast Historical Review* 4 (1989): 58-72.
Moore, Albert Burton. *Conscription and Conflict in the Confederacy*. 1924. Reprint, Columbia: University of South Carolina Press, 1996.
Moore, John Hammond. "Sherman's 'Fifth Column': A Guide to Unionist Activity in Georgia." *Georgia Historical Quarterly* 68 (1984): 382-409.
Morgan, Chad. *Planters' Progress: Modernizing Confederate Georgia*. Gainesville: University Press of Florida, 2005.
Mueller, Edward A. *Perilous Journeys: A History of Steamboating on the Chattahoochee, Apalachicola, and Flint Rivers, 1828-1928*. Eufaula, AL: Historic Chattahoochee Commission, 1990.
Nolan, Alan T. *Lee Considered: General Robert E. Lee and Civil War History*. Chapel Hill: University of North Carolina Press, 1991.
O'Donovan, Susan E. *Becoming Free in the Cotton South*. Cambridge, MA: Harvard University Press, 2007.
Oakes, James. *Slavery and Freedom: An Interpretation of the Old South*. New York: Vintage, 1990.
Parks, Joseph H. *Joseph E. Brown of Georgia*. Baton Rouge: Louisiana State University Press, 1977.
Percy, William Alexander. "Localizing the Context of Confederate Politics: The Congressional Election of 1863 in Georgia's First District." *Georgia Historical Quarterly* 79 (1995): 192-209.
Pioneers of Wiregrass Georgia. Vol. 8. Homerville, GA: Huxford Genealogical Society, 1988.
Phillips, Ulrich Bonnell. *Georgia and State Rights*. Washington, DC: Government Printing Office, 1902.

Potter, David. *Lincoln and His Party in the Secession Crisis.* New Haven, CT: Yale University Press, 1942.

Radley, Kenneth. *Rebel Watchdog: The Confederate States Army Provost Guard.* Baton Rouge: Louisiana State University Press, 1989.

Range, Willard. *A Century of Georgia Agriculture: 1850-1950.* Athens: University of Georgia Press, 1954.

Reidy, Joseph P. *From Slavery to Agrarian Capitalism in the Cotton South: Central Georgia, 1800-1880.* Chapel Hill: University of North Carolina Press, 1992.

_____. "States of Dependence and Independence in Civil War Georgia." In *Breaking the Heartland: The Civil War in Georgia*, edited by John D. Fowler and David B. Parker. Macon, GA: Mercer University Press, 2011.

Reiger, John F. "Deprivation, Disaffection, and Desertion in Confederate Florida." *Florida Historical Quarterly* 48 (1969-70): 279-98.

Revels, Tracy J. *Grander in Her Daughters: Florida's Women During the Civil War.* Columbia: University of South Carolina Press, 2004.

Riley, James A. "Desertion and Disloyalty in Georgia During the Civil War." Master's thesis, University of Georgia, 1951.

Sarris, Jonathan Dean. "Anatomy of an Atrocity: The Madden Branch Massacre and Guerrilla Warfare in North Georgia, 1861-1865." *Georgia Historical Quarterly* 77 (1993): 679-710.

_____. "An Execution in Lumpkin County: Local Loyalties in North Georgia's Civil War." In *The Civil War in Appalachia: Collected Essays*, edited by Kenneth W. Noe and Shannon H. Wilson. Knoxville: University of Tennessee Press, 1997.

_____. *A Separate Civil War: Communities in Conflict in the Mountain South.* Charlottesville: University of Virginia Press, 2006.

Scaife, William R., and William Harris Bragg. *Joe Brown's Pets: The Georgia Militia, 1861-1865.* Macon, GA: Mercer University Press, 2004.

Schott, Thomas E. *Alexander H. Stephens of Georgia: A Biography.* Baton Rouge: Louisiana State University Press, 1988.

Secrist, Philip L. *The Battle of Resaca.* Macon, GA: Mercer University Press, 2010.

Shankman, Arnold M. *The Pennsylvania Antiwar Movement, 1861-1865.* Rutherford, NJ: Fairleigh Dickinson University Press, 1980.

Siebert, William H. *The Underground Railroad From Slavery to Freedom.* New York: Macmillan, 1898.

Smith, Clifford L. *History of Troup County.* Atlanta: Foote and Davies, 1933.

Smith, John David, ed. *Black Soldiers in Blue: African American Troops in the Civil War Era.* Chapel Hill: University of North Carolina Press, 2002.

Speer, Lonnie R. *Portals to Hell: Military Prisons of the Civil War.* Mechanicsburg, PA: Stackpole Books, 1997.

Stampp, Kenneth M. *The Peculiar Institution: Slavery in the Ante-Bellum South.* New York: Vintage, 1956.

Standard, Diffee William. *Columbus, Georgia, in the Confederacy: The Social and Industrial Life of the Chattahoochee River Port.* New York: William-Frederick Press, 1954.

Stovall, Pleasant A. *Robert Toombs.* New York: Cassell Publishing, 1892.

Suarez, Annette McDonald. *A Source Book on the Early History of Cuthbert and Randolph County, Georgia.* Atlanta: Cherokee Publishing, 1982.

Swift, Charles Jewett. *The Last Battle of the Civil War*. Columbus, GA: Gilbert Printing, 1915.

Tatum, Georgia Lee. *Disloyalty in the Confederacy*. 1934. Reprint, with new introduction by David Williams, Lincoln: University of Nebraska Press, 2000.

Telfair, Nancy. *A History of Columbus, Georgia*. Columbus, GA: Historical Publishing, 1929.

Thompson, Wesley S. *The Free State of Winston: A History of Winston County, Alabama*. Winfield, AL: Pariel Press, 1968.

Tomblin, Barbara Brooks. *Bluejackets and Contrabands: African Americans and the Union Navy*. Lexington: University Press of Kentucky, 2009.

Turner, Maxine. *Navy Gray: A Story of the Confederate Navy on the Chattahoochee and Apalachicola Rivers*. Tuscaloosa: University of Alabama Press, 1988.

Venet, Wendy Hamand. *A Changing Wind: Commerce and Conflict in Civil War Atlanta*. New Haven, CT: Yale University Press, 2014.

_____. "From Gate City to Gotham: Sam Richards Chronicles the Civil War in Atlanta." In *Breaking the Heartland: The Civil War in Georgia*, edited by John D. Fowler and David B. Parker. Macon, GA: Mercer University Press, 2011.

Wallenstein, Peter. *From Slave South to New South: Public Policy in Nineteenth-Century Georgia*. Chapel Hill: University of North Carolina Press, 1987.

Ward, Geoffrey C. *The Civil War*. New York: Alfred A. Knopf, 1992.

Ward, Warren P. *Ward's History of Coffee County*. 1930. Reprint, Spartanburg, SC: Reprint Co., 1985.

Ware, Lynn Willoughby. "Enchantment and Ennui: The Experiences of the Crew of the CSS *Chattahoochee*." *Georgia Historical Quarterly* 70 (1986): 409-32.

Watson, Fred S. *Winds of Sorrow: Hardships of the Civil War, Early Crimes and Hangings, and War Casualties of the Wiregrass Area*. Dothan, AL: Hopkins Printing, 1986.

Weitz, Mark A. *A Higher Duty: Desertion Among Georgia Troops during the Civil War*. Lincoln: University of Nebraska Press, 2000.

Whitehead, Mary Grist, ed. *Collections of Early County Historical Society*. Vol. 1. Colquitt, GA: Automat Printers, 1971.

_____, ed. *Collections of Early County Historical Society*. Vol. 2. Tallahassee, FL: Rose Printing, 1979.

Whites, LeeAnn. *The Civil War as a Crisis in Gender: Augusta, Georgia, 1860-1890*. Athens: University of Georgia Press, 1995.

Williams, David. *Bitterly Divided: The South's Inner Civil War*. New York: The New Press, 2008.

_____. *I Freed Myself: African American Self-Emancipation in the Civil War Era*. New York: Cambridge University Press, 2014.

_____. *The Old South: A Brief History with Documents*. Macon, GA: Mercer University Press, 2014.

_____. *A People's History of the Civil War: Struggles for the Meaning of Freedom*. New York: The New Press, 2005.

_____. *Rich Man's War: Class, Caste, and Confederate Defeat in the Lower Chattahoochee Valley*. Athens: University of Georgia Press, 1998.

Williams, David, Teresa Crisp Williams, and David Carlson. *Plain Folk in a Rich Man's War: Class and Dissent in Confederate Georgia*. Gainesville: University Press of Flor-

ida, 2002.
Williams, David Salter. *From Mounds to Megachurches: Georgia's Religious Heritage*. Athens: University of Georgia Press, 2008.
Williams, Teresa Crisp. "'The Women Rising': Class and Gender in Civil War Georgia." Master's thesis, Valdosta State University, 1999.
Williams, Teresa Crisp, and David Williams. "'The Women Rising': Cotton, Class, and Confederate Georgia's Rioting Women." *Georgia Historical Quarterly* 86 (2002): 49-83.
Willoughby, Lynn. *Fair to Middlin': The Antebellum Cotton Trade of the Apalachicola/Chattahoochee River Valley*. Tuscaloosa: University of Alabama Press, 1993.
Winn, Bill. "Columbus' Last Battle: Peace Society May Have Aided City's Fall." *Columbus Ledger-Enquirer*, 19 April 1987.
Woodward, C. Vann. *Tom Watson*. Savannah, GA: Beehive Press, 1973.
Woodworth, Steven E. *Six Armies in Tennessee: The Chickamauga and Chattanooga Campaigns*. Lincoln: University of Nebraska Press, 1998.
Wynne, Lewis Nicholas. *The Continuity of Cotton: Planter Politics in Georgia, 1865-1892*. Macon, GA: Mercer University Press, 1986.

Index